JCSS Study no. 23

Arms Control and the New Middle East Security Environment

edited by
Shai Feldman and Ariel Levite

WESTVIEW PRESS
Boulder • San Francisco • Oxford

THE JER~~USALE~~

J~

Publication of the Jaffee Center for Strategic Studies, Tel Aviv University

This Westview softcover edition is printed on acid-free paper and bound in library-quality, coated covers that carry the highest rating of the National Association of State Textbook Administrators, in consultation with the Association of American Publishers and the Book Manufacturers' Institute.

Copyright © 1994 by Tel Aviv University, Jaffee Center for Strategic Studies

Published in 1994 in Israel by The Jerusalem Post, POB 81, Jerusalem 91000, Israel

Published in 1994 in the United States of America by Westview Press, Inc., 5500 Central Avenue, Boulder, Colorado 80301-2877, and in the United Kingdom by Westview Press, 36 Lonsdale Road, Summertown, Oxford OX2 7EW

CIP data available upon request
ISBN 0-8133-2221-9

Printed and bound in the United States of America

The paper used in this publication meets the requirements
of the American National Standard for Permanence of Paper
for Printed Library Materials Z39.48-1984.

10   9   8   7   6   5   4   3   2

Contents

vii

Acknowledgments

The Ginosar Conference on Arms Control and the New Middle East Security Environment was conducted within the framework of the Project on Security and Arms Control in the Middle East of Tel Aviv University's Jaffee Center for Strategic Studies. We could not have embarked on this project without the encouragement and consistent support of the late founder, builder and Head of the Center, Major General Aharon Yariv--a rare breed of an officer, gentleman and scholar, a man of great vision who was also blessed with the capacity to implement his dreams with wisdom, finesse, and endless energies. We were fortunate to have worked with General Yariv for many years. His recent death has left a huge void and we will sorely miss him.

Funding for the project was provided by the Ford Foundation. We are particularly grateful to Enid Schoettle, who at the time served as Director of the International Affairs Program of the Ford Foundation, for her support. We are also indebted to Steven M. Riskin, then-Program Officer at the Ford Foundation, for his assistance. Finally, thanks to Shephard Forman, current Director of the International Affairs Program, and to Geoffrey Wiseman, for their continued support.

Financial assistance for the participation of some of our American colleagues was provided by the United States Information Service. We are grateful to Martin Quinn, Cultural Attaché at the US Embassy in Israel, and to Anne Walter of the US Cultural Center in Tel Aviv, for their help in securing these funds.

Additional funding for the conference was provided by the IDB Bankholding Corporation Ltd. We are very grateful to Raphael Recanati and to Udi Recanati of IDB for their long-standing support for the Center's activities.

A large part of the administrative burden of holding the conference was shouldered by Sam Wiedermann. His commitment and devotion were indispensable in overcoming

1

numerous organizational problems involved in running a relatively large international meeting. Also, many thanks to Sharon Rudich who volunteered to be my research assistant during the summer of 1991 and returned to assist us during the conference. Thanks for their assistance are also due to Taly Shilo and Emily Landau of JCSS, who attended to the many details associated with the production of the conference and the book. The Ginosar conference involved particularly complex logistics because it was opened in Tel Aviv, held at Nof Ginosar on the shores of the Sea of Galilee, involved tours of parts of the country, and concluded in Jerusalem. This complexity could have become a nightmare were it not for the efficiency of Ilana and Shai Segev of Zabar Tourism Services and Tamar Muller of Ezoori Travel.

We owe a special word of thanks and an apology to Willy Kempel of the Austrian Embassy in Tel Aviv and to Alexander Konovalov of the USA-Canada Institute of the Russian Academy of Sciences in Moscow. Both provided excellent briefings at Ginosar--the former devoted his presentation to the then-proposed Chemical Weapons Convention and the latter to the evolving situation in the former Soviet Union. But because these timely briefings were soon overtaken by events, we decided not to include them in this volume.

Finally, particular thanks to Joseph Alpher, Director of the Center, for his editing suggestions and other help in bringing this monograph to print.

Shai Feldman
Director, Project on
Security and Arms Control
in the Middle East

Ariel Levite
Senior Research
Associate

Tel Aviv, June 1994

2

1.   Introduction

Shai Feldman

This volume incorporates the talks delivered at a conference on "Arms Control and the New Middle East Security Environment," held in Ginosar (Israel) in January 1992. The conference was organized within the framework of the Project on Security and Arms Control in the Middle East conducted by Tel Aviv University's Jaffee Center for Strategic Studies. Some 28 scholars from eight different countries, together with some 30 Israelis, took part in the conference deliberations.

When the Jaffee Center's arms control project was launched in 1990, the subject of arms control was foreign to all Middle East countries, including Israel. Having assessed that developments in the region would soon place the topic on the region's agenda, we saw an acute need to educate and socialize members of Israel's policy elite regarding the issues involved. For this purpose, the Ginosar Conference was designed to expose Israelis--scholars, government officials and senior members of the media--to international scholars and former officials well versed in the subject.

The objective of the conference was to air the experience gained in arms control in other regions--primarily but not exclusively in the US-Soviet and NATO-Warsaw Pact context--and to familiarize Israelis with this experience.   In addition, a significant effort was made to examine the effects of the new Middle East security environment that was emerging after the end of the Cold War, the breakup of the Soviet Union and the 1990-91 Gulf War, on the prospects for applying arms control in the region. From the outset, our interest in the subject was broad, encompassing not only arms reductions and non-proliferation, but also confidence- and security-building measures (CBMs) as well as the means for verifying compliance with the various agreements reached.

Meanwhile, developments in the region confirmed the expectations and assumptions guiding our project's design. And as it turned out, the Ginosar Conference could not have been more timely. Thus, soon after we met in Ginosar, the Middle East Multilateral Conference was held in Moscow, launching the complex deliberations of the working group on Arms Control and Regional Security (ACRS) in the Middle East. This produced immediate demand for education on the issues involved.

These unique circumstances also explain our decision to produce this volume despite the very late publication date. First, we feel we owe this to our colleagues, in Israel and abroad, who were not privileged to share our deliberations at Ginosar. Secondly, we believe that students of the Middle East might find it useful to have a picture of the factors that affected the prospects for applying arms control measures in the region when the multilateral process was launched. Finally and most significantly, our examination and editing of the texts convinced us that they contain significant insights and original analysis to merit publication.

Within this context, three reminders are extremely important. First, this volume does not comprise academic research papers. The speakers at Ginosar were asked to share their insights and experiences with us, and these were subsequently edited for the benefit of those who could not be there. The best indication of the quality of these insights is that most of them remain relevant to this very day. However, it is important to remember that the chapters of this volume comprise edited presentations. For the most part, these are think-pieces and briefs, and should not be held to the standards expected of academic research papers that are normally found in edited books or journal articles.

Secondly, while most insights remain relevant, it must nevertheless be emphasized that the presentations printed here were delivered in their original form in January 1992. Finally, most of our participants were employed in government, public or other institutions. Some have joined such institutions since the Ginosar Conference. In all cases they delivered their presentations at the conference in their private capacity. Thus, none of the comments they have made should be viewed as reflecting the institutions to which they belonged or that they have joined since the conference was held.

The conference presentations addressed five main topics. Anthony Cordesman and Barry Posen laid the foundations by elaborating the role of arms and military systems in the Middle East, and their implications for the prospects for arms control in the region. Cordesman's analysis questions whether the magnitude of the problem propelling interest in Middle East arms control--fear that the huge quantities of advanced weapons acquired by the region's states will result in great harm--is as serious as most observers believe. He argues persuasively that most of the region's military establishments manifest gross mismanagement and structural inefficiencies. Their governments insist on purchasing NATO-standard state-of-the-art weapons that are usually more advanced than anything the human and military infrastructure of these states can absorb. These systems are also very expensive, limiting the number of units that can be purchased. At the same time, advanced weapons are far more dependent than area weapons on the efficient functioning of the integrated command, control, communications and intelligence (C^3I) support system. Yet most of the region's states lack such efficient support systems, while their dependence on outside technical support presents a serious constraint on the use of military force. As a consequence, these states can derive much less output from their arms than their high military expenditures would otherwise indicate. In turn, this means that their armed forces can do far less damage than most observers expect.

Cordesman's analysis also questions the commonly held premise that the proliferation of advanced weapons is particularly worrisome. Indeed, he argues that "high technology conflicts have tended to be quick and decisive and to produce far fewer casualties than long civil conflicts or prolonged conflicts between military forces with only moderate capability." This is probably because precision weapons kill far fewer people around the targets they hit, thus resulting in fewer casualties than those associated with the use of 'traditional' area weapons. In any case, Cordesman's point illustrates that concern about casualty rates cannot be a credible motive for arresting the spread of advanced conventional munitions.

Cordesman also points out the dynamics of the many different conflicts throughout the Middle East. This has significant implications for arms control, because in contrast to Europe, where the existence of a single conflict allowed an assessment of relative military power, such a yardstick for ascertaining 'military balance' does not exist in the Middle East.

Barry Posen proposes a different yet complementary cause for the difficulty of calculating a military balance in the Middle East. He points out that conventional military systems are quite fragile and that the military forces of different states are very dissimilar--much more than they appear to the superficial eye. This is particularly the case when 'traditional' military establishments confront systems that are structured along a new format--the "Thorough Exploitation of Science and Technology (TEST)." Posen points out that it is "the integrated application on the battlefield of capabilities laboriously developed in peacetime, supported by a military, scientific and industrial infrastructure that is active not only in peacetime, but capable of direct participation, even in a short war, that gives the new format its remarkable capability."

Posen argues that the IDF is the only military force in the region that meets the characteristics of the TEST format. Thus it would be difficult to apply conventional arms control not only because it would not be easy to estimate a balance between military systems that do not meet TEST standards with the IDF, but also because Israel "would need to preserve this asymmetrical advantage over the Arab war coalition. This advantage was hard won; it would drastically reduce Israeli casualties in any future conflict. Hence, it is almost inconceivable that the Israeli military would give up this advantage in the framework of an arms control agreement."

The second issue addressed in the framework of the conference was the threat perceptions of Israel and the Arab states. Ascertaining these threats is exceedingly important, since the region's states are likely to view any future arms control agreement as an avenue for alleviating the threats they face. Ephraim Kam analyzes the Arab states' threat perceptions and points to a further difficulty facing the prospects for arms control in the region: the multiple sources of the threats perceived. For example Syria, while fearing Israel, also fears Iraq and Turkey. Indeed, as Kam argues, "during the last decade the threat cluster in the [Persian] Gulf overshadowed, at least for some Arab states, even the perceived Israeli threat." Thus Saudi Arabia's fears of Iraq and Iran seem greater than its concerns regarding Israel. These multiple sources of threats render difficult indeed the task of designing a new regional equilibrium through arms control or any other means.

Dore Gold analyzes Israel's threat perceptions, and points out that as a consequence of positive developments in the region-- such as the enduring Israeli-Egyptian peace, the Arabs' loss of their Soviet patrons, and the divisions in the Arab world manifested in the 1990-91 Gulf War--the threat Israel faces has lost its specificity. Nevertheless, these developments might reverse course, thus exposing Israel once again to the constant and basic vulnerabilities that result from the long-standing asymmetries characterizing the relationships between Israel and its neighbors. These include asymmetries in size and in potential for coalition formation, and the asymmetries in numbers and force structures between the IDF and the large Arab war machines.

The third part of our conference was devoted to a preliminary discussion of the prospects of arresting the arms race in the Middle East. Ariel Levite elaborates a rather pessimistic view of the prospects for arms control in the region. He points out the continued appeal of acquiring high performance and ever more exotic conventional weapons, and the increasing interest in the acquisition of ballistic missiles. He discusses the role of civil and active defense programs, possibly propelling the region's states to acquire ever more robust forces in order to maintain strategic deterrence. He emphasizes the spreading perception that the utility of chemical arsenals is limited, resulting in increased

7

interest in nuclear weapons. He also argues that perceptions that supplier regimes may be tightening controls might encourage the region's states to pursue preemptive purchases. Finally, he addresses the impact of the increased range of weapons in expanding the states' threat horizons: states which earlier did not figure in other states' threat assessments must now be taken into account, since for the first time they possess systems that can deliver munitions and do great harm to the assessing state.

Levite also argues that the character of most Middle East governments presents serious limitations on the prospects for applying arms control in the region. He notes the propensity of some of the region's states to adopt a rather flimsy attitude regarding the need to comply with agreements they have signed; the likelihood that, having undertaken such agreements with the full intention to comply, the regime might abruptly disappear and be replaced by a new government that does not consider itself bound by commitments undertaken by its predecessors. Finally, the rather careless approach that some of the region's states have adopted regarding safety and environmental issues, produces less responsible modes of storing weapons. This must affect assumptions that have traditionally guided the design and application of verification methods.

Patrick Clawson provides a provocative critique of the economic rationale for conventional arms control. First, he argues that most Middle East states are perfectly capable of sustaining their current high level of arms purchases. He demonstrates this point through the examples of Syria and Israel. He claims that Syria's newly-earned $2-3 billion in annual oil revenues compensates for its loss of previous Soviet subsidies for its arms acquisitions, and that Israel could increase its military spending by 50%, if it were willing to return to the levels of taxation it applied during 1986-87.

Clawson also argues that the conclusion of peace agreements in the Middle East would not necessarily lead the states involved to reduce their defense expenditures. This is because such accords will result in serious military dislocations, such as the loss of expensive facilities which would need to be substituted, and the need to gain the support of the respective military establishments by 'bribery.' Finally, Clawson argues that the incentive to reduce defense expenditures perceived by the region's states is in any case limited, since "lower military spending would not lead to greater economic growth." This is because the money saved is not likely to be channeled to investments that would generate economic growth, and because the economic impact of defense expenditures is not entirely negative. Clawson points out that economic growth in the Middle East requires structural reform, not more financial resources. He further argues that much of the foreign assistance that was channeled to the Middle East was politically motivated, and most probably would not have been provided without the rationale and requirements generated by the Arab-Israel conflict.

Christophe Carle presents a French perspective on the prospects for arms control in the Middle East. He notes that the gap between the US and French approaches to arms control have narrowed in recent years, partly due to the "increasingly common recognition that over time and in many cases, the spread of sensitive knowledge and its technological and industrial applications in the military realm are indeed inevitable." Carle also identifies greater American willingness to accept the French view that regards "some instances of proliferation as reflecting legitimate sovereign self-defense needs that result from genuine security concerns." On the other hand, France also moved closer to the US-led non-proliferation consensus by joining the NPT.

On the other hand, France remains critical of important aspects of Washington's approach to non-proliferation. Arms exports assume ever greater importance for the survival of the French military industries. It also sees the US approach as suffering a "gap between the advertised intention to implement restraints on the one hand, and the magnitude of agreed and foreseeable US sales to the Middle East and the Gulf on the other hand." In reality, the US, France and other European states share an identical but competing interest in marketing their arms for foreign sales aggressively, thus making the prospects for supplier restraint less than promising.

9

Carle also examines the implications of Israel's nuclear posture on the prospects for arms control in the Middle East, and questions the merits of Israel's continued nuclear ambiguity. He argues that the claim that an explicit Israeli posture would accelerate regional proliferation does not hold ground, since Israeli ambiguity did not constrain Iraq and Iran from launching their nuclear programs. He also predicts that such a change in Israel's posture would not be heavily criticized, since the world already regards Israel as a nuclear state: "The fiction of Israeli nuclear virginity is wearing so thin that no one takes it at face value anymore." In his view, Israel can in any case easily sustain external pressures since "there is no credible scenario for Israeli denuclearization in the foreseeable future. Neither is it possible to argue that Israel has any less reason than France to maintain a nuclear security-insurance policy over the long term." Yet the effects of continued ambiguity on the prospects for arms control are negative because "there can be no valid and credible arms control and disarmament without transparency."

The fourth focus of the Ginosar Conference comprised an effort to examine the experience of other regions in arms control. Jerome Paolini's presentation examines the possibility that the negotiations and agreement on Conventional Forces in Europe (CFE) might serve as a model for arms control in the Middle East. Paolini stresses that one of the most important lessons of NATO-Warsaw Pact arms control is that fundamental political preconditions are indispensable if concrete results are to be achieved. He argues that until such preconditions were achieved, "arms control had little to do with disarmament: it was about managing the nuclear arms race and attempting to foster strategic stability between superpowers." Indeed, the lesson of the CFE is that "arms control generates very few positive results when implemented without a political settlement of the confrontation at stake." Thus, the key to the CFE's success was that by the time the negotiations were opened, the strategic and political context in Europe had been completely altered following the advent of Michael Gorbachev.

Paolini also stresses a number of pertinent lessons that could be drawn from the experience gained with the CFE negotiations format: that arms control should be conceived as an element of a comprehensive peace process; that negotiations should be restricted to the region's states, even if the problems involved are relevant to extra-regional parties as well; and that negotiations should be conducted by sovereign states and should not follow an Arab-Israeli coalition negotiation format.

Paolini warns that "defining conventional stability in a truly multipolar negotiation would be very difficult." In his view, the experience with CFE suggests that conventional arms control should be negotiated separately from nuclear issues and that acceptance of the principle of asymmetric cuts is a prerequisite to success. Within this context, Israel might have to trade reductions in its air-power for significant cuts in the Arabs' ground forces.

Wlodzimierz Konarski follows with some lessons that could be drawn from the architecture and dynamics of the Conference on Security and Cooperation in Europe (CSCE). Konarski emphasizes the importance of a CSCE-type process and the confidence-building measures adopted in its framework, when conditions are not yet suitable for arms reductions. Indeed, he argues that without this CBM infrastructure, the later CFE arms reductions agreement could not have been concluded. He also stresses the importance of the rule of consensus in insuring the survival and endurance of the CSCE.

Konarski points out that the success of a CSCE-type process in the Middle East would depend on the political will of the region's states; on the extent to which they would regard the peace process as progressing at a rate that promises eventual success; on the adoption of a framework based on the principle of equal rights; and on the contribution of outside powers--primarily the US--to the framework's success.

Shekhar Gupta shares with the conference participants the experience of applying CBMs in the India-Pakistan context. These include competitions and sports between soldiers of the two countries; the establishment of 'hot lines'--aimed at preventing inadvertent escalation--between local commanders on the two sides

11

of the border; the conduct of so-called 'flag meetings' between commanders, aimed at resolving practical problems; and the agreement on non-attack of nuclear installations.

Gupta argues that confidence building would have advanced further had India not rejected Pakistan's proposal that a five-power (India, Pakistan, Russia, China, and the US) conference be held to discuss the nuclear issue in South Asia. He also recommends that India open its borders to Pakistanis, and that Pakistan allow the selling of Indian books and magazines. Ultimately, he says, "people from both countries have to sit down and clean up school textbooks reciprocally."

Gupta also makes a controversial point: "the first prerequisite for any serious confidence-building regime between India and Pakistan is that these two states go overt with their nuclear programs." Gupta argues that confidence cannot be built around ambiguity, because one cannot be assured who controls the weapons. Also, ambiguity does not allow the development of public awareness regarding the strategic and other consequences of nuclear weapons.

The final focus of our conference deliberations comprised an effort to examine various facets of the US approach to non-proliferation. Geoffrey Kemp places the efforts of the Bush administration to arrest proliferation in historical context, illustrating that while America's record in this context was impressive, its desire to support close friends and allies--Israel, Saudi Arabia and Iran--often propelled it to transfer state-of-the-art weapons.

Kemp argues that these conflicting pressures on US policy were only reinforced by the experience of the Gulf War: It "highlighted the dangers of what happens when a Saddam Hussein is allowed access to advanced military technologies. But at the same time it demonstrated that US military operations can derive much benefit from a close military assistance relationship with Saudi Arabia. Had it not been for the massive buildup of infrastructure in Saudi Arabia during the 1980s, Desert Storm might never have happened."

12

Kemp points out that these dilemmas continue to characterize US policy. Thus, a "successful global nuclear non-proliferation policy would make it more difficult to exempt friends and allies in the region from controls." But US interests in the Middle East, particularly in the Gulf region, would continue to require arms sales to key Arab countries.

William Keller follows by emphasizing the pressures exerted by the defense sectors of the advanced industrial countries to continue the export of arms. Given the post-Cold War cutbacks in the defense budgets of these states, and the resulting diminished demand for weapons from their respective arms manufacturers, production lines would have to be closed in the absence of compensating arms exports. Keller considers the result a "failure to bring together two different policy arenas--the defense industrial base community and the foreign policy community. Each has a separate legislative history, a separate stream of documentation, its own language, lobbyists, experts and expectations."

Keller argues that in the realm of defense industries, the most important recent development has been internationalization: "Companies from different countries have entered into strategic alliances, joint ventures, licensed production and codevelopment activities, and many other forms of joint R&D and dynamic technology transfer." In his view, "the result is a state of affairs in which advanced defense equipment and technology has proliferated beyond the control of any single state or group of states, with profound implications for the future of the Middle East."

Lise Hartman then analyzes America's role in efforts to arrest the proliferation of ballistic missiles. She argues that the US became concerned about the issue in the course of the 1980s, when US decisionmakers became aware of the possible impact of the proliferation of these weapons on Israeli security and the security of US troop concentrations in the region. By 1987, this concern--shared by a number of other missile producers--led to the joint articulation of the Missile Technology Control Regime (MTCR).

Hartman argues that producing ballistic missiles, especially for countries lacking an advanced industrial base, is difficult in and of itself. By making it hard to acquire key sub-components, the constraints imposed by the regime are intended to increase these difficulties, thereby also making the costs of missile production prohibitive. The real test of the MTCR has been the extent to which the various member states have been willing to translate its stipulations into domestic rules and regulations. In this context the relevant US legislation--the Missile Technology Control Act (MTCA)--has acquired an impressive record.

Zachary Davis then elaborates the mechanisms available to the US Congress in shaping America's non-proliferation efforts. These include the holding of hearings; requiring the administration to provide it with certain reports; attaching conditions to proposed military and economic assistance; assigning responsibility to existing or newly-created agencies within the federal bureaucracy; imposing sanctions on violators of US non-proliferation policy; and legislating various forms of support for multilateral efforts to control the spread of conventional and nonconventional arms.

The final presentation, delivered by Lewis Dunn, provides an American scholar's view of the impact of the nuclear agenda on the Middle East. Dunn points out that the global nuclear agenda is in the midst of fundamental change: nuclear deterrence is irrelevant to the challenges presented by the breakup of the Soviet Union. His assessment is that the nuclear status quo in the Middle East is unstable, since Arab states will not accept Israel's nuclear monopoly. Dunn also argues that if nuclear weapons spread in the Middle East, the region will become unstable, partly because the states involved may emphasize readiness at the expense of weapon safety.

Dunn recommends that Israel exercise unilateral self-restraint in the nuclear realm. He argues that such restraint would enhance the legitimacy of unilateral measures, including covert or direct military action, for blocking proliferation in the Middle East. Finally, Dunn acknowledges that the long-term solution to avoiding a multi-nuclear Middle East requires the political resolution of the Arab-Israeli dispute. But he warns that, given

14

current nuclear developments in the region, the time required for this resolution may not be available.

In conclusion, we hope that this volume will constitute a modest contribution to the embryonic literature available to scholars and practitioners regarding the prospects for arms control in the Middle East.

Part I

Arms Races and War

In the Middle East

2. Current Trends in Arms Sales in the Middle East

Anthony H. Cordesman

Before one can solve a problem, one has to understand it. This is as true of arms sales as of any other human activity. It is all too easy to condemn arms transfers to the Middle East for their impact in shaping regional conflicts, and all too easy to encourage arms sales as a means of encouraging regional stability. Neither approach is correct: sweeping efforts to embargo all arms transfers will not prevent conflicts; blank checks, even to friendly countries, will not bring security.

The problems that shape the arms race in the Maghreb, in the Arab-Israeli balance, in the Gulf, and in the Red Sea area cannot be dealt with by oversimplifying extremely complex problems or treating all nations alike. Both arms control and arms transfers must instead be tailored to an understanding of the dynamics of the military balance in each state and subregion of the Middle East, the reasons states are searching to improve force quality and force quantity, the motivations of seller as well as buyer states, and issues like proliferation.

Any effort to understand these problems must begin with an understanding of the multiple problems and limitations plaguing the available data. There are only three major sources of data on the overall patterns in the arms trade: the United Nations, the Stockholm International Peace Research Institute, and the declassified portion of the US intelligence community data base that is reported in part in CIA handbooks, in the Arms Control and Disarmament Agency's annual *World Military Expenditures and Arms Transfers*, and in Richard F. Grimmett's annual study for the Congressional Research Service, *Trends in Conventional Arms Transfers to the Third World by Major Supplier*.

Individual aspects of the work done on arms transfers by the United Nations and the Stockholm International Peace

Research Institute are excellent, but neither the UN nor SIPRI can hope to produce independent estimates of the broad patterns in arms transfers that are accurate. The Arms Control and Disarmament Agency's annual *World Military Expenditures and Arms Transfers*, drawing on inputs of intelligence estimates, is unquestionably the best source available on the overall patterns by individual state and region. Similarly, Grimmett's annual study draws on declassified data to provide the most up-to-date estimate in terms of overall transfers, although it does not provide anything like the detail of the ACDA document. Even these two sources suffer from multiple problems of data and analysis.

In spite of these problems, the most recently released US data on arms transfers to the Middle East do seem to provide a reasonably good picture of the overall flow of arms.

Total Regional Arms Transfers Through 1990

Data from the Arms Control and Disarmament Agency (ACDA) indicate that Middle Eastern countries spent some $180 billion on arms imports during 1978-1988, with $104 billion of this total being spent during 1984-1988.[1] The major states in the region consumed some 30-33% of the world's arms imports, versus 9-10% for NATO, 8-11% for the Warsaw Pact, 7-13% for East Asia, 11-12% for Africa, 10% for South Asia and Oceania, and 7-8% for Latin America.[2]

If the ACDA percentages showing arms transfers to the Middle East included Libya, Algeria, Tunisia, and Morocco as part of the Middle East, the annual percentage of world arms imports would always have exceeded 40 percent.[3] Six of the ten largest importers in the world are in the Middle East: they are Iraq, Saudi Arabia, Iran, Libya, Syria and Egypt.

Data analyzed by Grimmett of the Congressional Research Service (CRS), covering the period from 1983-1990,[4] indicate that the Middle East remains the largest arms market in the Third World. In 1983-1986, the Middle East accounted for over 61% of the total value of all Third World arms transfer agreements. During 1987-1990, the region accounted for 55.7% of all such agreements. The Middle East has also had the largest value of arms deliveries received by the Third World. In 1983-1986, it accounted for 62.5% of the total value of all Third World arms deliveries. During 1987-1990, it accounted for 50.8% of all such deliveries.

Several important facts about Middle East arms imports hold true irrespective of which time period is chosen during the period from 1960 onwards:

> **There are major differences in the pattern of new agreements and deliveries.** Deliveries lag agreements by up to half a decade, and often involve substantial changes in the agreement.
>
> **The lag between agreements and deliveries often makes it difficult to relate weapons deliveries and the buildup of Middle Eastern forces to the cause of the original arms order.** In general, however, most orders are driven by local conflicts within the region. Belligerents tend to rush orders during the conflict. Surrounding states place precautionary orders that often lag behind several years more.
>
> **There is a great deal of volatility in the total size of orders and deliveries in any given period.** For example, 1983-1986 reflects the peak of the Iran-Iraq War, the aftermath of Israel's invasion of Lebanon, and a period of sharp tension in the Maghreb. The period from 1987-1988 reflects a ceasefire in the Iran-Iraq War and a Gulf War where major imports could not be delivered in time to affect the Middle Eastern states in the Coalition, and Iraq faced an arms embargo, when military tensions between Israel and Syria were comparatively limited, and when the Maghreb states exhibited less tension and faced serious internal economic problems.
>
> **The role of given supplier states varies sharply over time.** US and Soviet flows have previously tended to vary according to the alignment of each power with given states in the region, while European suppliers have

21

experienced "boom and bust" sales patterns as they compete for major sales. More recently, developing country suppliers like China and North Korea have come to play a major role, while the Soviet Union and Eastern Europe have substituted concern over hard currency for concern over ideology.

Patterns of Conflict and Military Buildup

The war to liberate Kuwait between the United Nations-led coalition and Iraq is only one more conflict in a long history of the conflicts within the Middle East. Arms orders in the Middle East have been determined and shaped by a complex set of sub-conflicts which have swept across the region from Morocco to the Indian Ocean.[5] Virtually every state in the region has been involved in some form of local arms race, and many states are involved in what have become enduring internal and external conflicts.

Morocco, Mauritania, and Algeria have been involved in a complex political struggle for control over the destiny of the Spanish Sahara which has lasted well over a decade. In spite of various peace efforts, Morocco has remained at war with the Polisario--a movement which claims to represent the citizens of the Spanish Sahara.

The ambitions of Libya's leader, Colonel Qaddafi, have sustained an arms race throughout the Maghreb, which has affected many states outside it. Libya has played a spoiler role in most of the conflicts in the Middle East, has fought a series of wars with various factions in Chad, and has attempted to intervene in several other Subsaharan countries.

Egypt has become the "corner" of the Middle East. It must live with sustained tension with Libya, must continue to maintain its defenses against Israel, played a significant role in the Gulf War, and has increasingly become involved in the problems of the Sudan and its other Red

Sea and African neighbors, and fears the Islamic threat posed by Sudan and Iran.

The Arab-Israel conflict is now largely a struggle between Israel and Syria, but indirectly it involves every Arab state, and compels Jordan and Lebanon to play the role of front-line states. These conflicts between states have been exacerbated by the Palestinian uprising on the West Bank and Gaza, and by a Jordanian and PLO alignment with Iraq during the Gulf War. Although peace negotiations have begun, a lasting war of attrition between Israeli Jews and the Arabs in the occupied territories is equally likely. The various Palestinian movements are involved not only in a conflict with Israel, but often with Arab states and each other. There are splits within the PLO and other factions outside the occupied territories, splits within the factions supporting the PLO inside the West Bank and Gaza, and divisions between those Palestinians who support the PLO and the rising fundamentalist movements within the West Bank and Gaza.

Lebanon seems to be slowly emerging from nearly two decades of civil war between various Christian, Druze, Sunni, and Shi'ite factions. Although much of the country has come under central government control since Syria's defeat of General Aoun in the fall of 1990, some elements of the Lebanese civil war continue. Lebanon continues to be occupied by Syrian forces, and an Israeli-backed enclave has virtual autonomy in the south.

Syria continues to expand its forces despite massive economic problems, and the loss of much of its Soviet support. In addition to its conflict with Israel, it has been a constant rival of Iraq, an occasional rival of Jordan, and has supported outside movements such as the Kurdish independence movement in Turkey.

The combined heritage of the Iran-Iraq War and the Gulf War has severely weakened the military forces of the Gulf states. However, while neither Iran nor Iraq now poses an immediate threat to their Southern Gulf neighbors, both continue to seek arms and weapons of mass destruction, and may well go back to war with each other.

The Southern Gulf states have created a regional alliance called the Gulf Cooperation Council (GCC), and have attempted to strengthen their armed forces. However, the apparent unity of the GCC disguises rivalries between Bahrain and Qatar, Saudi Arabia and Oman, the key sheikhs of the UAE, and Saudi Arabia and Yemen.

North and South Yemen have unified, ostensibly ending decades of mutual rivalry. The new Yemen, however, is involved in a simmering conflict over the demarcation of its borders with Saudi Arabia, and Oman. There are continuing border clashes between Yemen and Saudi Arabia, and Yemen and Oman still deploy much of their military strength along their common border.

The Sudan is involved in a protracted civil war between the Muslim north and the Christian and animist South: a war in which Egypt, Libya, and several Gulf nations play an indirect role.

The long civil war in Ethiopia, between the dominant ethnic groups in the South and Arab-backed Muslim groups in the North, seems to have ended in 1991. Its Marxist regime and armed forces have collapsed, and the country is now governed by the Ethiopian People's Revolutionary Front (EPRF), the Eritrean People's Liberation Front (EPLF), the Oromo People's Democratic Organization and other smaller groups. It is far from clear, however, that the result will be order and stability; new civil conflicts may soon arise. Ethiopia remains involved in a low level struggle with Somalia for control of their common border area.

The civil war in Somalia between its northern and central tribal factions ended with the defeat of the Siad Barre government in 1991, but Somalia is now divided between regions controlled by the Somali National Movement in the North and the United Somali Congress in the south.

It no longer has unified armed forces, and may well return to a state of civil war.

The Casualty Effect

There have been shooting wars somewhere in the Middle East during virtually the entire period since 1945. Many have been small border wars or minor clashes which have gone virtually unrecorded. The present border conflict between Saudi Arabia and Yemen is a case in point. Some have been very intense high technology conflicts like the 1967, 1973, and 1982 Arab-Israel conflicts, the Iran-Iraq War of 1980-1988, and the Gulf War of 1990-1991. Others have involved protracted low technology conflicts for independence or between ethnic groups like those in North Africa and the Red Sea area--many of which have been extraordinarily bloody.

Upon closer examination several other insights into the problem of arms sales to the Middle East can be offered:

The pattern of conflicts within given states and sub-regions varies sharply over time, and low level conflicts often shift without warning into major struggles. It is almost a cliche to say that war is not predictable in terms of its timing, duration and intensity. This is particularly important because 1991 has to some extent presaged a period of exhaustion in many aspects of the Middle East arms race. The military forces of Iran and Iraq have been decimated by the Iran-Iraq War and Gulf War; the southern Gulf states are limited in their arms purchases by the cost of purchases made during 1990 and aid to the UN Coalition; the Red Sea states are financially exhausted by civil war and many have lost most of their regular forces to rebel groups; the Arab-Israeli arms race has been tempered by the economic problems of the major confrontation states; and the arms race in North Africa has enjoyed a temporary hiatus. These, however, are forces of coincidence, not forces of history.

There has been only a limited correlation between the volume of arms imports and cost of given conflicts. Casualties are more the product of political conditions than the volume of weapons. Civil wars, or conflicts involving civil strife, tend to be far more bloody than direct conflicts between states. Static wars, involving guerrilla conflict, trench warfare, or tactical conditions that prevent battles from reaching clear decisions, tend to be far more bloody than wars of maneuver.

Perhaps more importantly, in terms of some of the trends to be discussed later, is that so far there has been little correlation between the volume of arms imports, high technology and high casualties--in fact, high technology conflicts have tended to be quick and decisive and to produce far fewer casualties than long civil conflicts or prolonged conflicts between military forces with only moderate capability. This pattern has, of course been dependent on two critical restraints in past conflicts: the failure to make large scale and/or effective use of weapons of mass destruction; and the fact that high technology conflicts have not generally involved population centers, but have been restricted largely to counterforce attacks by opposing military forces.

The Burden of Military Expenditures

There is an inevitable interaction between arms sales and military expenditures. Upon comparison of the relevant statistics, it becomes obvious that five additional factors drive both the expenditure patterns and the flow of arms sales:

The first factor is the virtual institutionalization of most conflicts and tensions in the region. Expenditures tend to peak during the period before, during, and after actual conflict, but each successive military encounter generally fails to resolve the political problems that led to war. The resulting peace settlements and ceasefires tend to be limited or temporary. Major victories are rare, and are often fleeting when they do occur. Changes in regime and political system rarely produce any meaningful lasting change in external relations. The end result is that the factors leading to military spending and larger military forces rarely change over time.

The second factor is the catalyst effect. Major fighting in any given conflict tends to trigger an acceleration of the arms race throughout a broad part of the region. The Arab-Israel conflicts of 1967, 1973, and 1982 are obvious cases in point. So are the Iran-Iraq War and the Gulf War. The conflicts between Morocco and the Polisario, and Libya and Chad, have had more contained effects, but have indirectly impacted on the entire Maghreb and most of the Red Sea countries. Even major out-of-area conflicts like the Falklands War usually trigger new spending on advanced technology and new forms of force structure.

The third factor is technology. The Middle Eastern states are increasingly seeking to obtain and operate the most advanced tactical systems available to NATO and Warsaw Pact countries. Even when Middle Eastern countries lack the capability to absorb advanced technology effectively, they still tend to buy the most advanced weapons available. Virtually all the regional arms races between given countries or groups of countries are also races to obtain the most advanced weapons and military technology available.

The fourth factor is increasing real cost per weapon or force element. The acquisition of more sophisticated weapons and technology has produced sharp rises in real cost per weapon, or type of weapons, during the last decade. These increases in cost have been particularly severe since 1986, because of a more rapid increase in the real cost of weapons platforms, and the resulting need for more training and use of foreign technicians, the need for new military facilities and operations and maintenance

(O&M) and other support capabilities, and the need for more expensive munitions and military electronics. Further, most arms-importing states have found it far harder to get easy credit terms since the early 1980s. The US has sharply reduced aid to all states except Israel and Egypt, and the USSR has largely abolished both aid and barter transactions and long term credits.

The fifth factor is oil. While the real oil incomes of Middle Eastern states have fluctuated sharply since the massive oil boom following 1973, oil wealth has fueled the arms race throughout the region. It was the massive rise in oil prices after 1974, for example, that drove much of the arms race that followed. It was the collapse of oil prices in the mid-1980s that led to the dip in spending shown for many countries during the late 1980s--although recent rises in oil prices have eased this trend in some countries. At other times, the increase in military forces has been shaped by military assistance and sales from states outside the region. Examples include US military sales and assistance to Egypt and Israel, and Soviet-bloc sales to Algeria, Ethiopia, Iraq, Libya, Syria and Yemen.

Our analysis reveals that levels of military effort vary by subregion within the Middle East. The arms race in the Maghreb is limited in scale by the standards of the Gulf and the Arab-Israel conflict, although all the Maghreb states still spend enough to seriously damage their economies and long-term prospects for development. For example, Morocco's long war with the Polisario, and tensions with Algeria, have been particularly damaging. Libya's "spoiler" role throughout the region has consumed much of that country's vast oil wealth, and has forced its neighbors into high levels of defense expenditure. Egypt has suffered from being caught in a triangle of tension with Libya, instability in the Red Sea, and the failure to reach a comprehensive Arab-Israeli peace settlement. These external threats and pressures have deprived Egypt of much of the benefit of the Camp David Accords.

The states involved in the Arab-Israel conflict rank second in terms of expenditure, and first in terms of military manpower. The Arab-Israeli arms race has, however, undergone some significant structural changes over time. No longer can Egypt be regarded as a confrontation state. The Camp David Accords of 1978 produced the only major peace agreement in the area, with the possible exception of the accords between Oman and the PDRY in the mid-1980s. Jordan has also shifted from a leading military power to a "sideshow" caught in the arms race between Israel, Syria, and Iraq. Jordan's forces are still highly professional, but Jordan lacks the manpower and money to compete with its larger neighbors. The continuing disintegration of Lebanon has largely removed it from the regional arms race as an active state, but Lebanon remains a killing ground for its warring ethnic groups and is the scene of recurrent military intervention by Israel and Syria.

Israel remains far more capable of absorbing and operating advanced military technology than any other Middle Eastern state, but it has experienced serious problems in funding its forces in spite of massive US aid. Syria and Egypt made significant progress in improving their training and readiness between 1982 and 1987, but have since suffered from serious financing problems and have seen a significant overall decline in readiness and the ability to absorb and operate advanced military technology.

The most costly subregion in terms of military expenditure and arms imports is the Gulf states. Gulf states are able to afford large military expenditures and arms sales for states their size, although the southern Gulf states--Bahrain, Kuwait, Oman, Qatar, Saudi Arabia, and the United Arab Emirates--are severely constrained in manpower.

All the Gulf states have limited indigenous ability to fully absorb advanced military technology. Iran and Iraq should be most able to make effective use of their defense expenditures, but both face problems with "self-inflicted wounds." In spite of considerable oil wealth, the Iran-Iraq War has placed an immense financial burden on both Iran and Iraq, costing well over $70 billion in arms imports alone. Iran has not been able to recover from the mix of revolution and the loss of most of its military equipment due to a western arms embargo and defeats in May-August 1988, that cost it nearly 40% of its ground forces' equipment. Iraq's debt burden is one factor that led it to invade Kuwait, and its war with the UN coalition has cost it hundreds of billions of dollars worth of military equipment.

Bahrain, Kuwait, Oman, Qatar, Saudi Arabia, and the United Arab Emirates all lack the pool of trained manpower to develop large high technology forces, and all have imported more equipment than they can effectively use. In spite of the creation of the Gulf Cooperation Council (GCC) during the Iran-Iraq War, military cooperation exists largely in name. There is little standardization. Each of the small Gulf states develops its forces in relative isolation, and faces massive diseconomies of scale that rob its military expenditures of much of their effectiveness. Only Oman and Saudi Arabia can man their forces with native manpower, and they have serious manpower problems in terms of both quality and quantity. The Saudi Air Force is the only force in the southern Gulf that is moderately effective by western standards.

The Red Sea region spends less on military forces than the other three major subregions within the Middle East, but it may well suffer the most from actual fighting. The PDRY has wasted much of its national wealth in a civil war and in competing with Oman. The YAR has fought a low level civil war with Saudi Arabia. While the PDRY and YAR have merged, it is far too soon to determine what this really means.

The southern edge of the Red Sea region has been a politico-military disaster area. Ethiopia has been caught in a brutal civil war for more than a decade, and in low level border conflicts with Somalia and the Sudan. Somalia has plunged from tribal feuding, and conflict with Ethiopia, to its own civil war. The Sudan collapsed into a lasting civil war in the early 1980s, and shows no sign of recovery. In combination with famine and gross mismanagement of the economy, these tensions and conflicts have killed at least several million human beings over the last decade. While Ethiopia has recently emerged from its civil war with something approaching a democratic government, and the emergence of an independent Eritrea, it is far from clear that it will not splinter into ethnic enclaves or return to civil war.

What virtually all Middle Eastern states have in common is the fact that regional pressures have driven their military spending to levels far beyond what developing states can afford. It cannot be stressed too firmly that the expenditure of every country in the Middle East on military forces is so high that it seriously limits economic growth and the provision of key services ranging from education to improvements in infrastructure. These pressures are particularly severe in the case of non-oil exporting states like Egypt, Israel, and Syria. Even rich oil exporting states like Saudi Arabia, however, are spending far too much on defense, and this often drives them into debt or seriously distorts their economies by funneling too much of the nation's best manpower into military forces.

The pattern of defense spending in the Middle East also raises severe questions about the future. Most Middle Eastern states already have a serious military debt because of past arms purchases. In many cases they cannot properly service this debt-- particularly in the cases of Egypt, Israel, Jordan, Morocco, and Syria. Yet the constant pace of improvement in military technology quickly makes the inventory of Middle Eastern states obsolescent.

The end effect is that few Middle Eastern states can afford to maintain their present level of capability, and most cannot possibly afford to modernize their current force structure. This leaves them with a number of unpleasant choices: (a) losing readiness and capability relative to their rivals; (b) making major cuts in force size to fund a smaller and more capable force; (c) going even deeper into debt with no real prospect of ever fully repaying that debt; or (d) turning to weapons of mass destruction as a "cheap" way of trying to get equivalent military capability.

Equipment Numbers: The Issue of Quantity

The equipment trends provide what may be the best simple measure of both the trends in arms sales and the trends in military capability. While the equipment commodities counted vary sharply in quality, as does the capacity of individual countries to use it effectively, it is clear that most countries have increased equipment numbers steadily over the last decade, and are likely to continue doing so in the future.

To put tanks and aircraft numbers in perspective, the Middle East now has some 23,000 main battle tanks and 3,800 combat aircraft--totals which have dropped sharply since 1990 because of the Gulf War and the disintegration of the regular armed forces of Ethiopia and Somalia. In contrast, the total active strength of all the main battle tanks in the NATO Central Region is around 8,000, while the total number of combat aircraft is around 1,400.

Yet, even NATO's most developed countries have trouble providing enough manpower, support, and sustainability to make these forces fully effective, although they have a far more capable manpower and technology base than any Middle Eastern state with the exception of Israel. Given the total numbers of equipment in many Middle Eastern states, it is obvious that many countries confuse sheer mass with military capability, and the "glitter factor" inherent in being able to buy the latest equipment with the ability to operate it effectively.

The force structures of the North African and Red Sea states are particularly poorly balanced in terms of overall ability to operate total national equipment holdings. Only Algeria, Morocco, and Egypt rise to even the lower levels of mediocrity, and most of the states in the region have low overall military capability. Libya's capabilities to use its military equipment are probably the worst of any major arms buyer in the world--nearly one-third of Libya's equipment holdings are in storage or inoperable.

Israel and Jordan do set relatively high standards. Iraq improved significantly under the pressure of the Iran-Iraq War, but partially demobilized after the war and had never recovered its effectiveness before its forces were shattered in the Gulf conflict. Syria improved during the period from 1982-1987, but then began to suffer from serious financial problems. As for the Southern Gulf states, Bahrain, Kuwait, Qatar, and the UAE are all heavily dependent on foreign mercenaries, and have more modern equipment than they can use effectively in combat. Oman lacks large numbers of heavy weapons. Saudi Arabia is able to operate most of its air equipment with reasonable effectiveness by the standards of the Gulf region, but can use only about half to two-thirds of its army equipment.

Qualitative Factors Affecting the Balance

During the last decade, there has also been a shift from an emphasis on mass, or force quantity, to an emphasis on force quality. This shift has been driven in large part by Israel's success in its 1967, 1970, 1973, and 1982 wars with its Arab neighbors. In each case, Israel demonstrated that its edge in technology more than overcame any advantage in numbers. Further, in each case, the resulting impact of new technologies on the conflict accelerated the race in technology versus the race in numbers.

Outside conflicts and arms races also played a powerful role in influencing this shift from increasing quantity to increasing quality. The dependence of regional states on East and West, and particularly on the US and Soviet Union, inevitably led them to mirror image the growing emphasis on technology in their supplier states. The US use of technology in Vietnam, and Soviet use of technology in Afghanistan, demonstrated the potential value of new weapons and technologies--although each superpower decisively lost its respective conflict.

Virtually all of these systems can increase military effectiveness, yet most also present growing problems for virtually every Middle East country.

Rising real cost. While no precise statistics are available, it is clear that the cost of new military equipment is rising far more quickly in real terms than either central government revenues or defense budgets. This rise in cost is made worse by the fact that new major weapons systems require far more costly munitions or missiles, and must be integrated into a highly complex sensor, and command, control, communications, and intelligence (C^3I) systems. The average cost of most items of major military equipment rose by at least 50% in constant dollars during the period between 1982 and 1990, and continues to rise at this rate.

Rising foreign debt. As was touched upon earlier, most Middle Eastern states already have a military debt for past equipment purchases which they cannot properly service. They cannot afford to maintain their present force structure and continue to modernize their present equipment.

Growing problems with absorption of more sophisticated technologies. The problems that Middle Eastern states face in acquiring and absorbing such technology, and in dealing with such transfers to unfriendly states, are also accelerating. A decade ago, there was usually a 5-10 year lag between the initial deployment of major new weapons systems in US, NATO, Soviet, and Warsaw Pact forces, and any large-scale sale of such arms to the developing world. That lag is now being eliminated. Western Europe is selling aircraft, armor, and ships to developing countries at the same time it introduces such systems to its own armed forces. Russia is not only selling its new MiG-29 fighters to India, Iraq, and Syria; it is also selling coproduction rights to India. Soviet SS-21 missiles appeared in Syrian forces almost at the same time they became fully operational in Soviet forces in East Germany.

Need for highly sophisticated associated systems. In most cases, the effective use of advanced weapons requires sophisticated intelligence, warning, command and control, communications, targeting, and battle damage assessment systems. These complex systems are extremely difficult for developing countries to create, maintain, and operate. They also add a major new dimension to force costs--sometimes doubling the cost of maintaining a national air force and increasing the cost of land forces by 25-33 percent. Further, such systems are vulnerable to countermeasures and technical change-- creating new uncertainties and modernization costs.

Force cuts or force ineffectiveness. These pressures have led to force cuts in some countries like Israel, and awkward and ineffective compromises between force quantity and force quality in most other states in the region. All the larger Arab states have tried to maintain force size while radically altering the technology mix of their forces. This has often led the countries involved to buy high cost weapons or systems that they lack the resources and skills to properly operate; they can only buy the facade of capability without the mix of associated weapons, munitions, command and control systems, training aid, maintenance facilities and other military capabilities necessary to make them effective.

The further complication of uncertain financing. These problems have been further compounded by the erratic delivery of military aid and shifts in oil prices--often forcing states into debt to buy new technologies while still leaving them without the resources to make what they have bought effective. Further, the internal politics of many states prevent them from eliminating units, military functions, and bases which no longer are effective, to save resources for the forces they need. This produces bloated and inefficient structures at every level, and often leaves major amounts of equipment in storage or in hollow units that are little more than military parking lots.

Hollow forces. As a result, most Middle Eastern forces often appear to be far more threatening in terms of force strength and weapons numbers than they are in terms of actual military capability. Only a small fraction of the major combat units in most countries are really effective, and the overall mix of command and control, sensor and communications, and support and logistic systems necessary to make even these units fully effective are lacking. Skilled manpower shortages are endemic--often compounded by wretched personnel policies and management and poor pay for skilled other ranks and junior officers.

At the same time, the pace of technological change, and/or increase in weapons strength, has additional important side effects.

First, it keeps all Middle Eastern states, except Israel, highly dependent on outside technical support and limits the value of most local efforts to develop a national arms industry. In spite of claims to the contrary, most Middle Eastern states remain dependent on outside resupply and technical advice. Further, almost all advanced weapons production in the Middle East--with the exception of some production in Israel and Iraq--consists of coproduction or the assembly of imported parts. This does not increase independence: such plants do not transfer real production or industrialization capability. Further, the net cost of coproduced equipment is virtually always far higher in real terms than buying fully assembled equipment that is produced efficiently and as part of longer production runs.

Second, it keeps most Middle Eastern forces in a constant state of military flux, and prevents effective training and organization. Far too large a percentage of the force structure of most Middle Eastern states is devoted to receiving new equipment that has to be retrained and reorganized. Coupled with force expansion, the end result is almost constant turbulence. Officers, NCOs, and technicians are forever being rotated and retrained. Units are constantly changing in structure. In many cases this turbulence has gone on for over a decade, and many units have never enjoyed enough stability to operate as coherent forces.

Finally, this pace of change makes effective manpower management virtually impossible. The constant need to train or retrain, while expanding the base of trained manpower, leads to nearly chaotic conditions for career and skilled personnel with technical specialties. The basic problems of changes in force structure and equipment are compounded by generally low administrative standards. Personnel are often trained without adequate language skills or education. Trained personnel are mis-assigned. Insufficient career incentives are provided for trained personnel. Traditional discipline cannot adjust to the creation of highly skilled NCO and junior officers and the need for highly skilled enlisted men.

At the same time, no Middle Eastern country can ignore the need for modernization. The local threats in the region are generally too real. States in the Middle East, and the outside states with capability to project power into the region, face a massive problem in terms of "conventional proliferation." Not only must they match potential threats in terms of equipment numbers; but they must match the new weapons technologies that will be present in the forces of hostile nations.

This complex mix of trends may benefit a few of the wealthier Gulf nations, which can afford to use technology to partially compensate for their limited ground strength. At the same time, it is unlikely that even these states will achieve enough of a technical "edge" over the equipment in the forces of potential threat states to compensate for their superior mass.

The rest of the states in the region are likely to face serious financial constraints on funding anything approaching an effective balance of manpower and equipment strength, manpower and equipment quality, and the necessary infrastructure and support capability. Given past trends, many are likely to spend most of their money on major weapons systems and will fail to fund the rest of the investment necessary to make their forces effective.

The trend toward high technology has put great pressure on Jordan and Oman, which have relatively effective forces, but which are particularly hard put to keep up with the race in military technology. Iran also faces the problem of rebuilding an obsolete and low grade mix of equipment and the manpower, training, and support base necessary to use advanced weaponry. Even Israel may find much of its qualitative edge diminishing--at least in terms of pure technology. But Israel is likely to retain or even increase its qualitative advantage in actually being able to use its advanced military equipment since all of the surrounding Arab states face serious--if not crippling--fiscal problems in funding a high technology force mix.

Trends in the Proliferation of Weapons of Mass Destruction

It is hardly surprising, given these broad patterns in the arms race in the Middle East, that many of the major military powers in the region are already involved in some aspect of proliferation. The wide range of interactive incentives for proliferation have had a powerful effect, and the search for weapons of mass destruction is scarcely new to the region. Israel first began examining nuclear options in the 1950s, and Egypt used poison gas against the Royalists during the Yemeni civil war in the 1960s. Israel had acquired a significant stockpile of nuclear weapons by 1967. Egypt and Libya sought both nuclear weapons and long range delivery systems, and Egypt and Syria were heavily equipped with chemical defense gear when they attacked Israel in 1973.

Nevertheless, recent politico-military developments have interacted with the patterns shaping the conventional arms race to accelerate the regional search for weapons of mass destruction:

The rising cost of conventional weapons, and the need for a cheaper "force multiplier;"

The availability of systems, key parts and equipment, and technical advice from a steadily widening number of European, Latin American, and Asian suppliers;

Iraq and Iran's use of poison gas in their war, and Iraq's use of poison gas against its rebellious Kurds;

Revelations of the size of Iraq's nuclear, chemical, and biological weapons and long-range delivery system efforts, and about Iran's nuclear efforts, chemical and biological efforts, and purchases of long-range missiles from North Korea;

A series of revelations about the size of the Israeli nuclear effort, and the fact that Israel may be developing missiles with IRBM ranges;

Syria's response to Israel in the form of the development of a capability to produce and deliver nerve gas and other chemical weapons;

Possible Soviet use of chemical weapons in Afghanistan;

India and Pakistan's development of nuclear and chemical weapons and long range missiles; and

Libya's possible use of poison gas during the final phases of its war in Chad, and its creation of a massive facility for the production of weapons of mass destruction;

Algeria's acquisition of a nuclear reactor that seems useful largely for nuclear weapons development purposes.

The end result is that virtually every Middle Eastern country with a major technology base, or large amounts of oil money, has begun some form of effort to develop or acquire weapons of mass destruction and suitable delivery systems--although many of these efforts remain at the precautionary or contingency stage. This race to proliferate has interacted with similar arms races in other regions. For example, with efforts like those of Argentina and Brazil to develop long-range missiles and the capability to make nuclear weapons, with similar efforts at proliferation in Asia, with South Africa's nuclear weapons and long-range missile effort, and with the search of various Western European firms and the PRC to enter the market for missiles, nuclear components, and the equipment needed for chemical and biological weapons.

It is true that most countries in the Middle East have not openly deployed weapons of mass destruction, and that many of the efforts in those states that are seeking to proliferate are still in their early stages. It is also true that past estimates of the probable rate of proliferation of weapons of mass destruction have been notoriously over-alarming, and estimates of the effects of the use of such weapons--particularly chemical and biological agents-- also tend to be exaggerated. Nevertheless, this new aspect of the regional arms race is all too real.

The Role of Arms Suppliers

If the military balance in the Middle East has been shaped by local conflicts and the flow of arms imports into the region, it has also been shaped by competition among arms sellers. The high levels of arms imports to the Middle East reflect both the past competition among the superpowers and NATO and the Warsaw Pact, and the new competition among seller nations in the West, Communist Bloc, and Third World to sell to the Middle East market. There is an inevitable interaction between the conflicts and tensions in the region, and the role of key supplier states.

A number of economic forces have driven the efforts of seller states. The increases that have taken place in European sales since the mid-1970s have been driven by an increasing need to export to maintain the viability of national arms industries--a pressure that is likely to grow sharply as NATO countries cut their defense investment in reaction to the demise of the Soviet Union. The Middle East is a market that averages well over $20 billion a year, and is immensely lucrative. Like other countries, European sellers have been able to capitalize on the US loss of sales to Arab states because of America's ties to Israel, and European arms sales have also enabled their industries to increase their production runs and make their military production and research and development activities efficient.

The hard currency benefits of arms sales have had an increasing impact on communist or ex-communist states. Ironically, the end of the Cold War has had a mixed impact on the USSR/Russia. Since 1988, Moscow has been far less willing to help fund the arms imports of states like Libya, Syria, Iraq, Ethiopia, and the Yemens simply to confront the West. It has, however, shown an increasing willingness to sell to all buyers, and has increasingly insisted on cash payment. Arms have become Moscow's second largest export item after oil, and have provided important sources of hard currency to Eastern Europe. Similar trends have emerged in several East European states, particularly Czechoslovakia, Rumania, and Yugoslavia.

As has been touched upon earlier, arms sales have increasingly attracted the PRC, North Korea, and other Third World states, particularly Latin American countries like Argentina and Brazil. The volume of PRC and other Third World arms sales has nearly doubled since 1986, and the PRC, North Korea, and Brazil are now far more important arms suppliers to the region than the Eastern European states.

These trends have led several Middle Eastern states to take advantage of the growing number of suppliers to diversify their sources of arms supply. These states have included Iraq, Jordan, Kuwait and Saudi Arabia. During 1977-1990, Iraq increasingly sought advanced technology from the West that it could not obtain from the USSR. Jordan sought to play East against West to obtain the volume of arms it needs. Kuwait tried unsuccessfully to balance East against West to obtain added security against its neighbors. Saudi Arabia sought to find more reliable and less politically constrained arms vendors than the US.

Many states, however, with very limited technology transfer capability--such as the Southern Gulf states--have far too many suppliers for countries that are heavily dependent on foreign technical support. The excessive use of multiple suppliers leads to a lack of standardization and interoperability within their force structures, additional serious diseconomies of scale in training and creating effective military facilities, and significant additional costs.

The Impact of Aggressor or Destabilizing States

Ultimately, all of these trends really have meaning only to the extent they affect individual countries and individual confrontations, conflicts, tensions and arms races. It is easy to generalize about arms transfers to the Middle East, and then seek region-wide solutions to arms transfers and arms control. In practice, however, the Middle East arms race has been driven by the actions of a few key states in each subregion, and the other states have largely reacted.

North Africa

During the 1980s, the rise in arms imports in North Africa was driven by three key trends: the war in the Spanish Sahara; the rivalry between Libya and its neighbors; and the fact that while Egypt was at peace with Israel, the states around it were growing progressively less stable, and the failure to reach a broader Arab-Israeli peace settlement was compelling Egypt to maintain large forces.

As is the case with the other subregions of the Middle East, the arms race has been driven by a relatively small number of actors--in this case Algeria and Libya. Egypt's actions have been almost solely defensive since the Camp David Accords, and Tunisia has played a defensive role ever since independence. Mauritania is too poor to be a player, and Morocco faces both a potential threat from Algeria and Libya, and already has sufficient arms to complete its conquest of the former Spanish Sahara.

Supplier relationships have been equally important. The Soviet Union has dominated the transfer of arms to Algeria and Libya, and shaped the buildup of Egypt's military forces through 1974. The US and the West have shaped the forces of Morocco and Tunisia, and of Egypt since President Sadat's adherence to the Camp David Accords.

The end of the Cold War does not affect the tensions among the Arab states in North Africa, but it may change some of these supplier relationships. No longer are the USSR and Eastern Europe likely to provide Algeria or Libya with arms for ideological reasons, and the West has less reason to provide arms to Morocco and Tunisia. At the same time, however, the Maghreb is still an attractive market. If ideology is less of an incentive, hard currency is far more attractive to the USSR and Eastern Europe and may make them equally willing to sell.

The Arab-Israeli Confrontation States

The Arab-Israel conflict has been one of the enduring realities of the Post War era. A steady buildup in force strengths has taken place over a period of more than half a century. Although the increase in force numbers has been moderated during the last decade by the search for force quality discussed earlier, it is also clear that the quantitative buildup has scarcely ceased.

What is equally important is that there is no stable Arab-Israeli balance. The Arab states that actually commit forces to war shift with the conflict, and some conflicts--such as the 1982 war--involved a limited portion of the total forces of the countries engaged. This makes it almost impossible to set some threshold regarding what force levels are right, or what level of arms imports is "stabilizing" or "justified." This is particularly true because the conflicts and threats affecting this military buildup are scarcely limited to Arab-Israeli tensions. Jordan and Lebanon have often had ample reason to be concerned about Syria.

A fundamental shift in the regional balance occurred with the Camp David Accords. The Egyptian-Israeli peace treaty effectively took Egypt out of the Arab-Israeli balance, and the arms race in this subregion has since been driven largely by Syria and Israel. This shift has largely eliminated the risk of a catastrophic conventional war, since no credible combination of other Arab states can hope to directly threaten Israel--particularly after Iraq's shattering defeat in the Gulf War.

The country that has continued to drive the arms race in the region is Syria. It ordered $5.6 billion worth of new arms between 1987 and 1990, and took delivery on $14.5 billion worth of arms during this period. It has recently ranked tenth in new arms orders in the developing world, and eighth in deliveries. Helped by aid transfers from Saudi Arabia, Syria ordered $960 million worth of new arms in 1990. Its major supplier was the USSR.

In spite of occasional political rhetoric, Syria has relentlessly sought parity with Israel since 1974, while putting pressure on Jordan and gradually acquiring de facto military control over most of Lebanon. It has spent 11-23% of its gross national product, and 35%-48% of its central government expenditures, on military forces during every year since 1979. This has placed a crippling burden on its economy--even though some of this expenditure has come from foreign aid.

While its arms imports were only 69 percent of Israel's during 1974-1978 ($3.3 billion compared with Israel's $4.8 billion), they were 135 percent during 1984-1988 ($8.2 billion compared with Israel's $6.1 billion).[6]

In fact, Syria's military expansion has been limited almost solely by its weak economy and dependence on foreign aid. Syria was able to make major arms purchases during the early to mid-1980s, when military expenditures reached about $3 billion annually in current dollars. However, Syria faced growing problems after 1985 as the USSR increased its insistence on hard currency payments, and outside aid dropped. As a result, Syrian military expenditures dropped to $2.5 billion in 1986 and around $1.5 billion annually in 1987-1990. Syrian arms imports dropped to $1.6 billion in 1985 and $1.2 billion in 1986, then rose to $1.9 billion in 1987, and then dropped again to $1.3 billion in 1988.

Syria, however, obtained significant aid from Kuwait and Saudi Arabia as a result of its support for the Coalition in the Gulf War, and this has allowed it to revive its arms purchases.

The Gulf States

While the Arab-Israel conflict has been a driving factor behind the high level of arms imports in the region, so has the Iran-Iraq War and tension in the Gulf. Iran imported $14.5 billion worth of arms during 1983-1990, and Iraq imported $39.5 billion. Iraq was the Third World's largest arms importer during 1983-1986, and the second largest during 1987-1990. Iran was the Third World's fifth largest importer during both 1983-1986 and 1987-1990. During 1982-1989--the most intense period of the war--the total value of arms transfer agreements with Iran and Iraq was 39 percent of all arms transfers to the developing world.

Iraqi and Iranian arms imports rose by 30 percent annually from 1980-1984, when they reached a level equal to 25 percent of all world arms imports, 30 percent of all developing country imports, and 55 percent of all Middle Eastern imports. Iranian and Iraqi arms imports dropped by nearly 50% in 1985-1986, but rose significantly in 1987 and early 1988. They rose again in 1990, although both states faced an internal economic crisis.

It is important to note, however, that this arms race, fueled by imports, began long before the early 1980s, and has followed a consistent pattern. Iran's military buildup began in the late 1950s, but only became intense in the late 1960s. Until the fall of the Shah in 1979, it was supported largely by US sales, although there were some important British and Soviet deliveries. In contrast, Iraq's military buildup occurred after the fall of the monarchy and the collapse of CENTO, and was supported largely by the Soviet Bloc. Iran led Iraq during this period in manpower, equipment quality and air power. It had a decisive edge over Iraq, and supported the Iraqi Kurds in an uprising against the Iraqi regime. During 1972-1975, Iran and Iraq fought a de facto border war which Iran won by exploiting the Kurds. The end result was the Algiers Accord of 1975, forcing Iraq to concede control over the Shatt al-Arab to Iran.

During the late 1960s and through the mid-to-late 1970s, Iraq played a radical role in the Gulf, supporting many "independence" movements in the Southern Gulf. It threatened to seize Kuwait in the late 1960s, and was seen as the major regional threat to the West and conservative Gulf states. Iran, in contrast, aligned itself with the West, and supported Oman against the South Yemen-backed Dhofar rebellion on Oman's southern border. It built up massive military power, and dominated Gulf waters--seizing several islands and oil fields from the UAE during the last days of British military withdrawal.

The Iran-Iraq arms race stimulated the southern Gulf states--Bahrain, Kuwait, Oman, Qatar, Saudi Arabia, and the UAE--to build up their own forces. Oman and Saudi Arabia were further stimulated by a hostile Marxist regime in South Yemen, and Saudi Arabia faced problems along its border with North Yemen and growing radicalism in the Red Sea area--particularly in the form of massive Soviet arms transfers to a Marxist Ethiopia.

The mid to late 1970s saw some shifts in Iraq's behavior. The rise in oil prices made Iraq wealthy, and a new Ba'ath regime shifted its ambitions from ideology to regional power. Iraq began to import weapons and aircraft from Europe--principally France-- as well as the Soviet Bloc. It ceased to back most radical movements in the southern Gulf, and sought to build close relations with the southern Gulf states. At the same time, the Shah's regime gradually weakened after 1977, and collapsed in 1979. This suddenly put a radically xenophobic Islamic government in power under the Ayatollah Khomeini. He gradually forced a break with the US and the West, seizing American diplomats as hostages, and virtually cutting Iran off from any western source of major arms, munitions, and spare parts. At the same time, Iran rejected Iraq's efforts to reach a new political settlement, and aggressively encouraged Iraq's Shi'ite majority to rise up against the Ba'ath government.

In 1980, the internal turmoil in Iran reached a point that Saddam Hussein attempted to exploit by invading it. The Iraqi invasion initially enjoyed considerable success, the Shah's fall and purges of the Iranian military had crippled all of Iran's forces and left it unable to make effective use of much of its airpower and armor. Iraq's military machine was more political than effective, however, and the Iraqi offensive quickly bogged down. Iraq's efforts to split off Iran's southeastern territory--which contained both much of its oil and most of its ethnic Arabs--failed, and Iran had the time to mobilize a massive popular army.

During 1981-1982, Iraq was driven out of Iran and placed on the defensive. Iran not only liberated its own southeast, it cut Iraq off from the Gulf and from its major oil export facilities in the Gulf. An Iranian-Syrian alliance shut down Iraq's oil export facilities through Syria, leaving Iraq only a limited export capability through Turkey. Iran also developed a new network of arms purchasing offices, and was able to obtain arms from the Soviet Union, Eastern Europe, the PRC, North Korea, and many other states. It was never able to rebuild its armor or to either replace its US-supplied aircraft, or find the parts to render them effective. It was, however, able to obtain enough artillery and light armor to build up a force that threatened Iraq's survival during 1984-1987.

Iraq, in turn, virtually bankrupted itself buying arms during 1980-1988. It became dependent on Kuwaiti and Saudi financial aid, and only gradually was able to restore much of its oil export capability by expanding its pipelines through Turkey and creating a new pipeline that joined Saudi pipelines to the Red Sea. Although Iraq was able to buy far more arms than Iran, and had access to superior French and other European military technology, as well as massive Soviet and PRC deliveries, it remained on the defensive until 1988. It was only after Iraq virtually rebuilt and retrained its forces during eight years of war, and Iran could no longer mobilize its superior population in the face of massive casualties, that Iraq acquired a decisive superiority over Iran.

In the spring of 1988, Iran virtually collapsed--only months after threatening Iraq in the north. The Iranian Army was decisively defeated in a series of battles that ranged from Faw in Iraq to most of the key Iranian defensive positions on the central and southern border. Iran's army lost nearly 40% of its major equipment, and Iran was forced to agree to a ceasefire.

During 1980-1988, Bahrain, Kuwait, Oman, Qatar, Saudi Arabia, and the UAE attempted to build up their own forces to meet what they perceived as a major threat from Iran. They created the Gulf Cooperation Council, and attempted to create common forces and an effective military alliance. This cooperation largely failed, and there was no effective integration of forces, or standardization of training and equipment. They did, however, greatly improve their military dialogue, conducted some common exercises, and set up a token integrated land force, or "rapid reaction force," at Hafr al-Batin.

During this period, Saudi Arabia emerged as by far the most dominant southern Gulf state, although it was dependent on US, British, and French equipment and technical support, and its forces were still so small that it was dependent on US reinforcement in any serious contingency. This was demonstrated clearly during 1986-1988, when Iran retaliated against Iraq's air strikes on its oil facilities by threatening shipping and tanker movements to Kuwait and Saudi Arabia. Saudi Arabia, Kuwait, and the UAE were forced to seek US, British, and French naval intervention under the guise of US reflagging of Kuwaiti tankers.

In the period immediately following the ceasefire in the Iran-Iraq War, Iraq emerged as the military superpower in the Gulf--a country with a massive regional superiority in air and land power, in surface-to-surface missiles, and chemical weapons. At the same time, its debt exceeded $70 billion, and its leader's ambitions vastly exceeded his resources. During 1988-1990, Iraq gradually shifted from an alliance with the southern Gulf states to the position of becoming an active threat--putting growing pressure on them for forgiveness of debt, preferential oil quotas and prices, and additional aid. A crippled Iran slowly rebuilt its forces, and shifted its policies once Ayatollah Khomeini died and was replaced by a slightly more moderate government.

This situation became a global confrontation on August 2, 1990, when Iraq invaded and seized Kuwait. Iraq not only attempted to annex a country that had helped it survive the Iran-Iraq War, but it did so under the flimsiest of political pretexts. It also moved a corps to the Kuwaiti-Saudi border--which was defended by only one Saudi brigade--and made political threats to the UAE. The result was immediate American military intervention, the creation of a 32-nation Coalition, and a UN embargo of Iraq. Iraq ignored a later UN threat to use force, and in January 1991 the Gulf War began. This involved a devastating air campaign, followed by a brief and decisive land attack. Iraq was not only driven out of Kuwait; it lost about 40-50% of its major land weapons, saw its air force decimated and become non-operational, and lost most of its missiles and weapons of mass destruction.

Consequently, Iraq is now being forced to give up the rest of its missiles and weapons of mass destruction under UN inspection and supervision, and remains embargoed from any major arms shipments. While Iraq still has the largest military forces of any Gulf nation, it no longer poses an immediate threat to the other Gulf states. At the same time, Iran has revived much of its hostility to Iraq and has begun to rebuild its conventional forces and is seeking missiles and weapons of mass destruction. The end result is a situation wherein the southern Gulf states have been obliged to expand their forces and have no assurance as to their long term security from either Iran or Iraq. The Gulf War has temporarily checked aggression in the Gulf, but has done nothing to alter the fundamental pattern of the arms race.

The only practical way of dealing with this situation is to restrict arms sales as much as possible to both Iran and Iraq, with special attention to weapons of mass destruction, missiles and long-range strike aircraft, heavy armor, and amphibious and heliborne lift. At the same time, selective arms transfers are needed to build up the capability of the southern Gulf states to forge an effective deterrent to low and mid-intensity attacks and permit rapid reinforcement from the West.

Neither arms nor arms control alone are the answer. The only effective solution is to target arms control against Iran and Iraq while supporting selective arms transfers to build up the defense capabilities of Bahrain, Kuwait, Oman, Qatar, Saudi Arabia, and the UAE. At the same time, structuring the forces of the southern Gulf states to allow rapid deployment of US air power and heavy divisions by using the equivalent of forward air bases and prepositioned army equipment is the only way in which external reinforcements can offset the mid and long term threat of significant Iranian and Iraqi attacks on the southern Gulf.

The US and Russia need to recognize that their past efforts to make either Iran or Iraq into allies or "pillars" have been dismal failures. The US never benefited from its military support of Iran, and indeed was forced to intervene against Iran during 1987-1988. The Soviet Union never obtained any meaningful form of strategic advantage or support from its arms transfers to Iraq.

Unfortunately, the history of the arms race in the Gulf is essentially the history of outside rivalry, a failure to limit arms transfers to Iran and Iraq, and a failure to establish a viable deterrent in the southern Gulf. In spite of decades of continuing war and crisis in the region, the defeat of Iran in the Iran-Iraq War, and the defeat of Iraq in the Gulf War, it is far from clear that the pattern that has shaped these conflicts and crises will be broken.

The Red Sea and the Horn

The flow of arms imports to the Red Sea states has been lower than in the other subregions of the Middle East--although it has led to far higher casualties and human suffering than in the states with higher levels of arms imports and high technology imports.

This flow of arms imports has been dominated by the tensions between the two Yemens, tensions between the former PDRY and Oman, border tensions between the Yemens and Saudi Arabia, and the Ethiopian, Sudanese, and Somalian civil wars. In every case, there are overwhelming arguments against further major exports to any of the Red Sea countries. Over the last four decades, a combination of outside interference and the arms imports of these three countries have killed hundreds of thousands of civilians, have consumed much of the potential development resources available to their respective governments, and put a constant strain upon their economies--particularly in the case of the Horn, where the effects of war have often been compounded by those of famine.

While the wars in the Red Sea region have received far less public attention than those in other parts of the Middle East, their bloody and continuing cost makes this an excellent area for a boycott, or at least for serious supplier restraint. This is unlikely to end the conflicts in the region, but it will almost certainly do more to force lasting solutions along the lines of self-determination than the kind of intervention that characterized the rivalry between the United States and Soviet Union to arm rival factions and nations.

Arms Control, Strategic Interests, and Regional Stability: Conflict or Synergy?

Any analysis of the Middle East that focuses solely on military developments and the arms race is necessarily bleak and pessimistic. In fact, political developments in the Middle East are scarcely without hope. The Arab-Israeli peace talks may or may not produce any tangible benefits over the next few years, but a dialogue and peace process have begun. The military tensions between Israel and Syria have considerable inherent military stability, and the Palestinian uprising still seems more likely to lead to little more than tensions and incidents, rather than to another major military conflict.

The UN coalition's attack on Iraq destroyed most of the facilities to produce weapons of mass destruction in that state, and demonstrated that aggression in the Gulf will be met with determination and force. While the tensions in North Africa continue, Libya has shown some signs of moderating its conduct, and the peace negotiations between Morocco and Algeria show at least faltering signs of promise.

The ceasefire in the Iran-Iraq War has held, with little sign of any immediate renewal of the conflict. The supposedly "unstable" southern Gulf states continue to enjoy considerable stability. Ethiopia and the Sudan have at least some prospects for peace, and the civil war in Somalia does not seem likely to be as bloody as the other civil wars in the Horn.

Nevertheless, no one can look at the overall patterns of struggle and conflict in the region, and the patterns in military developments, without deep concern and a real sense of tragedy. There is no question that there is a real risk that far bloodier wars may occur than in the past. It is painfully clear that even if such wars do not occur, the resulting economic strains imposed by military forces are a major barrier to development and civil welfare that offer virtually no compensation in terms of industrial development or productive services. Finally, the political and economic strains in the region are combining to push many states toward at least the acquisition of a covert capability to proliferate weapons of mass destruction.

The practical problem is how best to alter this situation. One answer is clearly peace negotiations and international pressure to resolve conflicts and disputes through peaceful and legal means. A second answer is international arms control. A third is multilateral or unilateral action by supplier states to halt arms transfers to aggressor and destabilizing states. A fourth is to build up the forces of defensive states, and a fifth is to preserve the power projection capabilities of the United States.

None of these solutions is adequate alone. Peace negotiations will not resolve many regional disputes with any stability or security, and often will not even produce cosmetic settlements in the near term. There are still too many regional leaders, and ethnic conflicts, that cannot be contained by such means. Arms control can be destabilizing if it attempts to treat all states as being equal, and as having the same intentions and character. It threatens to produce agreements that either have no real meaning or which bind or restrict those states whose regimes conform to international law, while allowing other regimes to violate the letter and spirit of such agreements. Building up the forces of the weaker or defensive states without peace negotiations or arms control will often fail to produce adequate local forces, will not limit the regional arms race, and inevitably will lead to future wars.

What is required is a synergistic balance of all these efforts tailored to the specific needs and character of each subregion and country in the Middle East. The Maghreb is not the Levant, the Levant is not the Gulf, and the Gulf is not the Horn. Tunisia is not Libya, Israel is not Syria, and Saudi Arabia is not Iraq. If there is any central message that emerges from the preceding analysis, it is that peace negotiations, arms control, and efforts to build up or maintain local military forces must be carefully targeted to achieve specific ends.

This is why arms control requires informed subtlety, rather than ideology or good intentions. There is no question that efforts need to be made to contain the arms race, but sweeping efforts to halt all arms transfers or apply region-wide solutions that do not take account of regional differences simply do not track with the realities in individual Middle Eastern states. States that drive the regional arms race--Iran, Iraq, Libya, and Syria--need one kind of treatment. States that are weak or which require continuing arms transfers to maintain their security or move toward a peace settlement--Israel, Egypt, Saudi Arabia and the other southern Gulf states--need quite another.

The complexity of the arms control problem in the region is also illustrated by several points that have surfaced in the preceding historical analysis:

> **There is no clear correlation between the volume of arms transfers and the occurrence of war--except when arms go to aggressor or destabilizing states.** It is true that aggressor or destabilizing states are often major arms purchasers. So, however, are defensive states. In cases involving civil conflict--which have tended to be the bloodiest conflicts in the region--low to moderate levels of arms transfers have been more than adequate to sustain extremely high civilian and military casualties.
>
> **The arms race is driven largely by a few aggressive states.** There is a serious danger in treating the Middle

East as an entity, as distinguished from a group of very different countries. Over the last 40 years, a relative handful of states has driven the arms race to dangerous proportions. Since the Camp David Accords, these countries have clearly included Iran, Iraq, Libya, and Syria. Other destabilizing or aggressor states--at least in terms of civil or local conflict--have included Ethiopia, Somalia, the Sudan, and Yemen. Algeria and Morocco have long remained on the edge of such a category, and Morocco has waged a sustained war. In contrast, three of the region's largest arms purchasers--Egypt, Israel, and Saudi Arabia--have been defensive states. At least since the mid-1970s, their arms purchases have contributed largely to regional stability. A number of other states are both militarily weak and threatened by their neighbors: these include Bahrain, Chad, Jordan, Kuwait, Lebanon, Oman, Qatar, Tunisia, and the UAE.

Technological sophistication does not tend to produce wars with the highest civilian and military casualties. These come from relatively low technology civil wars. It is interesting to compare the Arab-Israeli wars after 1950, fought on military lines by well-equipped professional armies, with the civil wars in the Horn of Africa, fought largely on ethnic lines with low technology land weaponry. The modern Arab-Israeli wars have tended to be short, intense, and relatively low in casualties; the civil wars in Ethiopia, Somalia, and the Sudan were extremely bloody. Similarly, even the intense and destructive war to liberate Kuwait, fought with free-ranging air power, produced a decisive result and end to the fight with far fewer casualties that the World War I-like war of attrition between a low technology Iranian force and a moderate technology Iraq.

Even a total end to arms shipments would not prevent further war in most parts of the Middle East. The states involved are already armed to the point where a halt to arms shipments might often encourage war by creating a "use or lose" response, or allowing states that emphasize mass to overcome the qualitative advantage of their present opponents.

The key issue is not defensive versus offensive arms. All arms transfers tend to be destabilizing when they go to states that are seeking to expand their regional power and influence. There is no meaningful distinction between offensive and defensive arms when they go to aggressor or destabilizing states. These states are already so well armed that any improvement in defense frees offensive assets for offensive action. Similarly, states involved in civil conflicts can use virtually any form of arms against rival factions. Anti-aircraft guns are a classic example. While seemingly a defensive weapon, they make excellent weapons against personnel and light armored vehicles. Similarly, improved command, control, and communications systems have no offensive power in themselves, but can vastly improve the offensive power of air and armored forces.

At the same time, weapons of mass destruction, surface-to-surface missiles, long-range strike aircraft and modern main battle tanks are more destabilizing than other weapons. Controlling the type of arms transfers cannot prevent conflict, but some weapons unquestionably are worse than others. Aggressor states will find it far harder to threaten or attack their neighbors if they are denied modern armor, strike aircraft and long-range missiles, or weapons of mass destruction. At the same time, armor is the best defense against armor. A purely defensive air force lacks the deterrent impact of an air force with strike capability and the ability to support counteroffensive operations. A state that is militarily weak or lacks strategic depth can deter with weapons of mass destruction and long-range missiles.

There is little prospect that an uncontrolled arms race will result in a stable balance of deterrence or terror. With the exception of Israel, deterrence along East-West lines seems unlikely to enhance stability and the security of individual states in the Middle East. The history of Iraq--and the pattern of the arms buildup in Iran, Iraq, and Syria--offer little real prospect that such states would accept a stable balance of terror, or that sheer strength could sustain the peace. Similar patterns emerge in Algeria, Morocco, Yemen, and the Horn. Many Middle Eastern regimes will take risks, and will go to war.

Reducing conventional arms transfers, or selective controls on proliferation, may have counterproductive results. It is not possible to separate controls on one element of the arms race from the others. A given state's treatment of the five basic elements of the regional arms race--conventional arms, long-range strike systems, nuclear weapons, chemical weapons, and biological weapons--will be dictated by how it perceives its own interests. If conventional weapons are controlled or if conventional forces are limited, it may well seek weapons of mass destruction. If nuclear weapons are too expensive, it may seek cheaper conventional weapons. If chemical weapons are controlled, it may turn to more covert and easier-to-acquire technology like biological weapons. If it is denied long-range missiles, it may seek strike aircraft, and if both are denied, it may turn to the covert delivery of weapons of mass destruction. The arms race is fungible, and selective controls will tend to drive it along the path of least resistance.

Confidence-building measures can be helpful, but are not a solution. Confidence-building measures--like peace negotiations--are successful only to the extent that the states involved want them to be successful. If countries are edging toward peace, or at least "correct relations," then controls on exercises, scale and type of training, mobilization, force deployments, callups and the many other confidence-building measures that have been advocated over the years can be very useful. Not only can they defuse the military situation, but they build up dialogue and trust and lay the ground work for more serious forms of arms control and negotiation. It is obvious, however, that confidence-building measures will not limit states that are ready or nearly ready to go to war. Only major changes in force structure or disarmament can seriously affect many of the confrontations in the Middle East, and can make arms transfers less threatening.

Restraint by arms suppliers will also be helpful, but is likely to have a limited effect. The end of the Cold War creates a situation where East and West should be able similarly to end the rivalry to sell arms to given target states. This rivalry never produced either client states that served the seller's interest, or any clear benefits in terms of broader strategic interests. In many ways, it also failed to produce any profits. Preferential Soviet Bloc sales certainly cost the Soviet Bloc more than they produced in barter and soft currency transfers. Western intervention in the Gulf in 1987-1991, along with the high cost of other interventions and swings in oil prices, almost certainly cost western economies far more than the benefits derived from those arms sales that produced hard currency.

It is already clear, however, that East-West rivalry threatens to be replaced by a conflict between those sellers who are seeking to bring strategic stability and some degree of peace to the region, and those who are primarily interested in hard currency and profits. Some "rogue merchants" have already emerged. North Korea is a clear example of such a state, and the PRC threatens to become one. Russia and East Europe threaten to replace ideological sales with profit-oriented ones that will be equally damaging. Many western and neutral governments seem unable to bring any coherence to their arms sales--often declaring one policy while playing complex power games with individual countries, or turning a blind eye to the sales and operations of individual firms. Rhetoric to the contrary, some of the world's arms sellers have already rushed to seize the moral low ground of the arms trade.

None of these points argue against efforts like the Missile Technology Control Regime, the Chemical Weapons Convention, the Nuclear Non-Proliferation Treaty, the Biological Weapons Convention, or the new arms supplier conference. Quite the contrary, every effort to develop these agreements into more effective arms control arrangements and expand their coverage will help reduce the problem. The same is true of efforts to strengthen unilateral national controls on the flow of arms and military technology.

At the same time, the fact remains that the priority for arms control must be shaped by the priority for other strategic interests. Arms control does not mean simply halting all arms sales. It means shaping arms sales to achieve stability and/or peace. It means tailoring the flow of arms to strengthen those countries threatened by aggressor states, and clearly recognizing the fact that certain states are more destabilizing than others.

To be specific, it means ensuring that Israel remains strong enough to defend itself conventionally and to deter any threat from regional powers with weapons of mass destruction. It means keeping Egypt a strong and moderate force in the Middle East. It means building up Saudi Arabia and the smaller Gulf Cooperation Council states to create as effective a regional deterrent as possible. It means ensuring that Morocco and Tunisia have enough military forces to help contain Libya and deal with the risk of a reversal in Algeria's policies. None of these cases should involve a blank check. In each case, supplier states should carefully assess each individual transfer of arms and technology to see if the end result will be to enhance regional stability. Nevertheless, peace and regional stability depend on the use of continuing arms transfers.

So, finally, does maintaining significant US power projection capability. The US is the only state that can project enough power into the region to deal with mid and high intensity conflicts, and enough long-range strike capability to ensure that the process of proliferation can be met with military force when arms control fails or is only partially successful. American military presence is not an answer in itself, and arms control and regional deterrents will always be preferable. Where possible, American action should also take place as part of international coalitions and under the auspices of the United Nations. It will be at least a decade, however, before the various arms races and aggressor states in the region can be contained through arms control and regional deterrents. In the interim, the alternative to American power projection will be war, and an even greater risk of the use of weapons of mass destruction.

Notes

1.   Totals include Arab African states. Arms Control and Disarmament Agency (ACDA) totals do not include Algeria, Ethiopia, Libya, Mauritania, Morocco, Somalia, Sudan, and Tunisia.

2.   These percentages on arms imports are taken from various editions of ACDA, *World Military Expenditures and Arms Transfers*, Washington, GPO. The totals for the "Middle East" include data on Bahrain, Cyprus, Egypt, Iran, Iraq, Israel, Jordan, Kuwait, Lebanon, Oman, PDRY, Qatar, Saudi Arabia, Syria, UAE, and YAR. For historical reasons, ACDA totals do not include Algeria, Ethiopia, Libya, Mauritania, Morocco, Somalia, Sudan, and Tunisia. The source data do not permit adjustment of the percentages.

3.   ACDA is the Arms Control and Disarmament Agency. For the statistical rationale for this statement, see the arms import tables in ACDA, *World Military Expenditures and Arms Transfers, 1989* (Washington: GPO, 1990).

4.   Richard F. Grimmett, *Conventional Arms Transfers to the Third World, 1983-1990* (Washington: Congressional Research Service, CRS-9 1-578F, August 2, 1991).

5.   The reader should be aware that the author is defining the Middle East to include all of the Arab states, plus Israel, Iran, and Ethiopia. Mauritania is defined as an Arab state. The statistical information on the region is highly uncertain, and major differences exist among virtually all sources. Few countries in the region report any statistical information on their military forces or defense spending, and when they do it is heavily politicized and often inaccurate. The UN data on the arms race in the region is notoriously poor, and even the most authoritative sources are uncertain.   Unless otherwise specified, the economic and manpower statistics used in this chapter are taken from the CIA data presented in ACDA, *World Military Expenditures and Arms Transfers, 1987* (Washington: GPO, 1988); Central Intelligence Agency (CIA), *The World Factbook, 1987*, September 1987. The data on military forces are estimated by the author based on personal knowledge and background, but are adapted from two primary sources: The International Institute for Strategic Studies (IISS), *The Military Balance, 1988-1989* (London: IISS, 1988); and the Jaffee Center for Strategic Studies (JCSS), *The Middle East Military Balance 1987* (Boulder: Westview, 1988).

6.   The US ACDA, *World Military Expenditures and Arms Transfers 1989* (Washington: GPO, 1989), pp. 117-188; and US ACDA, *World Military Expenditures and Arms Transfers 1969-1978* (Washington: GPO, 1989), pp. 160-161.

3. Military Lessons of the Gulf War--Implications for Middle East Arms Control

Barry R. Posen

The history of both conventional arms control and Middle East politics suggests that it is likely to be extremely difficult to apply conventional arms control in this region. If anything, the lessons of the Gulf War are likely to make this task even more difficult, especially if the various disputants in the conflict have drawn from the war lessons similar to those elaborated here. To illustrate this, the purposes of arms control and the way those purposes have been achieved will be briefly assessed. Then, some of the inherent problems of **conventional** arms control will be discussed. Finally, the military lessons of the Gulf War and their arms control implications will be portrayed.

Arms Control Fundamentals

The most important objective of arms control, and perhaps the most politically salient during the Cold War, is to reduce the odds of war. There are two approaches to this objective, although they are not entirely distinct. The first is to reduce first strike advantages in crisis. The second is to reduce offensive possibilities more generally. One can think of military relationships in which first-strike advantages in crisis are reduced, but both parties nevertheless maintain offensive capabilities versus each other. The current separation of forces on the Golan Heights somewhat reduces first strike advantages in crisis, but Israel and Syria have not been deprived of offensive capabilities vis-a-vis one another, as any tour of the area will reveal.

The second objective of arms control is to reduce the cost of war. This has generally been approached through efforts to outlaw particularly horrific weapons, such as chemical or biological weapons.

The third objective of arms control--Bernard Brodie's favorite--has been to save money by reducing the cost of preparing for war. Often when Israelis express their support for arms control in the Middle East, they seem to indicate that they would like to preserve the current military "balance," but at a lower level of expenditures.

Historically, two broad groups of measures have been invoked to achieve these objectives. The first is constraints on number and types of weapons in inventories. In the realm of conventional forces, this has often degenerated into a preoccupation with "vulgar" parity, as was reflected in the Conventional Forces in Europe (CFE) talks. It is not at all clear why vulgar parity in numbers of major weapons systems produces equal security for two parties in conflict, or why it should substantially reduce each side's ability to wage offensive war. Nevertheless this solution has been accepted, perhaps faute de mieux.

The second group of measures has emphasized the elimination of "demon" weapons. In terms of offense and preemption the demon weapons have been tanks and fighter bomber aircraft. Attack helicopters are often lumped into this category as well.

More recently an interest has developed in confidence- and security-building measures. These have taken the form of redeployment agreements, which include military keep-out zones, transparency agreements for data exchange, mutual inspection, observation, and open skies proposals. Finally there are constraints on peacetime activity such as maneuvers and test mobilizations.

Inherent Problems of Conventional Arms Control[1]

In general, any two countries' conventional military forces are very dissimilar, much more so than nuclear forces. Even when the conventional forces of two countries look alike, further study often reveals that they are very different. These differences make conventional arms control much more difficult than arms control in the nuclear realm. Therefore, negotiators should take their time before deciding that a new arrangement of conventional forces, that would preserve their security as well as the existing one, can be found.

Another important characteristic of conventional forces-- again in contrast to nuclear forces--is that they depend on high levels of cooperation for their effectiveness. Conventional forces are functionally integrated organisms, and as a consequence, they are somewhat fragile. Conventional systems are not normally seen in this way; a 62-ton monster like a Merkava tank, is not commonly regarded as fragile. But they comprise institutions which can be struck in certain ways that cause them to shatter. Conventional forces were shattered in the past and those who plan forces both for offense and defense must bear this in mind. The whole system can be made to come apart: you like to take your adversary's force apart and you have to worry that he will find a way to take your force apart--to cause a catastrophic failure. When conventional forces fail catastrophically, you are left with very little.

Nuclear forces do not have this fragility problem. Some argued that they did, that the command and control could be destroyed, thus disarming the adversary by separating the weapons from the most senior political and military decisionmakers. But the headless chicken problem with nuclear forces--the grave risk that in the aftermath of a large nuclear attack, some of an enemy's surviving nuclear weapons could be fired chaotically, without clear formal authorization--ought to be enough to deter most reasonable people. This is because, in contrast to a disorganized conventional counterattack, the damage that even a disorganized nuclear retaliation could do would no doubt be extraordinary.

Yet another critical aspect of conventional forces is banal, but worth remembering. Conventional warfare is the most competitive activity known to the species. Nothing is derived from conventional forces automatically. If a state owns a few hundred tanks, throws them onto the battlefield and hopes for the best, no combat power will result. Moreover, if one's adversary thinks that this is all that has been done, no political effects can be produced.

Conventional forces must compete, and they compete in every dimension imaginable: technology, tactics, secrecy, camouflage, and intelligence. Necessarily, this competition is broad and deep. As a consequence of the fragility discussed earlier, and the fact that the activity of combat is so competitive, states in real political disputes, led by leaders who believe that they have to settle these disputes by war, will have very great difficulty defining by negotiation a military relationship that makes them feel equally comfortable and equally secure. Each side will suspect that the other is using arms control to find a more advantageous military relationship, implying that arms control is war by other means.

Even in the context of US-Soviet military competition, each side suspected that the other was using arms control as a form of military operation aimed at gaining some kind of unilateral advantage. It was hard to see how a special advantage could be gained in a world of thousands and thousands of nuclear weapons, many of which could not be struck by the most imaginative preemptive strike. Nevertheless, both sides feared that an advantage might be gained, causing tremendous complications for nuclear arms control. If such concerns caused substantial complications in nuclear arms control, they are bound to cause far greater complications for arms control in the conventional realm.

A final point about the inherent intractability of conventional arms control is that there often exists a trade-off between the two classic arms control goals of crisis stability and mutual deterrence--a tradeoff that does not exist in nuclear arms control. Crisis stability tends to be reinforced when the offensive aspects of military forces are reduced. In theory this should also enhance mutual deterrence, but in practice most military forces have some inherent offensive capabilities. If the caricature offensive systems such as tanks and fighter bombers are weeded out, the offensive game will change but not be eliminated. If a high-tech military competition is turned into a mass infantry army competition, the side that has the advantage in terms of manpower will benefit from that agreement.

Thus, the prospects of mutual deterrence are not necessarily improved by eliminating these demon weapons. Israelis regularly speak to this point when they observe that Israel can only generate small standing forces, while its adversaries can afford quite large standing forces. Looking more deeply into the problem, the disparity in numbers of mobilizable men of military age between the Arab coalition and Israel is substantial. Therefore, it would be absurd for Israel to enter an agreement that drives patterns of combat back to those of 1914-1918.

Military Lessons of the Gulf War

The Gulf War has revealed a major innovation in conventional warfare. A number of military analysts seem to share this view in one form or another.[2] The basic proposition is that the Americans achieved an innovation in "military format:" not just plans, ideas or technology, but the whole range of the fundamentals of combat power--recruitment, training, armament, and organization.[3]

During most of this century, the dominant military format in the western world has been the mass mobilization army. There are basically two kinds of mass mobilization armies. One is a light force, an infantry force, which characterized the 1914-1918 period. World War II witnessed a mass mobilization heavy force, which uses armor, artillery, and aircraft, but which is still basically an "area-fire" force. It deploys large numbers of relatively mediocre systems against equally large numbers of relatively mediocre systems. This is a caricatured kind of statement, of course, since there was substantial variance from force to force in that war.

In the mass mobilization format, high casualties are just a cost of doing business. None of the different theaters in World War II experienced the low casualties sustained by the UN coalition during Desert Storm. Even the United States Army experienced high casualties in World War II, and it believed in

65

capital substitution, mainly in its heavy reliance on artillery and fighter-bombers.

By contrast, the new force derives its combat power from science and technology. This does not mean science and technology in the narrow sense, limited to the types of weapons systems deployed. Rather science and technology are thoroughly integrated into every aspect of the generation of combat power: training, logistics, intelligence, command and control, and the actual engagement of individual weapons. They are applied to all types of conventional forces, ground, air and naval.

During World War II, such integration was exercised in anti-submarine warfare and in night strategic bombing. But it was not exercised in the normal activity of ground war and tactical air war. Indeed, such integration could not be observed in the normal activity of ground combat and tactical air war until the last stages of the American air effort in Vietnam.

The combat power of the system derives only in part from the excellence of particular weapons, the brilliance of particular commanders, or the wisdom of doctrine, all of which retain their historical importance. Rather, it is the integrated application on the battlefield of capabilities laboriously developed in peacetime, supported by a military, scientific and industrial infrastructure that is active not only in peacetime, but capable of direct participation, even in a short war, that gives the new format its remarkable capability.

Combat is a relative game, so it is important not to be fooled by individual stories of weapons and devices that do not work exactly as planned. The system of combat power created by the thoroughgoing exploitation of science and technology is vastly superior to the sum of its parts; it is a different system. It is so superior that in an engagement with military forces that superficially resemble them, particularly traditional, mass mobilization, heavy forces, such as those possessed by Iraq and Syria, and arguably even by the Soviet Union as of the 1980s, the results are likely to be vastly asymmetrical. The asymmetrical result experienced during the Gulf War was not a freak accident.

66

Rather, it was the consequence of a clash of two entirely different generations of military systems.

This new military system, which for want of a better term might be called *Thorough Exploitation of Science and Technology* (TEST) can literally destroy simple heavy weapons at whatever rate the adversary chooses to present them for destruction.[4] Clearly, there may be some level of quantitative superiority at which the mass mobilization heavy format becomes competitive with the TEST format. It is more difficult, however, to predict the interaction of two military forces both organized according to the TEST military format. At present, however, no region of the world experiences two competing TEST military systems.

The TEST format may not enjoy the advantages demonstrated during the Gulf War in all other types of combat. Thus the TEST format is unlikely to provide such advantages for counterinsurgency. Also, it is not clear that the format will have much application in warfare between conventional armies in difficult, thickly wooded terrain. But in the terrain characterizing Central Europe and the Middle East, the TEST format can be highly dominant.

One illustration of the TEST military format during the Gulf War was the battle against the "Integrated Air Defense System." After the 1973 Yom Kippur War there was much discussion regarding the reduced utility of tactical aviation in ground warfare. To some extent it was an odd time for this discussion to have developed because the American aerial experience in 1972 against the North Vietnamese mechanized forces illustrated clearly that air power was very effective. The Israel Air Force showed in 1982 that an air defense system could be attacked, and in retrospect the campaign foreshadowed what the Americans were able to do during the Gulf War.

This was achieved through the systematic application of science, technology, and money over several decades. Then, a huge and relatively speedy effort was made to gather intelligence on the Iraqi air defense system. All this intelligence was taken to the United States, where it was plugged into automated war gaming systems, and provided to real training operations like Red

Flag. With these computerized war games and instrumented training ranges, scenarios could be run and rerun. After all this careful planning, the integrated air defense system that military analysts feared for such a long time, was annihilated--driven down--in one day.

This is one of the biggest lessons of the war. Having won command of the air, air power can be used to affect the ground battle in ways that had never been exercised so effectively in the past. The US was superb at applying close air support in World War II. The allies had lots of airplanes and threw lots of them at the other side; the weapons themselves were not very interesting, and killed armor by virtue of the fact that a lot of mass was thrown at it. The picture is very different now; weapons systems can travel, find and annihilate individual items of adversary equipment.

There are two criticisms that can be leveled against the analysis offered above. First, in light of the great disparity in military resources between the coalition and Iraq, and given the disastrous leadership of Saddam Hussein, one ought not draw too many general inferences from the outcome of Desert Storm.[5] But precisely because of these factors one **can** draw certain kinds of inferences. Since Iraqi resistance was so weak, observers were permitted to ascertain the full force of the TEST format operating as close to its designed parameters as one ever observes in warfare. Thus, the peculiar circumstances of the war help us recognize the new pattern of warfare. At the same time, however, it is fair to point out the difficulties of distinguishing the relative weight of several likely causes of the lopsided coalition victory-- including the coalition's vast material superiority; Saddam's abysmal leadership; and the TEST format. More research and analysis is necessary to get a better fix on this issue.

TEST and the Prospects for Middle East Arms Control

What does this model indicate with respect to the Arab-Israeli competition and the prospects of conventional arms control in the Middle East? Israel is the only power in this region that even approximates the TEST military format. In fact it is the only other power in the world besides the United States that approximates this model. The European countries have not taken the full panoply of tactical-air and ground operations as seriously as have the Americans and the Israelis, although capabilities they have acquired in many areas are impressive. By contrast the Arab states are still in the realm of mass mobilization of heavy forces. Israel has achieved its TEST military format partly due to the nature of its own society and military, and partly through its privileged access to the US military industrial base.

This does not imply that the precise pattern of any future war can be predicted on the basis of the knowledge that Israel fits the TEST model. A future engagement with the Syrians might not be quite so lopsided as Desert Storm. While militarily capable, Israel lacks the material depth of the US military, and does **not** have access to all of the products of US science and industry, such as the F-117 stealth aircraft. Similarly, Syria may be a more competent version of the mass mobilization heavy format than was Iraq. Finally, the political circumstances of any future war may temporarily compress the action, denying Israel the luxury of six weeks of preliminary aerial bombardment. Nevertheless, the basic disparity between the Israeli TEST format and the Syrian mass mobilization heavy format is substantial, and is likely to influence strongly the pattern of any war that might occur in the not too distant future.

It is likely that any conventional arms control agreement that Israel would accept would need to preserve this asymmetrical advantage over the Arab war coalition. This advantage was hard won; it would drastically reduce Israeli casualties in any future conflict. Hence, it is almost inconceivable that the Israeli military would give up this advantage in the framework of an arms control agreement.

The desire to keep this advantage is likely to be further reinforced by another aspect of the Gulf War: the great damage to Iraqi society and the high casualties to Iraq's military forces that Saddam Hussein was and remains willing to accept.

Therefore from Israel's standpoint, deterrence of Iraq, Syria, or other such powers, is likely to be perceived as fragile, despite the superior Israeli military format. Israel is likely to believe that it must have a viable option to fight the Arab war coalition decisively. Hence the IDF is unlikely to support an agreement that would place it in a situation of quantitative parity with the Arab coalition, if that parity agreement permitted the coalition members to begin to compete with Israel in this new military format. The IDF is thus likely to be quite concerned if the Arab war coalition has access to equal or slightly superior numbers of advanced western weaponry. This concern would arise in stark fashion if outside powers were to try to "buy" an agreement through promises to provide the Arab countries, especially frontline states, advanced western systems. Although the hypothesis proposed here is that advanced western weaponry comprises only part of this format, it is difficult to imagine that the Israelis would wish to put this hypothesis to a test.

It also seems unlikely that Israel would support the severance of access to high technology for **all** parties in the region. Indeed, Israel has little interest in an arms control regime that might push its weapons inventories closer to technical parity, at lower levels of sophistication, with a notional Arab war coalition whose members seem to be less casualty-sensitive than Israel.

The Arabs, on the other hand, should have little interest in superficial parity with Israel. Iraq enjoyed superficial parity in tanks and artillery with the coalition, but this had little effect in determining the outcome of the confrontation. Superficial parity, such as that currently enjoyed by Syria versus Israel, provides a very weak reed for an Arab war coalition. It is difficult to ascertain how Arab states would define their military interest. The first question from their perspective is the makeup of their notional war coalition. Israel has always tended to define the notional Arab war coalition broadly. Yet most of the Arab states have experienced defection by prospective coalition members identified by Israel for "bean counting" (total order of battle assessment) purposes. In the CFE negotiations, all Warsaw Pact countries were counted as NATO's adversaries, even though the Poles and Czechs, and probably even the East Germans, did not contribute much to the overall strength of the Warsaw Pact. The formal-alliance-to-formal-alliance context of the negotiations facilitated this counting rule. But in the Middle East this would not be possible, since such formal structures do not exist.

It is not clear how Arab military leaders imagine redressing the condition of military inferiority that the Gulf War has revealed. If they think they have the potential to compete with Israel in this high-tech format by some combination of buying high-tech weapons and working hard to develop the entire system behind those weapons, then they might want to compete at formal quantitative parity. However, it is doubtful that they believe they can compete in this race. Thus, they are more likely to attempt preserving quantitative superiority, since this is their only plausible avenue to remaining even remotely competitive with Israel.

Thus, one lesson of the Gulf War is to reinforce the proposition that there is even more to disagree about in the world of conventional forces than there is in the world of nuclear forces. There are many mysterious differences between Arab and Israeli military forces, which each side will wish to either maintain or eliminate.

Additional Observations

One key component of the TEST military format is superior intelligence and command and control. The US was able to achieve an impressive theater capability during the Gulf War through the diversion of strategic intelligence assets, the concentration of tactical assets from around the world, and six months of preparation to net this capability together.

The reverse also occurred. Saddam Hussein was denied any imagery due to his inferiority in the air and the apparent unwillingness of those with useful satellite imagery to share it with Iraq. Once the war began, the US applied both hard kills and soft kills against whatever electronic intelligence assets the Iraqis had. Thus Iraq was rendered blind.

This has some important implications. It is plausible that the intelligence advantage in this part of the world redounds to whoever holds the high ground. This directly affects the military value of the territory in dispute here--the high ground on the Golan Heights and in the West Bank. These are very important intelligence assets; around most spots labeled "Tourist Vista" on Israeli tourist maps a forest of antennas can be found nearby. The reason is obvious; high ground is very useful in the world of electronic intelligence. Radio direction finding tends to work by line of sight, so height is very important. It is also not difficult to imagine that Israel enjoys a very elaborate national communications network that links together the intelligence supplied by these sources. Clearly this provides Israel a very good picture of developments around its borders, and a very useful real-time capability in the event of war. This capability approximates the intelligence assets assembled by the US so laboriously in the Persian Gulf.

It is difficult to imagine that Israel would agree to give up this capability. It is very useful for waging war so it is a problem for peace agreements.

Of course, it is possible to argue that much of this capability can be replaced by satellites. So far, however, the region's states do not possess reconnaissance satellites, although Israel is probably developing one: it has developed launch vehicles and has conducted experimental satellite launches. This also implies that satellite launch vehicles are very useful for conventional warfare. They provide some autonomy in the intelligence realm, and the utility of this was illustrated by Saddam Hussein's experience with intelligence denial.

Hence, controlling the proliferation of ballistic missiles in the region presents a problem. In order to be competitive in the intelligence realm, it is important to obtain access to satellite intelligence. Israel has an edge in this realm, and neither the Arabs nor the Israelis are likely to agree to a state of permanent intelligence dependency on outside great powers.

Finally two basic lessons from the ground war in the Gulf should be discussed, since they have implications for two favorite confidence-building measures. It should be recalled that many advocates of "defensive defense" in Central Europe were very interested in fixed fortifications, although usually of the expedient type. In the Gulf War, neither expedient field works nor hardened concrete bunkers deep in Iraq stood up very well to air attack either from "dumb" or precision-guided munitions. In fact both airplanes in bunkers and armor in earthworks were systematically annihilated by aircraft.

Since Israel enjoys a very superior air force that can easily obtain command of the air, and given the tremendous power that air forces have now demonstrated against fixed ground fortifications and against ground forces more generally, Arab military leaders are likely to prove skeptical of any agreement that would be aimed at tailoring defensively structured ground forces. It was well known that air power could be effective against ground forces on the move; that is where it always performed best. But it was not clear that air power could be effective against dug-in, fixed, defended ground forces. Yet the Gulf War revealed that air power can take these fixed ground defenses apart. Hence, the Syrians should not be very comfortable regarding the lines of fortifications between the Golan Heights and Damascus. As a result, any arms control agreement that strives for defensive specialization in ground forces would also have to eliminate Israel's aerial advantage. This would prove a rather demanding task.

The so called left-hook--the movement first west, and then north by the American 18th and 7th corps, out from the area just south of the Kuwaiti-Iraqi border--holds another important lesson. It is not just the flanking movement from right to left that is interesting, but the movement north into Iraq. In executing this movement, the Americans achieved quite an extraordinary pace. The 24th Mechanized Infantry Division moved over 300 kilometers in less than 36 hours.[6] Obviously this occurred against almost no resistance, but there were also no roads in that area. They saddled up a mechanized division--probably a 5000-

6000 vehicle operation in the US Army--and moved it at a rate of nearly 200 kilometers a day, across an area without roads. They then supplied it cross-country for several high intensity engagements. The Americans did not do as good a job at supply as they would have liked; there were some problems in this realm. But possible solutions have already been identified.

The experience of this very high rate of movement casts a shadow over a favored confidence-building measure--separation of forces. If a big armor-heavy force can be moved this fast, then to feel confident that the active Syrian Army could not launch a successful surprise attack, would require that it be employed somewhere behind Damascus. Alternatively, the agreement would have to permit Israel to preserve its ability to obtain command of the air.

Consequently, an Israeli might say, "Well, the current separation of forces is not big enough; we need a greater separation of forces. But we also need to ensure ourselves against the rapid movement that armored forces can achieve; thus the agreement must preserve air superiority." Of course you can also imagine Arabs saying, "When are these concessions to Israel's security needs going to stop? How many asymmetrical things do we have to agree to before the State of Israel feels secure?"

Closing Remarks

The news here, albeit based on a somewhat impressionistic analysis, is not good. The Persian Gulf War has further clarified the point made at the outset: conventional forces are very dissimilar. The assumption that such forces were similar and comparable could be made in the framework of negotiating CFE because of special political and military circumstances. But such an assumption is definitely false in the Middle East, and is unlikely to be acceptable to the negotiating parties.

Conventional forces that are superficially similar in structure, especially in the bean counts that are the favorite currency of arms control agreements, are vastly different in capability. Moreover the leaders of nation states, and their peoples, vary in their willingness to assume risks and suffer costs, and in the objectives for which they will assume risks and suffer costs. Competitors tailor their forces to control their own risks and to raise those of their adversary up to a level that they think will deter that adversary. States always believe that it takes more to deter their adversaries, and that they deserve to suffer fewer risks and lower costs. This adds further disparities to the structures of competing forces.

These basic Gulf War experiences reinforce the notion that arms control can only support a political settlement of the Arab-Israeli dispute; it cannot precede it. At any rate acceptance of arms control agreements that are necessary to backstop a settlement, is likely to require a truly remarkable degree of political will.

If the political dispute remains deep, it is difficult to envisage a control accord that provides enough benefits to all the parties. It is difficult to see how arms control can lead the way to a political agreement. Process arguments, suggesting that the very fact of negotiation is a contribution to the prospects for peace, are valid. But it is unlikely that the process itself will generate much good will. It may do little damage, but it is also possible that as the issues outlined earlier begin to surface, arms control may actually produce more ill will.

On the other hand, resource scarcity may encourage arms control in the Middle East. One traditional goal of arms control has been to save money, although this is the least popular objective among arms controllers. If money becomes tight in the Middle East, a much more practical kind of arms control may be achieved, perhaps on a tacit basis. One could argue that this has happened at various times over the course of the Israeli-Arab military competition. Thus, a tacit arms control agreement that involves a degree of "hovering in place" in the Middle East may be accepted by the region's states. In the short term, there is not much that the Arabs can do about their military inferiority. As long as this remains the case, Israel does not need to further improve its position. With some jawboning by the superpowers and a degree of sales restraint, one can imagine a cooling off period--a breathing spell, in which the intensity of the competition slows down. This may provide a window for more ambitious arms control schemes or political negotiations.

Notes

1.   For a lengthier discussion see my essay "Crisis Stability and Conventional Arms Control," *Daedalus* (Winter 1991), pp. 217-232.

2.   See for example Representative Les Aspin, "Desert One To Desert Storm: Making Ready for Victory," a speech before the Center For Strategic and International Studies, June 20, 1991; Norman Augustine, "How We Almost Lost the Technological War," *Wall Street Journal*, June 14, 1991, p. A. 8; Secretary of Defense Richard Cheney, *Annual Report to the President and the Congress*, February 1992, p. 6; Douglas L. Clarke, "What the Soviet General Staff Might Learn from the Gulf War," *Report on the USSR*, March 15, 1991, pp. 3-5.

3.   I borrow the notion of military format from the historian Samuel Finer, "State- and Nation-Building in Europe: the Role of the Military," in Charles Tilly, ed., *The Formation of National States in Western Europe* (Princeton: Princeton University Press, 1975), pp. 89-90.

4.   If a nation-state is incapable of putting a TEST military format into the field, and faces an enemy that does have this capability, it may simply be forced to put a mass mobilization military format into the field. Its task will then be to so perfect that format, and to so perfect its political and military strategy, that any military clash that occurs does so under circumstances that are most favorable. For example, it is plausible that in defense of difficult terrain, augmented by fortifications and obstacles, a large, motivated, and well-handled mass mobilization force could impose significant casualties on a TEST force. This prospect may be enough to dissuade a country fielding a TEST

76

force from launching an attack in any political crisis other than one deemed absolutely vital to its survival. This is, in effect, the Syrian strategy against Israel today.

5.   For an accounting of capabilities on the eve of war, see Barry R. Posen, "Military Mobilization in the Persian Gulf Conflict," pp. 639-654, *SIPRI Yearbook 1991: World Armaments and Disarmament*.

6.   Joseph L. Galloway, "The Point of the Spear," *US News and World Report,* March 11, 1991, p. 32.

Part II

Arab and Israeli

Threat Perceptions

4. The Threat Perception of the Arab States

Ephraim Kam

Most of the Arab states, if not all of them, perceive a relatively high level of threat, or set of threats, directed against them. This high level of perceived threat stems from several main sources:

Old historical disputes--like the one between Iraq and Iran.

A belief that certain local states are seeking to change the status quo ante, or even to expand their territory. This constitutes the focus of the Arab perception of the Israeli threat.

Asymmetry in the balance of power among neighboring states, such as between Iraq and Kuwait.

The absolute size of some local military forces, and the quality of the weapons systems they have acquired.

The frequent use of military force in Middle Eastern disputes.

Existing assets or resources upon which some of the regime states depend--such as oil and water--which increase their concern regarding possible external attempts to assume control.

The high level of superpower involvement in the Middle East which, in some Arab states, arouses fears of superpower military intervention against them.

Finally, the severe domestic problems in most Arab states, which can be exploited by both internal and external opponents.

By and large, the threats perceived by the Arab states evolve in three circles: inner, regional and superpower. The inner circle, encompassing internal threats to the stability of regimes, will not be dealt with here except for one comment: since the fear of internal threats is pervasive, and since Arab states are not pluralistic democracies, most of the Arab regimes allocate an important part of their armed forces for internal missions. The names given to these forces vary: the Republican Guards in Syria, Iraq or Egypt; the Royal Guard in Jordan; the National Guard in Saudi Arabia. However, their mission is the same: to defend the stability of the regime by elite units, equipped with the best weapons systems. These units are an important integral component of the overall order-of-battle--the best example is the role of the Iraqi Republican Guards during the war in Kuwait--and hence can address external threats as well.

The second circle, the regional one, comprises the main source of the Arab threat perception. Most Arab states believe that one or more Middle East states--non-Arab or Arab--poses a real threat to their national interests. This threat could be an assumed intention to occupy the state's territory, or part of it; to acquire control over its economic assets; or to undermine the stability of its regime or the structure of its society. Such threats could materialize mainly by the use of force, but also by subversive means.

Finally, the superpower circle: due to the intensive involvement of the superpowers in the Middle East, and especially because of their military presence there, some Arab states have been concerned about superpower military intervention--direct or indirect--against their assets. In this context, a distinction should be made between the US and the former Soviet Union.

Despite Soviet military presence in the Middle East, and the proximity of the Soviet Union to the region, pro-western Arab states were rarely concerned about direct Soviet military intervention against them. They were more concerned about Soviet subversion, and about Soviet assistance to Arab radical regimes against their interests. Obviously, the collapse of the Soviet empire has mitigated this perceived threat as well.

By contrast, the American threat has been perceived by the Arab radical states as a more acute and direct one; most of these states are, or were, concerned about the real possibility of American military intervention against their territory or regime. This fear can be explained by the Arab radicals' view of the US as the leading proponent of western imperialism, and the emotions, hatred and fears this has created in parts of the Arab world. Also, they perceive the US as willing, perhaps more than the Soviets ever were, to use force in order to advance its interests. Finally, they regard the US as supporting Israeli aggression against the Arabs. In these contexts, they note the experience of the main Arab radical states: Libya during the 1980s and early 1990s, Syria in 1982-3, and Iraq since 1990.

This chapter focuses on the regional circle, the perceived threats created by local states. Two sources of threat can be distinguished in this context: a threat created by Arab or Muslim states against their neighbors; and the perceived Israeli threat.

The *Arab-Muslim threat*. Generally, radical regimes in the Middle East create a sphere of threats around themselves. One sphere is especially important--the Gulf area, which has become the main source of threats toward many Arab states during the last decade, and for several reasons.

The main reason for the unique standing of the Gulf in this respect is the existence of two outstanding sources of military threat in this area--Iran and Iraq--that threaten each other as well as other states in the Gulf and beyond. Both Iraq and Iran are striving for regional hegemony. Iraq has demonstrated its willingness to use massive force against its neighbors, while Iran has declared its aspiration to export the revolution beyond its borders. An additional source of fears is the disparity in the military balance between Iraq or Iran on the one hand, and the other Gulf states on the other. As mentioned earlier, the attraction of oil reserves in the Gulf comprises a final source of such fears.

Given these factors, it is not surprising that during the last decade the threat cluster in the Gulf overshadowed, at least for some Arab states, even the perceived Israeli threat. Doubtless the events of 1990-91--the invasion of Kuwait, the revelations about the Iraqi nonconventional weapons programs, and the growing

Iranian nonconventional threat--we
states.

Beyond the Gulf sphere, th\
though less important, threat clusters.
African cluster, the core of which is th\
neighbors--Egypt, Sudan, Chad and Tunisi\
extent, the dispute between Morocco and Algeria. \
Sudan has been perceived as posing an Islamic re\
destabilizing threat, particularly toward Egypt. The \
during certain periods, is the cluster around Syria: Jordan, Iraq,
some communities in Lebanon, and perhaps Turkey. To this, one
may add a third cluster--in the Horn of Africa.

Radical regimes within these three groups periodically add
fuel to the fire by attacking a neighbor, exerting pressure on it,
concentrating forces near its border, or providing assistance to
internal opposition groups.

The second main focus of the Arab threat perception is
Israel. There are a number of reasons why the Israeli threat is so
prominent in the view of most Arab states. First, the Arabs
perceive Israel as a **military society**, which mobilizes a major part
of its resources for national security. In their eyes, Zionism, by
its nature, calls for territorial expansion at the expense of the
Arabs. They view Israel as believing that all the territory between
the Nile and the Euphrates was promised and belongs to the Jews,
and as striving to achieve this objective. Hence the drive for
territorial expansion is perceived as a constant component of the
Israeli and Zionist strategy and as intended to satisfy various
needs:

To gain strategic depth for the defense of the Jewish state.
In the Arabs' view, Israel demands secure borders only as
a pretext to occupying additional territories.

As a response to the Arab aspiration to establish an Arab
union in the Middle East, and in order to prevent the
establishment of a Palestinian state.

To create a buffer zone between Israel's Arab neighbors.

To absorb Jewish communities from the diaspora.

To control additional water resources, and perhaps other natural assets as well.

The Arabs believe that since 1967--despite the alleged dream of a "Greater Israel"--a change has taken place in the Israeli concept of the armed struggle: Israel has reached the limits of its capability to expand. The occupation of additional territories would further increase the Arab population under Israeli control, while Israel already faces growing difficulties in controlling the territories occupied in 1967. Hence the role of the Israeli military force is to help the absorption of the territories occupied in 1967, and to convince the Arabs to accept the existence of Israel and to end the struggle against it.

This means that the objectives of a future Israeli offensive will be limited to the destruction of Arab forces, without occupying further territories indefinitely, or occupying merely defensive positions. In Arab eyes, this does not mean that Israel will refrain from occupying territories in the future. But since it would be difficult to control these territories for a long time, Israel's objective would be to keep them temporarily for bargaining, and in order to remove threats from Israeli borders.

A second reason for the high level of the perceived Israeli threat concerns the Arab view that Israel is striving to maintain its **military superiority** over the Arabs by retaining a qualitative edge, thus offsetting the Arab quantitative advantage. This superiority is necessary both in order to accomplish the goals of Israel's strategy, and to convince the Arabs that they are unable to regain the territories, or to solve the conflict, by force. In order to maintain its superiority, Israel is viewed as prepared to attack Arab strategic assets that might jeopardize its superiority-- for example, the Iraqi nuclear reactor.

Third, Israel is seen as seeking to preserve its **Jewish character**, implying a threat to transfer the Palestinians from the occupied territories, and to intervene in Jordan in order to create a Palestinian state there.

Fourth, Israel's **defense doctrine** is based on offensive principles, denoting aggression against the Arabs. These principles include: deterrence--which means not only maintaining military superiority, but also carrying out military operations against the Arabs in order to sustain deterrence; taking the military initiative and launching a preventive attack, implying that Israel is ready to strike first, whenever it believes that an Arab state is planning to attack; delivering the battle across Israel's borders, meaning also that should Israel decide to attack Syria, it would penetrate through northern Jordan and/or Lebanon as well, and would attack expeditionary forces coming from Iraq or Saudi Arabia.

Fifth, **reliance on a superpower**. Israel has formed strategic relations and cooperation with the US, which sustain its threat toward the Arabs.

On the basis of this perceived threatening approach, the Arabs believe that Israel enjoys *strategic advantages* over Arab states. One such advantage is its overall military superiority over the Arabs. Though the combination of the relevant Arab forces is quantitatively greater than Israel's, the Arabs believe that Israel enjoys overall superiority over each of them separately in most aspects of the military balance.

Within this context they note that under existing political conditions--the Arab world is divided and Egypt remains outside any potential Arab war coalition against Israel--it is impossible to establish an Arab coalition that would enjoy overall military superiority over Israel. Also, Israel enjoys a qualitative edge over the Arabs because of its technological lead, the quality of its manpower, and its creative defense doctrine. These allow Israel to surprise the Arabs by unexpected moves.

Then, too, Israel has a substantial capability to attack targets deep within Arab states: its air force is the best in the Middle East; it is perceived as having acquired long-range surface-to-surface missiles; and it has good intelligence, which enables it to strike accurately. Furthermore, while the Arabs are divided, Israel acts under a unified command, and under one leadership with clear political objectives.

Finally, Israel is viewed as enjoying the strategic support of the US. The latter is seen as having created Israel, and as

86

providing it with military and economic assistance, as well as political backing. In this context the US is viewed as having helped Israel in the 1967 war, and as having prevented its defeat in 1973. To this one should add Arab perceptions of the support provided by world Zionism to Israel. By contrast, even during the golden era of the Soviet-Arab friendship, the support given to the Arabs by Moscow was problematic. Also, it was never viewed as having equaled the extent of American support for Israel. During the last few years it has become clear to the Arabs--especially to the radical Arab states--that they have lost the last vestiges of Soviet strategic backing.

In the Arab view, Israel's nuclear capability comprises a central component of its military-technological advantage. The Arabs strongly believe that Israel has acquired nuclear weapons, and not merely a nuclear potential. Most Arab leaders claim--and apparently believe--that due to international constraints, as well as its proximity to Arab targets, Israel would find it very difficult to actually use nuclear weapons. Hence they assume that Israel might use nuclear weapons only as a last resort, i.e., if confronted with an existential threat. The Arabs do not define clearly this last-resort situation, but generally three relevant scenarios are mentioned in this context: a significant Arab penetration through the 1967 borders; the incurring by Israel of a large number of civilian casualties; and a deep erosion of Israel's military capability during wartime, or even the development of a severe military imbalance between Israel and the Arabs, which might lead to an Israeli defeat in war.

In recent years--following the Israeli attack on the Iraqi nuclear reactor, and the revelations of the Israeli nuclear technician Vanunu--Arab concern about Israel's nuclear policy has increased. The Arabs also assume that Israel has developed a capability to produce tactical nuclear weapons in order to hit targets within a restricted area. Hence the Arabs have recently been mentioning the possibility that Israel might also use nuclear weapons under circumstances that do not involve existential threat. Such situations might include Arab military pressure during war, even if not expected to bring about an Israeli defeat; an Israeli

87

need to react to Arab use of surface-to-surface missiles or chemical weapons; or a need to stop a major Arab breakthrough in the nuclear field. In addition, the Arabs assume that Israel might use chemical/biological weapons as an alternative to nuclear weapons, should the use of the latter appear more problematic.

In the Arab view, however, some of these Israeli advantages are offset by a series of *strategic disadvantages*.

First, Israel is viewed as operating under constant limitations: a small territory lacking sufficient strategic depth; limited manpower; a troubled economy; concentration of most of the population and infrastructure in the coast area; high vulnerability of the rear; and high sensitivity to casualties.

Also, the IDF's reliance on reserve units is seen as exposing it to considerable difficulties. It creates a critical time-frame until completion of mobilization of the reserves, thus enabling the Arabs to attack an unmobilized Israel and achieve strategic surprise. In addition, reliance on reserves makes it difficult for Israel to conduct a prolonged war, which might undermine its economy.

Moreover, in the Arab view, Israel's qualitative edge has been partly eroded, especially since 1973: the Arab forces have learned from experience, and have improved the quality of the weapons systems they use; the heavy burden on Israel's economy increasingly limits the IDF's military buildup and training programs; the intifada makes it difficult for the IDF to accomplish its military missions; Israel's capability to launch a blitzkrieg has been reduced, and it faces growing difficulties in conducting prolonged war; and the Arabs' improved capability to use surface-to-surface missiles partly compensates for their air forces' weaknesses.

Consequently, during recent years there have been repeated Arab statements to the effect that Israel's capability to achieve its strategic objectives by military means has somewhat declined. In turn, however, the Arab states have not been able to develop a military option against Israel.

This set of assumptions leads the Arabs to expect an Israeli decision to initiate a war against one or more Arab states under several possible scenarios: should the military balance change considerably in favor of the Arabs, for example due to a significant strengthening of the Syrian armed forces, which might enable them to take a military initiative; or if there emerges meaningful military cooperation between at least two central Arab states, such as Syria and Iraq, Egypt or Jordan; or if an Arab state began to produce nuclear weapons, or achieved a breakthrough of consequence toward this objective.

A significant internal political change in Jordan could lead to Israeli intervention there, especially if the Hashemite regime collapsed, and/or if a major Iraqi expeditionary force entered Jordan.

A deterioration of the domestic situation in Israel, for example as an outcome of the intifada, might propel its government to divert domestic attention by initiating a military move against an Arab state.

Finally, growing external threats toward Israel might drive it to make a military move, for example in the event of increased terrorist penetration through Israeli borders; or due to a severe Egyptian violation of the peace treaty, especially if a considerable force was moved into the Sinai Peninsula; or if a threat to Israeli navigation in the Red Sea developed. An external threat could also be exploited by Israel to occupy water resources.

Thus far the Arab threat perception has been dealt with in general terms. There are, however, important differences among the specific views of the various Arab states, primarily Syria, Jordan, Iraq and Egypt.

Syria regards Israel as its primary enemy, against whom it has been engaged in a series of military confrontations. Most of the points noted above regarding the Arab perception of the Israeli threat apply to Syria. Moreover, Syria sees itself as standing in the front line against Israel, facing a threat that could be realized in the near future, for several reasons: the Syrians assume that the IDF continues to enjoy military superiority, especially in the air, although the gap between the parties has narrowed in recent years; the IDF is deployed in close proximity to Damascus; and the conclusion of the peace treaty with Egypt has enlarged Israel's strategic maneuverability with regard to Syria. Consequently, the latter must assume that it might find itself alone in war against Israel. At the same time, however, the current peace process has presumably somewhat reduced the severity of the perceived Israeli threat from Syria's viewpoint.

Simultaneously, Syria perceives additional possible sources of threat to its national interests: its neighbors, Iraq and Turkey, and the US. Iraq competes with Syria regarding hegemony over the Fertile Crescent and influence in the Arab world; and Syria and Turkey have an historic border dispute, as well as (like Iraq) a dispute concerning water distribution. Syria has also felt threatened by the US, partly due to the latter's support for Israel, and especially during the American involvement in Lebanon during 1982-83. In recent years, however, this threat has declined considerably. Indeed, it appears that in Syria's view these threats are rather limited, and that the probability that they will develop into a military confrontation is rather low.

Jordan views itself as facing an existential threat, perhaps more than any other Arab state directly involved in the conflict with Israel. There are a number of reasons for this perception. First, Jordan is surrounded by three stronger states--Israel, Syria and Iraq. The Hashemite Kingdom has undergone a series of military confrontations during the last 50 years, internally as well as with Israel and Syria. Secondly, for many years, Jordan was perceived as an artificial entity, lacking internal and Arab legitimization. Its population is small, and its economy is weak. And Jordan is deeply embroiled in the Palestinian problem--in the territories occupied by Israel as well as within Jordan itself.

Above all, Jordan, like Syria, perceives Israel as its primary enemy--and as a concrete threat that could be realized in the near future. It perceives some in Israel as seeking to solve the Palestinian problem by establishing a Palestinian state in Jordan, whether by a military move or by transferring the Palestinians from the territories to Jordan. Jordanian leaders believe that Zionism regards Jordan as the weak point in the arena in which Israel seeks to expand. In addition, Israel is viewed as a strong local power which, following the conclusion of the peace treaty

90

with Egypt, can direct all its military strength to the east. Jordan cannot counter many of Israel's military advantages, it cannot defend the long common border, and it is incapable of coping with Israel's total air superiority.

Jordan also perceives Israel as capable of penetrating its territory in order to attack other Arab forces: to invade Syria through north Jordan, or to attack Iraqi expeditionary forces inside Jordan. Thus, Jordan portrays itself--although it is not clear whether its leaders really believe this--as a great wall facing Israel. In this view, Israel's objective is to break through this wall in order to reach the oil fields and the holy cities in the Arabian Peninsula.

The other threats facing Jordan--created by neighboring Arab states--are of a lower magnitude, although they are still significant. The Jordanians attach special importance to the Syrian threat. This, in light of Syria's military strength, its concept of "Greater Syria," its involvement in the Palestinian problem, and finally, in light of the memories of the Syrian invasion of northern Jordan in September 1970.

The Iraqi potential threat toward Jordan--which has never been realized--is also perceived by Amman as a deterrent factor against Israel and Syria.

Unlike the cases of Syria or Jordan, in *Iraq*'s view the main threat it confronts is apparently not Israel, but two other external threats: the traditional threat, Iran; and more recently, the American threat, which was perceived as a potential danger for years, but has grown into an acute one since 1990.

Iran comprises the main constant threat perceived by Iraq. This has deep-rooted causes: historical disputes between the two parties; religious aspects, since half of Iraq's population is Shi'ite; border disputes, which concern control of the Shatt al-Arab waterway and of key defensive points along the border; the struggle for regional hegemony; Iranian military power, built by the Shah; the robust manpower as well as economic potential of Iran; the proximity of Iranian forces to Iraqi strategic positions; and finally, Iran's ideology of exporting its revolution.

Yet in its public statements, Iraq presents Israel as the main threat to its national security. Even during the war with Iran, Iraqi leaders claimed that Israel was the primary enemy of the Arab nation, and that Iraq regarded the Palestinian issue, rather than its war with Iran, as its main problem. The Iraqi assumptions behind this perception are that Israel presents a threat to overall Arab vital interests, for which Iraq regards itself responsible. And Iraq perceives Israel--in cooperation with the US--as a direct threat to its drive for regional hegemony. Israel's attack on the Iraqi nuclear reactor is viewed in this context.

Finally, the *Egyptian* case is interesting in light of the peace treaty Egypt concluded with Israel, and because following the decline of the Israeli threat, Egypt does not perceive other direct major threats.

Due to its senior inter-Arab and regional position, Egypt expands the definition of its threat perception. In Egypt's view, its national security is linked to the security of the entire Arab world, and any threat to an Arab state presents Egypt with a threat as well. Hence all focal points of regional instability pose threats to Egyptian national security: the Arab-Israel conflict; the Gulf wars and the Iraqi and Iranian threats; Lebanon; and terrorism. In this context, Egypt is especially concerned, in recent years, by the growing Iranian threat to stability in the Gulf, and to its own national interests as well.

In its immediate environs, Egypt perceives three sources of threat. The first is Qaddafi's Libya, perceived by Egypt as a subversive actor undermining important Egyptian interests, especially in Sudan as well as within Egypt itself, and as presenting Egypt with a limited military threat, compelling it to allocate containment forces.

The second is the potential threat to Nile resources, particularly in Sudan and Ethiopia. Iran's deep involvement in Sudan, and its radical Islamic regime, have recently added another dimension to Egypt's concern regarding its southern neighbor. Hence Egypt's view that the situation in Sudan concerns its national security.

Finally, Egypt perceives the freedom of navigation in the Red Sea as threatened by radical elements as well as by Israel.

Clearly, Egypt's perception of the Israeli threat comprises the most interesting aspect of this complex. Officially the Egyptians emphasize that they are committed to the 1979 peace treaty. However in their view the Arab-Israel conflict is a central source of instability, and creates threats to Arab states with which Egypt is bound by special relations and common defense agreement. Moreover Israel's constant military buildup, and its considerable military superiority over Egypt, appears to pose a threat.

Egypt apparently does not expect to be attacked by Israel in the foreseeable future. Yet in its view this potential danger continues to exist. Although the direct Israeli threat has been considerably reduced, Egypt continues to take into account that it could find itself at war with Israel in the distant future--due to circumstances such as an Israeli initiative to reoccupy the Sinai Peninsula, or a deterioration in relations stemming from the failure to solve the Arab-Israel conflict.

In closing, two comments are in order regarding the general Arab threat perception. First, over the years there have been changes and fluctuations in the degree of threat perceived by the Arabs. These permutations are affected by changes in the military balance between the threatening and the threatened parties, and by changes in the regimes of threatening states--e.g., the revolution in Iran. These reactions are also affected by regional political changes, such as the formation of a new Arab coalition or the deterioration of an existing coalition.

Finally, despite the high level of perceived threat, most Arab states--the only possible exceptions being Jordan and some of the smaller Gulf emirates--do not regard their existence as threatened, in the same fashion that Israel perceives the Arab threat. They perceive threats to their important interests and assets, and sometimes to parts of their territory, but not to their existence as political entities. Possibly this is due to their assessment that they are strong enough to defend themselves, and/or because they assume that international constraints will prevent an enemy from attempting to liquidate their existence.

5.   Evaluating the Threat to Israel in an Era of Change

Dore Gold

Threat analysis comprises the foundation of any national security policy. It is critical for military establishments that must assess the types of weapons systems needed to counter their adversaries' specific capabilities. Thus the process of drafting defense budgets usually begins with an evaluation of the threat to national interests. And since national defense consists of more than material matter, threat analysis is also tied to the military strategies and combat doctrines that states choose to acquire in order to gain adequate protection.

As arms control enters the military considerations of Middle Eastern countries, national arms control agendas must also be established on the basis of an evaluation of regional threats. Instead of adding weaponry to counter an adversary's most dangerous deployments, arms control, as a component of national strategy, seeks to neutralize the strategic advantage of potential enemies through diplomacy.

Thus, implicit in any arms control agenda is a correct identification of the central components of the military power of adversaries. Moreover, from each state's perspective, a successfully implemented arms control strategy should shift the focus of any future military competition to areas where it enjoys inherent advantages by virtue of relatively constant elements of its national power, e.g., access to the sea, capacity to make alliances, geographic dimensions, population, resources, and technology.

Yet threat analysis has become considerably more complex on the global level as well as in the Middle East. For example, from America's viewpoint, the main existential threat posed during the Cold War, that served as a central and constant assumption in national planning, simply ended in 1989. Equally important, the subsequent demise of the Soviet Union removed the

specificity of the military threat for the purpose of US military planning. Based on the Iraqi paradigm, the main threats to US interests abroad were defined in 1992 in terms of regional "hegemons." But it is not clear which country will be the leading candidate for this role in the 1990s: Iran, North Korea, or, again, Iraq.

Unlike the case of the US, the existential threat to Israel did not simply vanish in 1992, but it did lose its specificity. For purposes of planning, the principal threat to Israel in the aftermath of the 1979 Egyptian-Israeli peace treaty was a potential conventional Arab war coalition along Israel's eastern front, led by Syria and reinforced by Iraq, Jordan, and possibly Saudi Arabia. Yet 13 years later Syria had lost its Soviet patron; the prospects of an Iraqi strategic reserve for Syria had declined following the Gulf War; Syria and Jordan were engaged in bilateral peace negotiations with Israel; and Saudi Arabia was participating with Israel in multilateral talks aimed at resolving Middle East regional issues.

Clearly, many of these developments could change course. Syria might not regain a superpower patron, but as Iran's nonconventional weapons programs advance and its strategic reach improves, the Syrian-Iranian connection may offer a partial regional alternative to the Syrian-Soviet relationship.

Iraq had shown in 1990 that the loss of a Soviet patron could allow regional powers greater freedom of maneuver. And while Baghdad's access to advanced weaponry was restricted from 1992-93 by UN sanctions, it could not be ruled out that, later in the decade, Iraq would break out of its present isolation and obtain advanced weaponry.

The peace process was a hedge against war, but it chiefly addressed the **hostile intent** of Israel's neighbors and not their **military capability**. Indeed in 1979, Israel traded land in exchange for a termination of the state of war with Egypt, the establishment of a formal peace, and the exchange of ambassadors--it did not obtain a reduction in the offensive capability of the Egyptian armed forces. In fact, the modernization of Egypt's army was accelerated by the United States following the conclusion of Egyptian-Israeli peace.

In the 1990s this development was important for Israel to recall in light of the internal fundamentalist challenge faced by Egypt. In the event that the Mubarak regime were toppled, its latest-generation, American-equipped army could conceivably become the most dangerous threat facing Israel. Indeed, any new peace agreements would have to take into account extant threats of the post-settlement period, including the possibility that peace treaties would be rejected by the successors of the present leadership in Arab countries.

Thus, taking a decade-long view, existential threats to Israel remain quite possible, but the identity of the state that might lead a future war coalition is by no means clear.

Accordingly, any Israeli threat assessment would have to be highly flexible, taking into account different combinations of several possible regional adversaries and the capabilities they might be able to field.

A second source of complexity in making any Israeli threat analysis is related to the changing types of weaponry that are being deployed or developed in the Middle East during the 1990s, particularly ballistic missiles and nonconventional weaponry. The proliferation of these systems and technologies raises the possibility that the threats of the 1990s will differ substantively from the threats that Israel planned to deal with over the past 40 years. This would merely multiply the uncertainty regarding the identification of the country that is likely to become Israel's primary military threat.

For example, should Israel shift its primary security concerns from the armored divisions of its neighboring adversaries to more distant nuclear-tipped ballistic missiles, given the far-reaching implications of such a change for the structure of its defense budget and its national military strategy? Before answering this question, the manner in which Israel has traditionally viewed the main threats it faces should be recalled. Moreover, it is important to consider whether this traditional definition continues to guide Israeli thinking in the 1990s.

Current Perspectives on Traditional Israeli Threat Assessments

The Palestinian uprising, or intifada, that began in December 1987 has in many ways distorted the way threats to Israeli security have been appreciated. The common images in the electronic media of the Israeli-Palestinian struggle altered the accepted definition of the Arab-Israel conflict from a war between Israel and neighboring Arab states to an intercommunal rivalry between Israel and the Palestinians. Arab military establishments in neighboring states seemed, at best, to be no more than background noise.

For a short while, Saddam Hussein's invasion of Kuwait and his threats to Israel restored the perception of the Arab-Israel conflict as an inter-state war, but even in this case, certain distortions emerged regarding the manner in which Israel's central security challenge was perceived. In January 1991, Iraqi Scud missile attacks on Israel left an impression of a fundamental change in Middle Eastern warfare from the classic conventional battlefield to a new type of military balance based primarily on long-range ballistic missiles.

These impressions of a changing Arab-Israel military balance were not shared by most of those responsible for Israel's security. Neither the Palestinian uprising nor the ballistic missile are viewed as the **primary** challenge to the state's security; neither poses an existential threat to the Israeli state.

Since its creation, Israel has had to contend with the prospect of having its territory overrun by coalitions of much larger Arab state armies. The formative event that molded the emergence of Israel's national security doctrine was the invasion by five Arab armies on May 15, 1948, following the declaration of Israel's independence.

The war began with Egypt advancing up to Ashdod in the west and to the southern outskirts of Jerusalem in the east. Transjordanian forces nearly cut Jerusalem off from the coast and took the eastern half of the city. The Iraqi Army occupied western Samaria and reached Rosh Ha-Ayin, near Tel Aviv.

Israel threw back many of these invading forces and in some cases carried the war to the enemy's territory, but from that time onward the IDF considered that its primary task was to protect the country from the threat of a massive conventional attack. This view of the main threat to Israel prevailed up to the 1991 Gulf War. "The true problem," explained Lt. General Dan Shomron, the IDF's chief of staff at the time, "the [real] threat to our existence is not the Scuds, but the large ground and air forces [of Israel's military adversaries]".[1] Similarly, in 1993, Major General Amram Mitzna, Head of the IDF Planning Branch, said: "Our main mission is to defend against conventional war machines. Surface-to surface missiles, however modern, are not a threat to the existence of the country as long as they [carry] conventional [warheads]. But tanks, aircraft, infantry, and other armor are a threat."[2]

Israel's view of this central conventional threat includes an assessment of the basic numerical asymmetries favoring the Arab states. Thus, the head of IDF Research and Development, Brig. General Dr. Yitzchak Ben-Yisrael wrote in 1993: "At the foundation of these matters, it can be assumed that the overall air threat against us will be, as today, five times larger than the entire Israel Air Force...also, on land, we will continue to suffer from a numerically large gap [favoring the Arabs]."[3]

This constant quantitative inferiority of Israel vis-a-vis its neighbors is made even more pronounced by several fundamental structural asymmetries that political developments will not change:

Asymmetry in numbers and force structure. Israel's total population numbers approximately five million, including some 800,000 Arab citizens who are not drafted into the Israel Defense Forces. Syria has a population of nearly 12 million. Jordan's population numbers 3.4 million; its eastern strategic partner, Iraq, has a total population of over 18 million (including four million Kurds). While Egypt is at peace with Israel, should there be a change in regime in Cairo, its population of over 53 million would have to be taken into account in any assessment of the numerical balance between Israel and its neighbors.

In purely military terms, the large Arab population base permits Israel's neighbors to maintain relatively large military establishments. The IDF can field 12 armored divisions as well as an additional four mechanized or infantry divisions. The Syrian Army has 12 divisions, most of which are armored or mechanized. Moreover, Syrian divisions are in many cases reinforced, containing four brigades each instead of the usual three brigades found in most Middle Eastern armies. The Jordanian Army is organized around four divisions. To the east, Iraq has been able to retain some 30 divisions after the Gulf War; Iraq's expeditionary forces have participated in past Arab-Israeli wars (1948, 1967, 1973) and up to one third of the Iraqi order-of-battle could be expected to become engaged in a future Arab-Israeli confrontation. In this context, it is noteworthy that Iraq is not taking part in the current peace process begun in 1991 in Madrid. Libya and Iran also do not take part in the present peace efforts; thus, their contribution of some expeditionary forces must be taken into account along several alternative fronts.

What makes the numerical asymmetry particularly difficult for Israel is the basic difference in the force structures of the region's military establishments. While most of the formations in the Israel Defense Forces are reserve units, the Arab military forces comprise **standing** active service divisions. This difference produces Arab-Israel force ratios that are radically to Israel's detriment prior to the mobilization of its reserves. During the summer of 1973, for example, Israel could deploy only 60 tanks against Syria's 800 tanks in the Golan Heights.

Israel does not publish the number of active service divisions that it deploys along its borders at times of relative quiet; the International Institute for Strategic Studies, however, suggests that Israel deploys three divisions along its frontiers--less than the size of the Jordanian Army. Even if all these forces were fully deployed against Syria (assuming the absence of threats along Israel's other fronts), Syria would enjoy a 4 to 1 advantage against Israel in active service divisions. This quantitative superiority gives the Arab states considerable inducement to attempt a surprise attack before Israel mobilizes its reserves. It also elevates the importance of early-warning for Israel's overall national security. Not surprisingly, a former IDF chief of staff, currently deputy defense minister under the Rabin government, Mordechai Gur, concluded in 1989: "In fact, the main military element of instability in the Middle East is the huge geopolitical gap between the standing armies of the Arab world and Israel."[4]

Asymmetry in coalition formation. The asymmetry in numbers is exacerbated by the asymmetry in potential coalition formation. Despite the existence of strong inter-Arab rivalries, since 1948 the Arab states have managed repeatedly to form multi-state war coalitions against Israel. Thus despite their historic enmity, Syria permitted one third of Iraq's army to traverse Syrian territory to join its forces fighting in the Golan Heights in 1973. Jordan permitted Iraqi forces through in 1948 and 1967, while allowing Egyptian commando battalions into the West Bank on the eve of the Six-Day War. Jordan allowed Iraqi reconnaissance aircraft through its airspace in 1989 and shared intelligence with Iraq over Israeli air traffic. Egypt operated Jordan's main early-warning station in 1967. In addition, Arab states have been able to combine their talents through joint exercises. Thus coalition formation allows Israel's main adversaries to count on reinforcement from afar as well as on the integration of allied military capabilities in selected areas.

Even secondary coalition partners can have considerable impact on the Arab-Israeli military balance. Saudi Arabia's primary military adversaries are Iraq and Iran, not Israel. But in the event of a threat from an eastern front coalition involving Syria, Iraq and Jordan, Saudi air movements, especially in and around the air-base at Tabuk, may force Israeli air planners to take into account the possible involvement of the Saudi Air Force, thereby reducing the number of aircraft available for operations against Israel's primary military adversaries. Thus, even limited Saudi air engagements and menacing deployments of Saudi Arabian F-15 air superiority fighters south of Israel's borders would force the IAF to shift aircraft from missions against Syrian or Iraqi surface-to-air and ballistic missile launchers to missions defending Israeli airspace.[5]

Israel has no similar regional allies. In the past it has developed cooperative ties with "periphery states," like Iran under the Shah and Turkey, but it could never convert these relationships into active wartime alliances. In any event, the fall of the Shah in 1978 transformed Iran from a passive regional ally of Israel to a potentially hostile adversary, through its strategic support for Syria and its assistance to terrorist organizations in Lebanon. While Syria has had significant differences with Turkey in the past, the Syrian military is almost entirely deployed in the country's southwest--six divisions are oriented toward Lebanon while the rest are stationed in and near the Damascus-Golan front.

Asymmetry of size. The territory of pre-1967 Israel, together with East Jerusalem, is approximately 20,770 square kilometers. In contrast, Syria is spread over some 185,680 square kilometers, while the area of Iraq is about 438,446 square kilometers. The strategic significance of size can manifest itself in several areas. First, the Arab states generally have more airfields than Israel, providing them with an incentive to attempt a surprise attack of the type conducted by Israel against Egypt in 1967.

Secondly, it is far easier for the Arab states to disperse important strategic assets than it is for Israel. Moreover, due to their advantage in potential coalition formation, in their case dispersal can extend to neighboring states as well. In wartime, this makes Israel far more vulnerable. In peacetime, it makes the verification of arms control agreements far easier to conduct in Israel than in a country like Iraq.

Third, Israel's small size means that many of its most vital civilian and military facilities are located near its borders, hence are within striking range of conventional armies. When Jordan controlled the West Bank in 1967, its artillery opened fire on the IAF's Ramat David airbase. Its artillery could also reach Tel Aviv and residential areas of Jerusalem. Israel could only threaten similar assets in the Arab states through the use of airpower. Geography thus comprises yet another factor reinforcing the importance of conventional military balances and the interest of Israel's potential adversaries in conducting a strategic competition with Israel in the area of conventional arms.

In sum, these asymmetries mean that the central strategic challenge for Israel is countering the potential conventional military superiority of its Arab state adversaries--individually, but especially in coalition. In the short term, it is difficult to predict which country will be the coalition-leader and which countries might participate in coalition warfare. Syria's military options have been constrained by the collapse of its Soviet patron while Iraqi military power has been set back for several years.

In addition to an analysis of basic vulnerabilities, an appreciation of the long term threat to Israel must take into account ways in which its potential adversaries' capabilities are evolving. In fact, recent procurement trends in the Arab world indicate that conventional arms races in the region are intensifying rather than abating, despite the growing interest of Arab military establishments in ballistic missiles.

Following the end of the Cold War, the excess capacity of the former Soviet Bloc military industries has led to a radical reduction in the price of military hardware. Correspondingly, this has permitted considerable improvements in the military capacity of Syria and Iran.

Thus the Director of IDF Intelligence, Major General Uri Saguy, noted in April 1993: "In the conventional field, Syria has improved and is improving its tank fleet very impressively. If and when Syria completes the procurement transactions that it has already signed, all of its armored divisions will be equipped with the latest model T-72 tanks. Today, Syria has over 4,000 tanks and 300 self-propelled guns that provide it with an enhanced offensive capability in land battles."[6]

It is also noteworthy that since the Gulf War the Syrian buildup has not only involved the modernization of existing combat formations but the expansion of Syria's ground order-of-battle; Syria added a new armored division to its ground forces in 1991. In contrast, Israel has not enlarged its force structure.

The Iraqi situation is more complex than that of Syria. So far, Iraq has not been able to import excess Soviet-bloc weaponry at reduced prices. But that has not stopped its indigenous efforts to expand its conventional forces. According to US assessments, Baghdad has progressed considerably in restoring its conventional military capability: "Much of Iraq's military-industrial infrastructure has been rebuilt. Iraq now has the capability to manufacture ammunition, infantry weapons, mortars, and artillery. Iraqi factories can also produce most spare parts for some weapons systems and vehicles. Clearly Iraq has the military capability to conduct short-term offensive operations against Kuwait and Saudi Arabia. To counter such an Iraqi attack effectively would require a coalition effort."[7]

An Israeli appraisal of the conventional military threat must take into account not only Iraq's present military capabilities, but also what Iraqi military power will look like by the latter part of the decade, especially after UN restrictions on arms trade with Baghdad are removed and the Iraqi market opens up to sagging European and Russian defense industries.

During 1992-93, there was a tendency in the US as well as in Israel to emphasize the growing threat of Iran, particularly due to its support for terrorism as well as its investment in developing ballistic missiles and weapons of mass destruction. Given that Iran is not contiguous to Israel, but rather is located some 1200 kilometers away, to declare Iran Israel's primary future threat would necessarily mean to redefine the way Israel views its central military challenge.

But in 1993 the IDF was not convinced of the advisability of stressing the Iranian military threat. Israeli military spokesmen were careful to note that Israel does not see itself as Iran's primary target in the Middle East; instead, Iranian interests were seen as directed first and foremost toward the Persian Gulf. Thus, Major General Saguy warned that placing too much emphasis on Iran could make the Iranian threat a self-fulfilling prophecy.[8]

Arab-Israeli Asymmetries and the
Future Threat to Israel

The traditional asymmetries between Israel and the Arab states are particularly important to recall in an era wherein the threats to Israel have lost their short term specificity. Assuming that some forms of political-military competition will continue in the Middle East even if peace treaties are reached, it is reasonable to expect that Israel's remaining adversaries will seek to exploit its most salient vulnerabilities as part of any competitive strategy.

Thus in the absence of a clear identification of the enemy, Israeli security planning should be driven as much by an appreciation of the constant and basic Israeli vulnerabilities, as by the search to define the direction of the next military threat. Regardless of whether it would have to face a restored Iraq, a militarily assertive post-Mubarak Egypt, or a Syria buttressed by new regional allies, Israel would need to cope with an adversary that utilizes the substantial quantitative superiority that each of these countries could conceivably assert.

For purposes of arms control, Israel has a basic interest in processes that seek to address, above all, these sorts of conventional military superiority. Moreover, Israel's adversaries are not likely to choose to move away from an option of conventional military superiority to a military competition based chiefly on more qualitative weaponry like ballistic missiles.

Missiles alone cannot win wars--any more than any form of conventional firepower can decisively determine the outcome of armed conflict. "Armor is the main decisive factor on land," noted the IDF's Chief of Staff, Lt. General Ehud Barak, in September 1992. Not surprisingly, the search for improved ballistic missiles by Syria and Iran in 1992-93 has been accompanied by an intense conventional military buildup.

Thus, from the perspective of Israel's adversaries, ballistic missiles are not an alternative to conventional military superiority. Rather, they can serve as an instrument for the reinforcement of such superiority in the following ways. First, as the Gulf War demonstrated, ballistic missiles can cause tremendous social dislocations. In the event of a simultaneous conventional ground attack, these dislocations could conceivably upset the Israeli reserve mobilization, forcing Israel's small standing army to withstand vastly superior numbers of Arab standing formations for an extended period of time. In short, instead of having to withstand an attack for 48 hours, Israel's standing units might have to hold their ground for up to 72 hours. If Arab coalition forces outnumber the IDF by a ratio of eight to one before the reserves arrive, and by only two to one once mobilization is completed, the clear implication is that ballistic missiles may allow Arab leaders to extend the period of acute Israeli quantitative inferiority. In the event of an Arab breakthrough, this extension could be translated into considerable territorial gains that would not be obtained by the Arab forces had Israeli reserves been able to reach their positions in time.

Second, ballistic missiles reinforce conventional balances as a counter-deterrent to Israeli air superiority. Historically, Israeli airpower served as a qualitative response to the quantitative advantage of Arab ground forces; for example, during the 1969-1970 War of Attrition, deep penetration strikes of Israeli F-4 Phantoms countered an Egyptian advantage in artillery that reached ratios of 10 to 1.

With superior airpower, the Israel Air Force could threaten the civilian and military infrastructures of Arab states that decided to launch conventional warfare against Israel; but with inferior air forces, Arab states could not reciprocate with a similar threat. Given their assured penetration of Israeli air space, ballistic missiles expose Israel's civilian rear to the same type of threat with which it has deterred Arab states, thereby creating a counter-deterrent. Thus the advent of surface-to-surface missiles has by no means altered Israeli judgments about the centrality of conventional warfare in the Middle East.

The former commander of the Israel Air Force and of the IDF's Planning Branch, Major General (res.) Avihu Ben Nun, concluded recently that in a future nuclearized Middle East, mutual deterrence will raise the importance of conventional military balances.[9] This follows the US and Soviet approaches to the importance of the conventional battlefield in Europe during the 1970s, once nuclear parity between the superpowers was established.

Conclusion

Despite the evolution of warfare in the Middle East during the 1990s, there is little doubt that Israel will continue to look at the imbalance of conventional forces as the core strategic problem that its armed forces must plan for in the years ahead. Seeking conventional superiority is the natural choice for Israel's adversaries given the structural asymmetries that exist between Arab states and Israel in population, potential coalition partners and size.

In light of its adversaries' traditional war aims--to reduce Israel in size, or even ultimately to achieve its elimination--the outcome of military confrontations in the Middle East will continue to be determined by the movement of conventional forces. Missile warfare is more likely to be utilized in tandem with conventional military power rather than as a substitute for traditional land warfare.

Israel's arms control agenda, like its long-term defense planning, must take as its point of departure the need to counter the quantitative advantage of Arab states in conventional warfare. This entails reaching understandings that reduce the likelihood that this advantage could be exploited to achieve surprise attack. At the same time Israel must maintain the qualitative advantages that are necessary to assure that the military balance is preserved.

Notes

1.   Lt. General (res.) Dan Shomron, "Personal Report on the Gulf War," *Yediot Aharonot*, September 8, 1991.

2.   *Defense News*, January 18-24, 1993.

3.   Brig. General Yitzchak Ben-Yisrael, "Back to the Future," *Ma'arachot* (Hebrew), March-April 1993.

4.   Mordechai Gur, "Destabilizing Elements of the Middle East Military Balance," in Dore Gold (editor), *Arms Control in the Middle East* (Boulder: Westview Press, 1990), p. 14.

5.   Regarding the sale of the F-15 XP to Saudi Arabia, Major General Herzl Bodinger, Commander of the Israel Air Force, noted that the sale "will require us to divide our force differently among the missions that the Air Force has to take care of." *Yediot Aharonot*, September 27, 1992.   Implicit in his remark is the commitment of more Israeli aircraft to counter increased Saudi capabilities and a corresponding reduction in the number of aircraft for other missions, e.g., participation in the land campaign, SAM suppression, and the destruction of SCUD launchers.

6.   Ron Ben Yishai, interview with the Director of IDF Intelligence, Major General Uri Saguy, *Yediot Aharonot*, April 5, 1993.

7.   United States Central Command, *Posture Statement*, presented to the 103rd Congress by General Joseph P. Hoar, Commander in Chief, United States Central Command. p. 21.

According to US congressional sources, "Iraq has managed to reconstruct 80% of the military manufacturing capability it possessed before Desert Storm.... Iraq is manufacturing T-72 tanks, artillery munitions, and even short range ballistic missiles. See Hearing before the Committee on Foreign Affairs, June 29, 1993, Opening Statement by Congressman Tom Lantos.

8.   *Yediot Aharonot*, April 5, 1993.

9.   Address given at Yom Dado--Conference in Memory of Lt. General David Elazar, Jaffee Center for Strategic Studies, Tel Aviv University, May 17, 1993.

Part III

The Prospects for Arms

Control In the Middle East

6. Prospects for Middle East Arms Control in the Aftermath of the Gulf War

Ariel Levite

At the outset of this chapter, two preliminary remarks are in order. First, much of the presentation is not totally original in terms of factual contents. Yet it ventures to cast certain pertinent issues in a somewhat different analytical light. Secondly and more importantly, the conclusions presented here are highly tentative. This is due to the mental tension that inevitably exists between a realist conviction and strategic perspective on the one hand, and the incurable optimism which must drive anyone who wishes to reside permanently in Israel, on the other hand.

The point of departure for this presentation is a belief that when providing a regional perspective to a prominent arms control discussion group, there is some utility in attempting to air a somewhat pessimistic outlook on the prospects for arms control, even at the expense of being somewhat provocative. Hopefully, such an approach will stimulate others to address the same issues and might expose weaknesses or flaws in the analysis, or introduce additional factors that could generate more reassuring conclusions. Old hands at the game may be able to enlighten us as to what could be done in arms control in the Middle East given the peculiarities and complex problems of the region.

The Prospects for a New Arms Race

Turning to review the pertinent Middle East strategic picture, there are many reasons for being concerned about the resurgence of a Middle East arms race, especially after the Gulf crisis and war. Briefly, the adverse legacies of the Gulf War include the following factors:

The lure of conventional arms. The Gulf War erupted after a period in which there appeared to be a stalemate in conventional arms technology, and it was widely believed that a qualitative breakthrough could not be attained through the use of conventional technology. Then came the Gulf War and demonstrated clearly that there was a remarkable new potential for qualitative upgrades in the realm of conventional technology. Not that the potential was absent prior to the Gulf War. It had been there for quite a few years; but it was the "CNN factor"--the impact of bringing home directly impressive images of high-tech weapons performance--that ultimately convinced many people of their utility. The case for such weapons may consequently have been overstated, but the broader perception nonetheless remains that a new potential for attaining a strategic and operational edge has been created by recent developments in the conventional realm.

The practical implication of this development is that we are going to see, indeed can already see, acceleration in the global and regional spread of various exotic conventional weapons systems and sub-systems. This is happening, first and foremost in the area of air power and related weaponry, such as all weather/day and night reconnaissance, electronic warfare, and command and control, as well as precision-guided munitions of all sorts. This proliferation comes after the decade of the 1980s in which the decline in oil prices and diminishing East-West tensions somewhat slowed down this weapons proliferation trend.

The utility of chemical weapons. The second relevant factor is the diminution in the utility of chemical weapons. During the Gulf War the Iraqis did have such weapons in abundance. What they had, however, they elected not to use. Many explanations have been offered for this phenomenon. Two common elements cut across them: a realization of their limited utility in the battlefield, particularly against relatively well-protected soldiers, and a growing awareness as to the price tag associated with their use, especially in comparison to their potential utility. Use of chemical weapons is more than ever likely to entail heavy political costs and risks, and their use is likely to provoke costly retaliation.

On the one hand this is a positive development, since it implies the success of efforts to raise the threshold for using nonconventional weapons. But the corollary bad news is that chemical weapons may no longer be perceived as an adequate warfighting or deterrence solution. Those who once settled for chemical weapons for these purposes are therefore unlikely to be content with them in the future. Increasingly, they are likely to seek more potent weapons, which, if and when used, could prove politically or operationally decisive. There were some early indications of such a realization already in the aftermath of the Iran-Iraq War. But more recently there has been increasing evidence that this line of logic is creeping into the thinking of many in the Third World.

The lure of ballistic missiles. There is a well known discrepancy between the actual operational impact of conventionally armed ballistic missiles--in terms of the physical destruction they wreak and the number of people killed on impact--and the psychological influence such missiles have. Ballistic missiles have proven to be superb instruments of terror, especially for long range projections of terror in the classic sense of terror strategy, namely when used against civilians. The point is that in the Middle East and for that matter in South Asia as well, it is simply misleading to assess ballistic missiles primarily through the methods of operations research. It is true, as operations research suggests, that ballistic missiles are inferior weapons systems in comparison to modern combat aircraft since their capabilities are dwarfed by those of aircraft and their mission costs are significantly higher. But using ballistic missiles as a weapon of terror involves an entirely different utility calculus. And part of the enhanced current appetite for ballistic missiles in the Middle East can be traced to this special calculus.

Some demand for ballistic missiles was already evident before the war, hence only its growth and acceleration can be said to derive from the dissemination of the "lessons" of the war. The fact that even old and inaccurate ballistic missiles have proven to be so potent, and to enjoy penetrability advantage--which for the time being is virtually guaranteed (especially when used in large numbers) has impressed many people in our region and beyond.

The impact of civil and active defense programs. Massive investment in civil defense and active defense is not only perfectly legitimate in and of itself, but is also a natural outcome of the Gulf crisis and war trauma. It nonetheless triggers alarm in some circles, and may serve as another incentive for a new arms race. A common theme in recent Arab strategic analysis explicitly refers to the massive Israeli investment in active defense as well as in protective gear for the entire population, as a major threat. Egyptian publications express anxiety that these developments will erode whatever fragile balance of terror presently exists between the Arabs and Israel. The practical conclusion these analysts draw is that the Arabs need more ballistic missiles, as well as more effective and powerful warheads and other related systems, if they wish to retain their strategic deterrent capability. This conclusion ties in with our earlier observation regarding the diminution in the utility of chemical weapons. Together, these factors encourage the search for a more powerful combination of delivery capability and strategic weapons--namely chemical weapons, and more importantly, nuclear ones.

The impact of suppliers' regimes and the prospect of arms control arrangements. The spread, expansion and tightening of global arms control treaties, suppliers' regimes, and the mere prospect of regional arms control is anathema to some parties in the region, who fear that these will adversely affect the possession or acquisition of assets they value. Take as an example the prospect of a Chemical Weapons Convention (CWC) being imposed on the region before peace prevails. What implications might it have? The practical implication some regimes in the region will draw from the prospects of early CWC application is that they must offset it--that is, prepare for it in a sense other than what the convention's sponsors had intended. There are various ways to do so, and we will probably see quite a few of them taking place. These will range from attempts by some regimes to conceal assets they presently possess, to beginning development of weapons other than chemical ones, to expediting research, development and procurement of whatever other weapons systems they can produce before these agreements take effect--all the way to resisting acceptance of arms control agreements as long as possible, particularly in those areas that are of utmost concern. Early indications in these directions are already evident, for example, in the rush to acquire missiles, especially missile production technology, when faced with the prospect of an even tighter MTCR and possible regional missile production and procurement freeze, which some Arab states view with considerable alarm.

Overlapping threats and the expansion of the threat horizon. Finally, a most dramatic consequence of the Iraqi use of medium range ballistic missiles in the course of the Gulf War has been a direct and unambivalent expansion of the region involved in arms races and arms control. Until 1991, some kind of arms limitations regime--conventional, missile, or other--could conceivably have included only Israel and its surrounding countries. This is clearly no longer the case. With the introduction of ever longer range ballistic missiles as well as combat aircraft with air refuelling capabilities, the region--or at least the zone of relevance for purposes of arms control--has stretched to encompass many additional countries, with all the attendant consequences.

Consider, for example, the case of India. At a recent conference, a leading Indian strategist presented India's threat perception to include Pakistan and the PRC, in addition to Saudi Arabia, because India is within range of the Saudis' CSS-2 IRBMs, and Saudi Arabia is an Islamic country with obvious ties to Pakistan. As a consequence of the overlap of conflicts between the periphery and the core, both in the Middle East and between it and adjacent regions, the region--which however defined was never considered very small--is becoming broader and broader in a more concrete and immediate sense. This trend is clearly being reinforced by the disintegration of the Soviet Union which, above and beyond its potential contribution to further proliferation, has created five Islamic Republics on the borders of the Middle East. Considering the potential spread of Islamic fundamentalism, one can hardly be indifferent to threats that could emanate from it to countries in the region. Developments in the periphery of the region in both the Gulf (Iran) and the Maghreb (Algeria) only reinforce these concerns.

To conclude this section, while there have been many positive developments in the global arms control agenda, its prospects in the Middle East region must be viewed separately. On the bright side, a political dialogue has started in the Middle East, a process for discussing regional arms control issues has been launched, and the trends described above could serve as rather powerful incentives to rush into arms control accords in the region. Still, the overall arms control picture does not look bright. This is primarily due to another cluster of factors which complicate the picture and intensify pessimism regarding prospects for an early breakthrough in arms control negotiations in the Middle East.

Asymmetries and Conflicting Priorities in Arms Control

Geoffrey Kemp recently noted a number of strategic asymmetries between Israel and the Arabs that are of paramount importance relative to arms control. These, to recap briefly, include asymmetries in resources, geography, demography and availability of regional and extra-regional allies. Another key asymmetry is to be found in the type and stability of regimes. This point has considerable relevance above and beyond the arms control sphere. But when we talk about arms control in the Middle East, it has considerable significance in at least three different contexts.

First, how do states treat commitments they undertake; how bound do they feel to honor them? The Iraqi example is extremely instructive here. It demonstrated that the attitude toward honoring commitments by certain regimes could be governed solely by narrow and short-term expediency considerations. This state of affairs is frightening, because in the context of an arms control exercise which inevitably touches on sensitive security issues, a state will trade a tangible security asset for something less tangible only if it believes that there is reasonable confidence that the other side(s) will feel obligated to adhere to the terms of the deal. Verification mechanisms are inherently of limited utility; presently available enforcement mechanisms are even weaker; and the ability to retaliate against violators or to embark on compensatory actions in response to them may be constrained for anyone but the major powers. Certainly Israelis are acutely aware of this predicament.

Enforcement mechanisms have proven rather successful in the case of Iraq, at least in the short run, due to a rare combination of factors, particularly the fact that the Iraqis made a serious blunder. In any event, this is but one element of asymmetry pertaining to type and stability of regimes.

A second but related concern is that even when regimes that undertake commitments indeed intend to honor them, they may abruptly disappear from power and be replaced by regimes that do not feel bound by their predecessors' obligations. It suffices to look at Algeria, not to mention the Soviet Union, to realize the fluidity of the regimes in such societies, and to consider how quickly they could be transformed fundamentally from one character to something dramatically different. This prospect is really frightening; it recalls the worst memories of the Iranian revolution, and beyond.

A third regime-related concern and asymmetry can best be illustrated in the context of the evolution of thinking about the Chemical Weapons Convention (CWC). When the CWC was originally envisaged, and after some thinking had gone into the question of verifying it, the US was approached to explore how one actually stored chemical weapons, and to provide specifications of what a typical installation was supposed to look like. This procedure seemed satisfactory until the Gulf War. One of the striking revelations of the Iraqi experience was that certain states may be willing to compromise chemical weapons storage standards, at the risk of endangering their own population. This makes storage possible practically anywhere. What does this attitude imply for the verifiability of a treaty?

117

The experience with Iraq in the biological, nuclear, and missile areas is no less sobering. And Iraq is by no means an isolated case. Consider, for example, North Korea and several other countries where matters are only slighter better. The point is that nondemocratic regimes are capable of doing things that at present would be totally unacceptable, indeed inconceivable, in a democratic country. This clearly raises a serious concern, standing in the way of attaining ambitious arms control agreements in these areas and cases where reciprocity really matters.

To conclude this discussion regarding the type and stability of regimes, it is worth recalling the unprecedented breakthroughs in arms control attained elsewhere over the last couple of years. These have largely taken place in and between countries that have been or have become more open, democratic and westernized. If these broader political developments had not taken place and, conversely, the prospects of fundamentalism had loomed large, then breakthroughs of similar magnitude in arms control would have been largely inconceivable. This is a rather sobering thought when considering the prospects for similar breakthroughs in Middle East arms control.

In addition to the multiple asymmetries in the Middle East, there are other differences between the present situation in the region, and that which existed in other regions and facilitated substantial progress in arms control. These pertain to lack of familiarity of the relevant regional constituencies with arms control issues, and even more importantly, to the absence of established informal channels of dialogue on arms control. In other conflicts or contexts, academics were at least initially able to conduct an exchange of ideas on arms control, whether in the framework of the Pugwash forum or elsewhere. Although at first these discussions were treated with considerable cynicism, they gradually evolved into much more respectable and influential exercises. To date, this has not yet proven possible in the Middle East. Not only are diplomatic ties between the parties presently non-existent, but even sustained academic arms control exchanges have not yet proven possible. There are sporadic exchanges under foreign auspices, whose utility should not be belittled in any way.

But they are hardly a substitute for an intimate, sustained informal/academic dialogue to accompany and expedite a more formal exchange.

All of these factors assume even greater importance when one considers the regional arms control agenda and the different-- at times diametrically opposed--approaches to arms control by various regional parties. At present, one of the major stumbling blocks to Middle East arms control is precisely the opposing preferences between Middle East parties regarding the suitable approach, as well as priorities for dealing with regional arms control issues. To begin with, there is considerable tension between a global and a regional approach to Middle East arms control--some parties favor one approach (at least in some areas), whereas others favor the opposite. To give an example, Israel has already expressed willingness to endorse the Chemical Weapons Convention, but insists that the nuclear issue only be addressed regionally by establishing a Nuclear Weapon Free Zone (NWFZ). Most Arabs, on the other hand, insist on a global arrangement--the NPT--as the first step in Middle East arms control. Similar differences exist in other areas as well. It is quite clear why vital national interests govern and dictate these preferences, and these differences will therefore inevitably prove extremely difficult to bridge, especially given the linkages the various parties introduce.

A related problem associated with the preferences for global versus regional arrangements pertains to suppliers' regimes--such as the MTCR or the Australia Group--as well as the UN Arms Transfer Register. These raise obvious objections of one kind or another from all Middle East parties, whether because they also restrict the transfer of dual-use technologies, because they do not directly affect or include indigenous production, or because they fail to include all relevant suppliers and recipients.

Assuming that a consensus will somehow emerge to deal with arms control issues on a regional basis, it will still be necessary to overcome the aforementioned problems associated with the definition of the region. And even if this problem could be resolved satisfactorily, it will still be a truly formidable challenge to guarantee that all relevant parties in the region join the arms control process and subscribe to the arrangements it produces.

Then, of course, there are the problems of conflicting priorities on the sequence for dealing with the different categories of arms (e.g., conventional versus nuclear) as well as the linkages between them, such as between ballistic missiles and missile defense, between ballistic missiles and aircraft, as well as long range artillery.

Finally, there are also the obvious differences between those in the region who emphasize the precedence of political accommodations in the context of the bilateral peace tracks, over multilateral arms control arrangements, and others who favor either simultaneity or the reverse order. For Israel the choice is clear-cut, since it can hardly contemplate far-reaching territorial concessions at the same time that it undertakes significant arms control commitments and prior to the emergence of genuine political accommodation and reconciliation. It therefore insists on military and politically significant CBMs as the first step in the arms control process. For Egypt, having no additional territorial demands from Israel, the obvious choice is virtually the reverse, namely nuclear arms control. Others in the region find themselves somewhere in the middle between the two approaches, with Jordan, Syria, Lebanon and the Palestinians initially closer to the Israeli pole, and several other Arab states closer to Egypt's approach.

Where does this analysis leave us? A realist would probably be inclined to conclude that in the Middle East, arms control is somewhere between the impossible and the unnecessary: impossible without trust, and unnecessary with it. This may not be the sole or inevitable conclusion. There may be more reassuring aspects that this analysis has downplayed or overlooked. But the probability of short-term success in attaining arms limitation arrangements clearly does not appear high. This conclusion should not, however, in any way discourage us from embarking on this important regional process. In the short term it may well produce many side benefits, some of which may be very important (i.e., in the political domain). In the longer term, it may pave the way for more substantial arms control accords. This is where short-term pessimism should be tempered with longer-term optimism.

7. Military Spending and Economic Development in the Middle East

Patrick Clawson

This presentation attempts to support three unconventional theses: first, Middle East states can afford to sustain the arms race at current levels; secondly, a peace accord would not bring lower military spending; and third, lower military spending would not lead to greater economic growth.

Sustainability of Military Spending

Some analysts have argued that few Middle East states can afford to maintain their present level of military might and that, because money is tight, a tacit arms control can be achieved in the Middle East. To illustrate the contrary case, consider the instance of two countries with large militaries, namely, Israel and Syria. Each of these states could sustain its present level of military spending, if not a higher level.

Syria's military spending, including arms imports financed by aid as well as domestic expenditure, is now only around $2.5 billion a year. That is quite a drop from the $5 billion a year average in the period 1980-83. (Note that the usual source on comparative military spending, the US Arms Control and Disarmament Agency's *World Military Expenditures and Arms Transfers*, does not systematically include arms imports in its expenditure figures, so it shows lower amounts for Syria than those noted here). Syria financed its military spending during the period 1977-87 entirely with foreign aid. In that time-frame, Syria received about $42 billion in foreign aid. This financed the $21 billion in military imports and left $21 billion to use for domestic military expenditures. In fact, those domestic military expenditures were $17 billion. In other words, foreign aid was sufficient to finance 100% of Syria's military imports and 100%

of its domestic military expenditures, with money left over. This Syrian drive for strategic parity was made possible by Moscow and Riyadh.[1]

Since the mid-1980s, aid to Syria has dropped. Aid from the Soviet Union has dropped steadily since 1985. Aid from Arab countries dropped, except for the substantial $2 billion in extraordinary aid in 1990-91 as a result of the Persian Gulf crisis. There are few prospects that aid will soon rise to the high level seen in the late 1970s and the early 1980s.

Russia is self-absorbed and is therefore unlikely to send Syria much aid. The limit on Russian aid to Syria is political, not economic; Russia has the capacity of providing aid at the previous levels if it wanted to. There is much nonsense written about the dire straits of the Russian economy. Consider two facts: First, in 1991, despite the strong demand for imports in Russia, it actually ran a current account surplus with the rest of the world of about $2 billion. Secondly, the International Monetary Fund estimates that if Russia were to conduct its trade with other republics of the former Soviet Union at world market prices, Russia would be running a surplus on the order of $50 billion a year, because Russia now exports oil to the other republics at prices well below world market prices. If Russia converts all of its trade to world market prices, it would have the world's second largest current account surplus after Japan. In short, Russia is going to have a lot of resources in the future which it could use to finance Syria if it decided to. The poor prospects for Russian aid to Syria are not because of limited Russian resources, but because of lack of Russian interest.

Saudi Arabia is also unlikely to provide large amounts of aid to Syria because of Saudi internal economic problems. Saudi Arabia is running a large budget deficit, primarily because of its low tax burden. The Saudi government does not have the internal legitimacy to collect taxes from its citizens. In addition, Riyadh makes large welfare payments. Consider just its policy of subsidizing wheat farmers: the Saudis are spending $2 billion a year on their price supports for wheat, keeping the price so high that farmers grow enough to make Saudi Arabia the world's fourth largest exporter of wheat. The Saudis are also spending large sums on arms, but that is not the principal source of their budgetary problems.

Given that the amount of aid Syria obtains from its traditional allies is going to be low, how can Syria sustain its current level of military spending or increase that spending? The answer, in a word, is oil. By late 1992, Syria was producing 480,000 barrels of oil a day. Domestic consumption was around 80,000 barrels a day. That means Syria was already exporting 400,000 barrels of oil a day. The Syrian government expected to increase its exports of oil to 600,000 barrels a day by 1993. That target seemed overly ambitious. A conservative estimate would be that Syria continues to export 400,000 barrels a day.

Through 1991, Syria accrued relatively little financial advantage from its oil exports, because it had to agree to very generous terms in order to attract western oil companies, i.e., it had to let the oil companies use the first few years' oil receipts to pay for the costs of exploration and development of the oil fields. During this period, revenue left for the Syrian government was low. But beginning in 1993, the Syrian government's revenue from oil was expected to be much higher. A minimum estimate would be $2 billion a year, and a more likely forecast is $3 billion a year. This is an enormous amount of money for an economy the size of Syria's. By comparison, total Syrian imports in 1988 were $1.6 billion; as stated earlier, total Syrian military expenditures are $2.5 billion a year. In other words, the Syrian government will have the funds necessary to increase its military spending sharply. It will be able to maintain its existing military apparatus, which has been deteriorating somewhat in recent years, and it will have the funds with which to entice suppliers who are prepared to sell it weapons or to upgrade its existing weapons platforms.

This economic projection explains why President Assad is feeling so confident economically. Since the Gulf crisis broke out, the Syrians have sent a number of signals that they are not terribly interested in western investment, and that they are not particularly concerned about opening up their economy to reform.

Turning to Israel, the argument is quite different but the conclusion much the same: the country can afford to spend more on the military. The Israeli military has been reducing its expenditures both in real terms and relative to GNP. The cuts relative to GNP are quite impressive. Using the IMF's rather expansive definition of military expenditures, Israel's military spending was 18.3% of GNP in 1986/87, but only 12.2% in 1991. Israel could afford to reverse that trend, even in the absence of additional US aid--for it certainly seems likely that US aid will not increase and may decrease, even in nominal dollars.

Here we might suggest two income sources that could finance a return to the higher level of military spending. First, Israel's tax burden fell by 8% of GNP during the same five-year period, i.e., 1986/87 to 1991. While it would be unpleasant for the Israeli public to return to the tax levels of 1986/87, it would be possible, and that would finance an increase in military spending to 50% above its current level. Secondly, Israel has one of the highest levels for transfers and subsidies in the developing world: 14.3% of GNP were spent in 1990/91 on transfers and subsidies. This does not include the portion paid for by contributions to the National Insurance Institute; including that amount raises the total to 20% of GNP. Israel could, if necessary, reduce its transfers and subsidies to half their current level, which would generate enough to increase military spending by 50%.

Peace Accords And Military Spending

Peace accords would not bring down military spending for three reasons. First, in Israel at least, the military may insist that large sums be spent to replace lost facilities and to adjust to the new situation. Several analysts have commented on the importance of Israel's listening posts on the Golan. If Israel were to lose access or have degraded access to those facilities, the military would insist that these capabilities be restored. Spy satellites, for example, would require incredible amounts of money. In addition, loss of access to the Golan may mean that

125

new training facilities and new POMCUS areas would have to be found. Buying the land and building the facilities would not be cheap.

Secondly, and equally important, all the Middle Eastern countries expect that a peace agreement will be accompanied by a peace bribe. The precedent set by Camp David was that in order to get peace, you have to bribe the military establishments to agree to peace accords. Those establishments are generally opposed to such accords. They are by bent skeptical of the goodwill of the enemy. They will not be supportive of a peace accord unless they feel that their country's military capabilities would increase as insurance, just in case the goodwill is not really there. Moreover, the military is by profession likely to believe that a strong military posture is the best defense, and that the peace accord could weaken this posture. This is rather obvious for Israel, for whom a peace accord may involve reduced access to the Golan, but it is also true for other countries; for instance, the Syrian military may well pressure President Assad to increase Syrian military spending if Syria loses some of its access to Lebanon.

The third reason military spending may not diminish is that military leaders will face a personal career problem in the event of a peace accord--their prestige in society may well decline. In such an environment, military leaders will push for generous compensation. This will be the case not only in dictatorships but also in democratic societies like Israel. Military figures tend to have considerable prestige in the Israeli public eye; if we recognize that Israel has a delicate political balance, it seems plausible that the political leaders will seek to keep such prestigious figures happy with the direction of government policies.

Military Spending and Development

There is a vigorous debate in the economic literature about whether military spending hurts economic growth. It is certainly

126

striking that some of the most rapidly growing nations, such as South Korea and Taiwan, maintain large military forces.[2]

It is not surprising that military spending has little effect on growth. After all, most kinds of spending are not expected to affect growth. Economic growth is unlikely to be affected if consumers buy compact disk players instead of videorecorders. Similarly, it makes little difference if one government spends its money on the military while another spends its money on a social security system to take care of its elderly and disabled. Perhaps the country with a large social security system could be called kinder and gentler, but there is no reason in economic science to call it more efficient or more likely to grow.

The only difference would come if military spending had one of two effects: either it reduced spending on government services necessary for growth, like education or roads; or it increased overall government spending, thereby requiring higher taxes and/or a heavier debt. But there is little evidence that military spending has either of these effects. Countries that spend heavily on the military do not necessarily spend less on necessary services, nor do they necessarily spend more on the government overall; to a large extent, they simply spend less on such items as social security and subsidies.

Furthermore, while most observers focus on the negative effects of the military on the economy, it also has some positive effects. For instance, the military provides useful training. The military may take youths who would otherwise do little, and provide them with good work habits and with training in the use and maintenance of advanced equipment. Another positive effect of the military may be to stimulate employment in countries suffering from Keynesian-style insufficient aggregate demand. This author's study of the Syrian military suggests that the effect of military spending was to boost the local economy by providing more employment, by training Syrians in skills useful in the civilian economy, and by increasing demand for goods and services.[3]

The case for the theory that military spending places a heavy burden on Middle East economies rests on the assumption that a reduction in military spending would lead, dollar for dollar, to an increase in investment. Unfortunately, even here the evidence is ambiguous. Economic growth throughout the Middle East declined in the 1980s despite an increase in investment in some countries and a decline in others. The evidence shows that Middle Eastern states used capital poorly: they were not able to grow enough, using borrowed funds, to repay their loans. The best measure of how well a country uses its resources is how much capital is required to produce each additional unit of output--what economists call the ICOR (Incremental Capital Output Ratio). Middle East ICORs have averaged around 5.0 in the 1980s, which means that each additional unit of output requires twice as much investment as in the newly industrialized countries that require only 2.5 units of new capital.

What Middle Eastern states need to get their growth going is structural reforms, not more resources. The ICOR data provide striking evidence that the Middle East could do better. It does significantly worse than other areas with similar income in the efficiency with which capital is used. Furthermore, the 1980s have seen a spectacular increase in the amount of capital needed to produce an extra unit of output. In 1973-80, the ICOR was 3.2 in Egypt and 3.0 in Jordan; in both countries, it rose to 5.6 in 1980-87.

Precisely because the Middle East's key economic problems are internal rigidities rather than a lack of resources, there is remarkably little evidence that aid has helped it. As Victor Lavy and Eliezer Sheffer have argued, "an abundance of aid in the [1970s] did not build a more prosperous future and is responsible for the countries' current economic misery." They explain this phenomenon by arguing that, "when foreign resources are abundant, governments tend to want to spend a lot fast--often overinvesting in large-scale, low-return projects that are difficult to abandon when economic conditions change."[4] Khaled Sherif has made a parallel argument, namely, that foreign aid to Egypt provided additional resources for public enterprises that proceeded to rack up large losses, a process which in addition undermined private sector producers who could have made a profit providing the goods that the public sector companies produced at a loss.[5]

Hope springs eternal, and economists typically argue that foreign aid could promote development if it were used in support of sound economic policies.[6] The flaw in the argument is that foreign aid can provide the resources which permit governments to avoid making the hard decisions about changing past profligate practices--or as the World Bank admitted in its 1991 *World Development Report*, "sometimes aid can permit countries to postpone improving macroeconomic management and mobilizing domestic resources."[7] When interviewing government officials in Jordan in July 1990, this author asked what they would recommend be done with an additional $500 million in aid were it to become available. The typical response was that extra aid of that magnitude would hurt Jordan's economy because it would create irresistible pressure for government wage increases that would require correspondingly higher private sector wages, thereby undermining the competitiveness of Jordanian industry. Moshe Syrquin of Bar-Ilan University has argued with respect to Israel that aid "permitted inefficiencies to go on, reforms to be postponed, and eventually generated additional aid 'requirements.'"[8]

Furthermore, aid flows to Middle Eastern counties would not have been the same in the absence of conflict. Without the Arab-Israel conflict, aid to the Levant would have been largely driven by the usual reasons countries receive aid, which is because they are poor and because they are following economic reform programs, as in Eastern Europe. The Middle East does not merit as much aid as Africa and South Asia on either score. So let us compare aid to the Middle East with aid to Africa and South Asia, using data published by the World Bank on "official development assistance," which excludes military aid. In 1989, per capita aid averaged $8.70 worldwide, while Israel received $264 per capita; Egypt, $31; and Jordan, $72 (no data are available for Syria).[9] By contrast, the much poorer states of South Asia received $5.40 per person, and Sub-Saharan Africa received $27.70 in aid per capita. Again, recall that these data refer only to official development assistance, which excludes military aid.

In conclusion, military spending is paid for in part by aid which would not otherwise be available; reduced military spending will not necessarily release funds for civilian purposes. To the extent that more spending on civilian purposes is possible, it is not apparent that money will create more growth; if military spending comes at the expense of consumption, then reduced military spending will only change the nature of consumption without affecting growth at all. Furthermore, whatever negative effects are created by military spending, they are at least in part offset by the positive influences of the military in training labor and providing employment.

Notes

1.   Patrick Clawson, *Unaffordable Ambitions: Syria's Military Build-up and Economic Crisis* (Washington: Washington Institute for Near East Policy, 1989).
2.   The basic case that military spending helps development is Emil Benoit, "Growth and Defense Spending in Developing Countries," *Economic Development and Cultural Change*, Vol. 26, 1978. The basic response is Sadet Deger, *Military Expenditure in Third World Countries* (London: Routledge, Kegan and Paul, 1986).
3.   Clawson, *Unaffordable Ambitions*.
4.   Victory Lavy and Eliezer Sheffer, *Foreign Aid and Economic Development in the Middle East* (New York: Praeger, 1991), pp. 5 and 145.
5.   Khaled Sherif (of American University in Cairo and the World Bank), presentation at the Carter Center conference, "Economic Development in the Middle East," November 29, 1990.
6.   A case made strongly by Lavy and Sheffer, *Foreign Aid*.

7.   *World Development Report 1991*, p. 48. That page is devoted to a debate about whether aid has a positive or negative effect on growth. Interestingly, the main arguments for aid refer to financing of specific projects, not of policy reforms.

8.   At a seminar held by the Israel International Institute, quoted in *The Financial Times*, June 27, 1989.

9.   World Bank, *World Development Report 1991*. To be fair however, the world total is low because China and India receive aid equal to $2.00 and $2.30 per capita respectively. The world average without China and India is $14.40 per capita.

8. Proliferation and Arms Control in the Middle East: A French Perspective

Christophe Carle

Not so long ago, arms control as a regional remedy for weapons proliferation was but a glimmer in the eyes of a few analysts. Since the Second Gulf War, it has entered the agenda of policymakers, although any tangible prospects for agreement, let alone implementation, still appear a long way off. The following is an overview of the n. st salient aspects of arms proliferation in the Middle East, and an assessment of the measures which have been proposed to deal with it. Special attention will be paid to France's approach to the problem, at least inasmuch as any distinct French policy can be discerned regarding proliferation and non-proliferation matters.

On non-proliferation issues in general, France's attitude has traditionally been derided by many foreign observers as a peculiar blend of defeatism and hypocrisy. Defeatism was denounced largely because of the view often held in France that some degree of proliferation was inevitable if pursued with enough determination by Third World states. Hypocrisy was also often condemned because of France's long refusal to adhere to the NPT, which added fuel to the fire lit by those who liked to accuse France of being a free-rider in non-proliferation and international security arrangements.

The gap between French policy and the largely American-led non-proliferation community has narrowed considerably, however. There are several reasons for this assessment:

First, there is an increasingly common recognition that over time and in many cases, the spread of sensitive knowledge and its technological and industrial applications in the military realm are indeed inevitable. The broad though vague endorsement of some future form of regional arms control is symptomatic of the realization that some proliferation has already taken place, and

132

that some further proliferation will not be avoided, notably in the Middle East. This entails the need for post-proliferation policies-- roughly the same as what Anthony Cordesman calls "living with" proliferation. However, there is a fundamental tension between such realistic recognition and the newly-invigorated American trend of 'non-proliferation fundamentalism' which stresses not only powerful legal measures, but also preventive or punitive military action against selected proliferators. Thus, on the one hand, Cordesman informs us of the emergence of sensitive technologies, all of them marvelously new and effective; he warns that the spread of such technologies is for all practical purposes unavoidable. But on the other hand, he maintains that anyone caught dabbling with them should be dealt with most severely.

Second, the gap has also narrowed between American non-proliferation "correctness" (by analogy with the vogue for "political correctness") and the traditional French predisposition to see some instances of proliferation as reflecting legitimate sovereign self-defense needs that result from genuine security concerns. As Lewis Dunn has pointed out, there is an increasingly common view, at least within the circles of non-proliferation specialists, that not all proliferation is necessarily a bad thing. Israel is the most obvious and consensual case in point.

Third, France's old misgivings about non-proliferation measures, and the NPT in particular, as reflecting the hegemonistic bipolar structure of the international system, have of course dwindled with the end of the Cold War. Similarly, the hangover from France's own experience as a nuclear threshold state and as the prototypical n^{th} nuclear power has dissipated. And, France's commitment to join the NPT has put an end to customary declaratory contortions from Paris. It reflects France's long-standing self-interest in limiting proliferation, particularly in the nuclear field.

Yet these important elements of growing convergence do not imply that all is quietly consensual on the non-proliferation front. As a matter of universal principle, France continues to manifest a persistent reluctance to endorse discrimination against other states for seeking the technological levels attained by oneself. Hopefully, this can lead France to intercede within the non-proliferation community in support of a more political approach to proliferation-prevention, as well as remedies that are based on addressing genuine security concerns rather than on sanctimonious chastising or on the threat of military clobbering.

Meanwhile, France is clearly joining the non-proliferation fold. But unfortunately, so far it has shown neither the imagination nor the determination nor the clout to make any original contribution of its own to resolving arms proliferation problems and underlying regional security issues, notably in the Middle East.

The peace process has thus far illustrated that France, like other European states, has become a bystander in the Middle East. There are a number of reasons for this: first and foremost, the predominance of the American role among external powers. Also, France has been affected by preoccupations with developments in the European community, in Eastern Europe, and in the post-Soviet region. Part of the reason for the absence of French initiative in relation to the Middle East also lies in the mesmerizing effect for a weakening government of turbulent domestic politics and the prospects of parliamentary and presidential elections in 1993 and 1995. In addition to personal predispositions, this produces an inclination toward maneuvering rather than setting a far-sighted course on just about any issue, including the Middle East.

On **conventional weaponry**, the importance of weapons transfers to the French military industry is well-known and hardly needs to be restated. The notion of restraint on such transfers is not entirely new in France, given its brief participation with the US and the UK in the ill-fated Near East Arms Coordinating Committee under the Tripartite Declaration. The Mitterrand disarmament plan, issued shortly after the May 1991 Bush Initiative, made advocacies similar to its American counterpart, except for the French emphasis on global restraints, as opposed to the Bush plan's primary emphasis on the Middle East. The subsequent meeting of the five permanent members of the UN

134

Security Council (the P5) reflected the balance of power within the group. Naturally, it endorsed the American preference by addressing the Middle East as a matter of priority. In any case, it was not clear how the French view of global restraints was supposed to translate into practice.

The recent American record on conventional arms transfers to the Middle East is frequently criticized in Europe. The gap between the advertised intention to implement restraints on the one hand, and the magnitude of agreed and foreseeable US sales to the Middle East and the Gulf on the other hand, is too obvious to be ignored by media and other commentary. However, the basis for this criticism is itself questionable. The United States merely enjoys the mixed blessing of receiving by far the largest share of post-Gulf War Middle Eastern demand for armaments, much to the chagrin of France and other potential exporters.

Indeed, even as the P5 talks on arms transfers were going on, Europeans and Americans alike were actively seeking a larger share of the arms market. American statements on the issue have been broadly publicized, and highlight the shift from an advocacy of restraint by then Secretary of State James Baker to a more assertively salesmanlike position voiced by then Secretary of Defense Richard Cheney. Likewise, such officials as then Prime Minister Edith Cresson or Defense Minister Pierre Joxe stressed France's traditional position, according to which an independent French defense policy requires a strong armaments industry, which in turn requires exports.

Similarly, French arms industry representatives have recently argued for speedier and augmented local procurement of equipment such as the Mirage 2000-5 or the Leclerc main battle tank, not so much on the grounds of the requirements of the French Armed Forces, but rather in order to bolster export opportunities. Other Europeans applied the same sort of reasoning. Still aglow with pride at John Major's initial proposal for an arms trade register, the British were nevertheless concerned that massive US sales to the Gulf region might hamper Saudi Arabia's fulfillment of its Al-Yamamah-2 agreement with Britain. Overall, the dominance of the United States in the Middle East arms markets has left European producers hoping that congressional restrictions might provide opportunities for European exports. The dashing of such hopes leaves them trying to make a meal out of the crumbs left behind by the US; European arms manufacturers are also actively seeking new and expanded markets in Asia.

So far, therefore, the outlook for restraints on Middle East arms transfers from the US, Europe, and the P5 in general is mediocre. Optimists argue that the mere fact that discussions on the subject are taking place at regular meetings of the five is evidence of promising goodwill and of results to come. But this assessment is too complacent; it charitably overlooks the meager results attained to date. The language of the Paris and London P5 declarations could be translated into plain English by stating that "what I sell to my friends is stabilizing; what others sell to my friends may not be destabilizing but certainly needs to be notified and discussed; and what others sell to my foes is definitely destabilizing."

The net result is that if an arms trade register were fully operative today, it would do little else than record hefty military sales to the Middle East. Similarly, any data provided for a production register by United Nations members would have to be regarded with the utmost caution and suspicion.

Notably, however, in the wake of the Gulf War the idea of arms transfers restraint has elicited a markedly favorable echo in French public opinion. The trauma caused by the war against Iraq was perhaps not on a par with the American experience with Iran, but a similar syndrome was apparent. Promptly forgetting the past circumstances of the Iran-Iraq War, French public opinion reacted with considerable dismay at the sight of French troops confronting the substantial French equipment of Iraqi forces. Yet the determination of arms sales policy in France remains highly centralized. The systematic controls exercised on arms export matters are the exclusive domain of the specialized military and civilian bureaucracy, and the final say rests exclusively with the prime minister and the president. This has prompted proposals

136

for enhanced democratic accountability on arms sales vis-à-vis the National Assembly, but thus far without much success.

The issue of **ballistic missiles** has of course become even more salient after the Gulf War. France is one of the seven original adherents to the Missile Technology Control Regime (MTCR) guidelines, and in spite of some occasional quibbles with the United States, the French have undertaken the role of permanent contact point for the expanding number of MTCR states. Indeed, France has refrained so far from suggesting distinct proposals in the realm of missile proliferation.

Instead, the 1991 Mitterrand plan confined itself to reasserting the importance of adhering to the MTCR's principles. It also called for a future global agreement to facilitate international cooperation in the peaceful uses of space technology. But the plan was parsimonious on the subject, and no precise indications were provided regarding status, structure or content of such an agreement.

Taking into account its limited objectives, the adherence of a growing number of countries to the MTCR nevertheless attests to the largely unexpected vitality of the regime. Still, the missile race in the Middle East continues; the MTCR does not comprise--and cannot be a substitute for--arms control. Compliance with the MTCR by Middle East states (such as Israel) would affect their missile and technology export policies, not their actual missile deployments. Israel's recent adherence to the MTCR is more likely to affect Israeli technology transfers than Middle East security per se. There remain complicating factors such as supplies by non-MTCR states (China and North Korea, notably), and indigenous production (now being reinforced in Iran). More recently, another complicating factor must be taken into account: ballistic missile defense.

On this subject too, the outlook is ambiguous. Israel has every good reason to wish to protect its territory, population centers and other sensitive areas with ballistic missile defenses (BMD). The newly discovered vulnerability to SSMs during the Gulf War more than confirms this requirement. But the deployment of BMD also comprises another step in the Middle

East arms race. BMD acts as an incentive for potential adversaries to build up their ballistic missile forces both in quantity and in quality: if fewer missiles will be able to penetrate, it makes sense to acquire more and better missiles, and to seek "a bigger-bang" per warhead. This incentive to saturate or circumvent BMD exists as long as ATBM/ABM technology is anything less than 100% efficient. This will remain the case for the foreseeable future.

Whatever imperfect protection BMD can provide remains nonetheless attractive, and other states in the region can be expected to try and secure defensive systems in the years to come. One problem here is that BMD incorporates some of the most sophisticated missile technology, notably in terms of guidance and propulsion. The spread of such inherently dual-use technology can very well have the ulterior effect of spilling over into offensive SSM technology and development in the Middle East.

For Israel, these issues are very immediate, and they are compounded by complex procurement problems. From the viewpoint of a country like France, with its very expensive R&D infrastructure and relatively small-scale production of sophisticated military equipment (the Rafael fighter is the latest example), it appears debatable whether Israel is wise to embark on its highly costly Arrow program. Whether the fate of the Arrow will be similar to the Lavi's is yet to be determined, but for the coming years there appears to be a strong case for arguing that an improved Patriot in the hand is better than an Arrow in the bush.

On **chemical weapons**, verification problems remain considerable. Granting that a less than 100% effective accord is better than none at all, it is difficult to be optimistic with respect to the future impact of the new CWC.

Implicitly or explicitly, the **nuclear issue** is becoming unavoidable in the analysis of Middle East security and prospects for arms control. There are essentially three reasons for this. First, from a global perspective the ending of the Cold War and of the bipolar ad-absurdum nuclear race is prompting a thorough reassessment of the role of nuclear weapons in international security. Even the long-standing particularities of France's nuclear posture are not immune to such a review. The second reason is the resulting reemergence of the proliferation issue. This has been catalyzed by widespread surprise at the extent and intensity of Iraq's nuclear efforts. But it also reflects the fundamental focus of nuclear politics ever since the World War II Manhattan Project: "who is to have a bomb?" Thirdly, the nuclear question is bound to remain central in Middle East security because of Israel's own special status in this regard. Extensive and intimate cooperation between France and Israel on nuclear matters when both comprised threshold states makes it all the more appropriate that the issue be addressed here.

At heart, there is no credible scenario for Israeli denuclearization in the foreseeable future. Neither is it possible to argue that Israel has any less reason than France to maintain a nuclear security-insurance policy over the long term. The reason for this involves the intrinsic geographical, demographic, and quantitative conventional military imbalances between Israel and the surrounding states. It is also justified because neither Israel nor anyone else can be absolutely confident that no other Middle Eastern state will embark upon the nuclear route at some point.

With respect to the relationship between Israel's present nuclear posture and the prospects for arms control, it should be noted that a variety of arguments are usually advanced to justify Israel's policy of nuclear ambiguity. Not all of them can be examined here, but a brief overview of some of their main tenets indicates that they are certainly questionable, particularly in their implications for stability and for any future form of arms control, however remote.

It is often argued that an acknowledgment of Israel's nuclear capacity would trigger off rapid proliferation efforts by Arab and Muslim states. Any breach of ambiguity, it is held, would goad such states into action that they had not hitherto taken in nuclear R&D and ultimately in nuclear deployment. The Arabs, it is argued, would rush into action, spurred on by the humiliation of a less ambiguous Israeli nuclear posture. But this argument ignores the fact that the Arabs have always felt humiliated by their successive defeats by Israel. Indeed, Iraq

139

hardly waited for any Israeli nuclear transparency to launch its own nuclear program. And Iran now appears to be reinvigorating its nuclear efforts, irrespective of Israel's declaratory policy. Nuclear rivalry has long existed in the Middle East.

Ambiguity is endowed by its many advocates with de facto non-proliferation virtues it does not really possess. Political, financial, technological, industrial, and import-restriction constraints explain Arab nuclear abstinence and failures far better than does Israel's carefully veiled declaratory nuclear posture.

It is also often argued that any step toward nuclear explicitness would make Israel the target of unredeemable international opprobrium beyond the Middle East. No doubt there would be displeasure expressed abroad. But since when has Israel not been able to withstand foreign criticism? Moreover, that criticism would not be as harsh as many seem to fear, for the simple reason that the fiction of Israeli nuclear virginity is wearing so thin that no one takes it at face value anymore. Moreover, in official and unofficial non-proliferation circles, it is a matter of almost universal consensus that Israel has good reason to maintain a nuclear capacity. Any rational observer in or out of government can only conclude that Israel is for all practical purposes a nuclear power. The only alternative would be if Dimona and Israel's nuclear posture comprised merely an empty shell--and constituted contemporary history's most successful hoax!

The relationship between Israel's nuclear stand and arms control in the Middle East is more intricate. It has been convincingly argued that, as the East-West experience has amply shown, substantial progress on political accommodation is a sine qua non for any tangible arms control or disarmament in the Middle East. This does not invalidate the contributions that security discussions between Israel and its neighbors might make in parallel with the political aspects of the current--or any other-- peace process. Even in the worst junctures of the Cold War, Americans and Soviets at least spoke to one another. The limited objective of partially managing a regional arms race can be furthered by attempting to institutionalize some form of discussions by Middle Eastern states regarding sensitive security issues and mutual threat perceptions. Beyond such cautious aims, actual arms control discussions must presuppose considerable progress on the political front. Only when such progress is achieved or underway will Israel's nuclear posture come into question.

In that hypothesis, another lesson from the East-West experience becomes applicable: there can be no valid and credible arms control and disarmament without transparency. The implications for Israel are crucial because of the political (and logical) impossibility of instilling any confidence, or of freezing--let alone reducing--military capacities whose very existence is not acknowledged by one or several of the parties involved. Secrecy and ambiguity are inherently incompatible with arms control in the Middle East, as the secrecy surrounding the nuclear efforts of Iraq or North Korea illustrates all too clearly.

Even if a "comprehensive Middle East settlement" is achieved, structural imbalances and inevitable uncertainties about future risks would compel the region's states to maintain substantial military capabilities. Among these, there are solid reasons for arguing that Israel should have some form of a "minimal" nuclear deterrent. One of the challenges of future Middle East security discussions and eventual arms control will thus be to incorporate the Israeli nuclear factor into a politically acceptable and militarily stable Middle East security regime. In this context, the option of exchanging territories for a peace that includes an Israeli nuclear "insurance policy" cannot be disregarded. But no such acceptability or stability can be envisaged if Israeli nuclear ambiguity remains steadfast over the long term.

The gradual and cautious stripping-down of ambiguity regarding Israel's nuclear capability, **as warranted by political conditions**, will thus prove inevitable. But it will face the hurdle of acquired Israeli habit. If that habit is not overcome, Israel will put itself on a par with other proliferators, and its allies will appear increasingly conniving and complacent in the view of other Middle Eastern states. Currently, there is an increasing inclination in the post-Cold War international community to raise the Israeli nuclear issue with greater openness. It would be wise for Israel not to underestimate this tendency and to be fully prepared. Israel should also prepare for the fact that once arms control fully enters the Middle East agenda, nuclear ambiguity will manifest diminishing results.

Another obstacle to very gradual modifications in Israel's nuclear stance is presented by the NPT. In its present form the Treaty puts Israel (as it does India or Pakistan) in the uncomfortable dilemma of either denuclearizing completely, or hanging on to ambiguity come what may. On this issue the ball is not in the Israeli court, and the challenge is to reconsider the value of a treaty that is irrelevant where the issues are most crucial to security, i.e., where nuclear proliferation de facto has already taken place. It would be wonderful if the naturally conservative tendency of governmental and non-official specialists toward treaties and institutions would allow some measure of imaginative adaptation to changing realities. It would also be helpful if a new NPT signatory such as France (with a prior tradition of not shying away from unorthodox advocacies) were to contribute to this process. So far, unfortunately, there are no grounds for optimism on either count.

Part IV

The Experience of

Other Regimes

9. CFE as a Model for Arms Control in the Middle East

Jerome Paolini

The negotiations on Conventional Forces in Europe (CFE) were initiated in early 1989, and were successfully concluded by the Paris Treaty of November 1990. To suggest the CFE as a model for arms control in the Middle East requires a brief review of the history of arms control and disarmament. From a French perspective, two very important lessons can be drawn from the experience gained since the beginning of the Soviet-American discussions on nuclear arms in the mid-1960s: first, that arms control in the East-West and European frameworks has brought little actual disarmament; and second, that fundamental political preconditions are indispensable if concrete results are to be achieved in this field.

Between the two world wars, the European powers initiated negotiations aimed at achieving disarmament on the continent within the framework of the League of Nations. These efforts failed because Germany's goal was rearmament and the cancellation of the Versailles Treaty of 1919: the political premises for any substantial negotiations on arms reductions were simply absent.

After World War II, and following the failure of early attempts at general disarmament within the UN framework, the US invented a new form of disarmament called "arms control" and finally convinced the Soviet Union to enter into direct, bilateral negotiations in the nuclear sphere. But arms control had little to do with disarmament: it was about managing the nuclear arms race and attempting to foster strategic stability between superpowers with growing arsenals. By the time certain military activities were ultimately forbidden by treaty, they were either no longer an obstacle to the continuation of the arms race (e.g., the Limited Test Ban treaties of 1963, 1974 and 1976) or were impossible to realize technically (e.g., the ABM Treaty of 1972). Although academics and officials still advocated actual reductions in nuclear arsenals as a distant goal, the arms race remained intentionally protected by the SALT treaties of 1972 and 1979. Again, during the 1970s and 1980s, arms control was nothing but a palliative for disarmament, simply because the political conditions--the state of the East-West confrontation--prevented any substantial breakthrough. For the same reason, conventional arms negotiations between the two alliances in Europe (the MBFR talks) lasted almost 15 years without any result.

Beginning in 1985 these political conditions changed radically with the emergence of Michael Gorbachev. By this time even the Reagan administration joined the critics of the arms control process as it had evolved during the Cold War. Thus, with the 1987 INF treaty the complete elimination of an entire category of nuclear arms--ground launched ballistic and cruise missiles with a range of 500-5000 km--was achieved for the first time. Because the political premises of the process were altered dramatically by the end of the Cold War, arms control in the traditional sense transformed itself into actual disarmament.

The completely altered strategic and political context on the continent allowed the opening of the CFE negotiations. The stated goal was to drastically reduce conventional forces between the Atlantic and the Urals for the first time in European history. As Perestroika unfolded in Moscow, ultimately dismantling the Soviet system altogether, the initial thrust of the negotiations could be maintained and the Paris Treaty finally signed. But soon thereafter, the fundamental political change which had allowed this historic agreement to be concluded, overtook the entire process.

The collapse of the Soviet Union and its transformation into a loose Commonwealth of Independent States (CIS), the revival of the nation state and its interests in Europe, and the termination of the East-West confrontation, have now jeopardized the stable, manageable framework in which the CFE negotiations took place. Thus the window of opportunity for real disarmament in Europe, which opened in 1985 after two decades of arms control, was closed in 1991 because the speed of political change

146

far exceeded the diplomatic structures and the negotiation framework inherited from the Cold War. As a consequence, the reconstruction of a new European order, both at the political and institutional levels, became a prerequisite for progress in further disarmament.

The history of arms control and disarmament in the East-West context, leads to the first and foremost lesson of CFE for the Middle East context: arms control generates very few positive results when implemented without a political settlement of the confrontation at stake. If arms control is sought in isolation from conflict resolution, negotiations might even damage the parties' interests. And finally, since the political premises of arms control in Europe and the Middle East are so different, CFE cannot be considered an easily transposable model. At best, a few lessons from CFE should be drawn in case Middle East states decide that the political conditions are sufficiently mature to launch serious arms control negotiations. These involve the more technical aspects of the CFE negotiations.

One useful parallel stems from the negotiation format adopted for CFE. First, CFE was not only devised as a way to reduce conventional forces in Europe but also as an element of the overall transformation of the security order on the continent. Indeed, it was conceived as an integral part of the CSCE process, a comprehensive peace framework dealing with economic aspects, human rights and military security. Similarly, Middle East arms control should be conceived as an element of a comprehensive peace process. But it is important not to push this analogy too far. The CSCE was created by the 1975 Helsinki Accords with the unstated goal of managing the bipolar status quo in Europe. It is only the downfall of communism in the Soviet Union and Eastern Europe that finally transformed the CSCE into a negotiation framework capable of overcoming the Cold War status quo. The lesson here is that institutional processes are critically dependent on political contingencies and their purpose can vary greatly over time.

Another possible application to the Middle East stems from the regional character of CFE. The negotiation zone was carefully defined as covering the European continent from the Atlantic to the Urals, including the European part of the former Soviet Union. But the European experience relevant to the Middle East is that the strictly regional dimension of arms control negotiations is very difficult to implement in practice. If CFE was indeed a regional affair, it nevertheless had a global dimension, both because the issue at stake was global--the bipolar confrontation on the continent--and because of the political and military weight of the two superpowers participating in the talks. Similarly, it may not be entirely wise to limit arms control in the Middle East to an exclusive regional framework when the issues are clearly not confined to the region's states.

The third and final point concerning the CFE format is that negotiations were conducted among sovereign states, in a multipolar mode. These negotiations were intergovernmental and did not directly involve the two antagonistic alliances--NATO and the Warsaw Pact. Indeed, the CFE treaty survived the dissolution of the Warsaw Pact precisely because it was signed by individual states. In the Middle East, arms control negotiations should follow this example in order to avoid an Israeli-Arab bipolar format and to ensure that inter-Arab security problems and imbalances are incorporated.

Although the CFE talks were not an alliance-to-alliance negotiation, the criterion adopted for achieving real reductions in conventional arsenals in Europe followed the simple rule of parity at reduced levels between NATO and the Warsaw Pact. This criterion is simple and straightforward, thus easily applicable. But in the Middle East no such clear rule is conceivable. Defining conventional stability in a truly multipolar negotiation would be very difficult. It would be necessary to decide whether to attempt constructing parity between all countries involved or to define specific limitations for each participating state according to its minimum defense needs. In the latter case, defining these needs in a fashion not threatening to others would be very complicated. These issues are extremely difficult--as reflected now in the follow-on negotiations to CFE--since in the new political environment in Europe the parity criterion between alliances no longer applies. This issue would arise in even more complex form in the Middle East.

Regarding the more technical and military aspects of the CFE negotiation and treaty, two interesting aspects might be particularly relevant to arms control in the Middle East: that CFE focused on conventional arms, and that the treaty established the notion of deep but mostly asymmetrical cuts.

The CFE mandate of 1989 stipulated that negotiations exclusively encompass conventional armed forces, including aircraft and helicopters. Nuclear arms and delivery vehicles, naval arms and chemical weapons were excluded. Applied to the Middle East where--just like in Europe at the time--conventional imbalances are at the heart of the problem, this mandate would seem to be judicious. Indeed, from Israel's perspective the sheer size of Arab armies, as well as the problem of disparity between standing armies and ground forces relying on the call-up of reserves, are critical aspects to be addressed by arms control. On the other hand, Arab interests could be taken into account in the CFE model, since negotiations could include air forces, where Israel has a clear qualitative edge, while excluding surface-to-surface missiles that can compensate air force imbalances.

Thus, conventional stability in the Middle East could be achieved in the form of an agreement in which Israel would obtain deep cuts in Arab ground forces and armor, by accepting a compensating reduction in its own air power. But the technicalities of negotiating the swapping of aircraft for tanks are extremely complex. Ascertaining the respective weight of air power and ground forces in the Middle East balance is very difficult. It is not easy to decide how many T-72s are worth a Kfir or an F-16, or the manner in which anti-tank helicopters should be included in the calculation. Moreover, given the magnitude of Arab conventional capacities, Israel would probably have to pay a very high price in terms of air power reductions to obtain significant cuts in opposing ground forces. All these problems were debated in CFE, and the parties concluded that it was impossible to achieve an agreement that swapped western air power reductions for cuts in Soviet armor. This would probably apply in the Middle East as well.

CFE negotiations also pointed to the difficulties in drawing the line between conventional and nuclear forces once negotiations are actually implemented. CFE was of course limited to conventional arms, and the nuclear dimension was totally absent from the provisions of the Paris Treaty. But negotiations were nevertheless directly influenced by the foremost issue in European security at the time: the future modalities of nuclear deterrence on the continent. As soon as the talks began, the Soviet Union attempted to include nuclear arms indirectly by requesting reductions in dual-use launchers and singling out nuclear-capable surface-to-surface missiles and strike aircraft earmarked for nuclear missions.

Indeed, the CFE goal of conventional parity at lower levels raised a considerable debate on the future of the American nuclear presence in Europe. Since the beginning of the Cold War, NATO had stressed that western nuclear forces were partly justified to compensate for the overwhelming Soviet superiority in conventional ground forces. Consequently, it became inevitable that the following question would be raised: should conventional imbalances disappear through effective arms control, why would nuclear deterrence in Western Europe still be needed? The lesson here is clear: the linkage between nuclear and conventional forces, be it political or military, cannot be severed during negotiations on conventional arms control. Thus, directly or indirectly the nuclear dimension would become a key issue of any CFE-type negotiations in the Middle East. This does not imply that Israel would necessarily have to engage in an intricate and complex exchange of its nuclear capacity for deep cuts in Arab ground forces. But it does mean that any breakthrough in conventional arms control in the region will be linked to some form of clarification concerning the Middle East nuclear equation.

Turning to the principle of asymmetrical cuts, the most important breakthrough of CFE was that, for the first time since the beginning of the Cold War, the Soviet Union and its Warsaw Pact allies recognized their massive superiority in ground forces

150

over NATO. The West had argued for years that, given the overwhelming disparity in numbers and the lack of strategic depth of Western Europe vis-à-vis the Soviet Union, any form of conventional disarmament on the continent would have to be asymmetrical. The same applies to Israel in the Middle East: the absence of strategic depth and an overwhelming Arab quantitative superiority in ground forces. Given these imbalances, it would indeed be essential for Israel to reject the concept of linear reductions in a conventional arms control negotiation with its neighbors. As was the case in Europe, the goal should be Arab recognition of Israel's quantitative inferiority and the establishment of considerably greater cuts for Arab forces than for the IDF, particularly in light of the critical difference between Israel's reserve forces and Arab standing armies.

Although the comparison between CFE and prospective conventional disarmament negotiations in the Middle East seems extremely pertinent in this respect, the specifically Euro-centered aspects of CFE should not be forgotten. In fact, two important points lead to the conclusion that the transposition might not be as pertinent as it seems at first sight. First, negotiations for CFE-type asymmetrical cuts between Israel and its neighbors could neither be feasible nor desirable, if conventional arms control in the region is to address inter-Arab imbalances and instabilities as well.

Secondly, the deeply asymmetrical results of CFE in Europe were essentially caused by the gradual collapse of the Warsaw Pact while negotiations were conducted. Of course the Paris treaty itself is based on achieving parity between NATO countries and Warsaw Pact states, hence much greater cuts for the Eastern side to match the parity criterion (fixed at 10-15% below the NATO level of 1990). But the net advantage for the West was generated by the fact that the Soviet Union lost all its Eastern European allies with the demise of the Warsaw Pact after the treaty was signed. The changing political context in Europe wrecked the very notion of parity, putting the Soviet Union in a situation of net inferiority in ground forces on the continent vis-à-vis NATO and its former Eastern European allies. These

151

exceptional circumstances are unlikely to be duplicated in the Middle East.

Beyond this, it is also very doubtful that Israel's strategic interests in conventional arms negotiations could be addressed through unilateral gains of the magnitude achieved by the West in CFE. Verifiable and enduring arms control agreements must address security interests of all parties involved in the negotiation. This implies that if conventional stability in the Middle East is to be achieved through arms control, the Arab threat perception vis-à-vis Israel as well as inter-Arab imbalances will have to be addressed. Thus, although some lessons can be drawn from the CFE experience, transposition to the Middle East as such is simply impossible.

In sum, the East-West experience in arms control and disarmament in general, as well as CFE in particular, strongly suggest that three major lessons must be considered when envisaging future prospects and modalities for security negotiations in the Middle East:

1. **The primacy of the political context**. Without prior resolution of the root causes of the Middle East entanglement, real disarmament cannot be achieved. Clearly, this does not mean that a security dialogue should not be entered into. But it must be clear that short of a political settlement, the outcome of such a dialogue can only be a mere palliative to disarmament.

2. **Any negotiation format must be specifically adaptable to the region**. CFE was a specific answer to a specific geopolitical situation on the European continent. The complex multipolarity of the Middle East does not lend itself to such a simple bipolar arrangement and would necessitate the definition of appropriate and distinct frameworks and goals for arms control. Such a definition must be made by the Middle East parties themselves.

3. **Significant arms control cannot avoid the nuclear question**. Nonconventional weapons and imbalances, and nuclear ones in particular, are an integral part of the regional security equation, in the Middle East as in Europe. Without some form of

clarification by all parties involved, and particularly by Israel, it would be illusory to pursue conventional stability on its own.

This may appear to be an impossibly tall order. But the requirements outlined above only amount to what should be considered the three strategic pillars of long term Israeli security: the settlement of the Palestinian question, a strategic nuclear deterrent, and participation in a stable, permanent, and institutionalized security negotiation for the Middle East.

10. The Architecture and Dynamics of The Conference on Security and Cooperation in Europe (CSCE)

Wlodzimierz Konarski

The first part of this presentation will mainly concern the way the CSCE works, its advantages and disadvantages, and obstacles. Then, a few ideas about the military security aspects and arms control aspects of this CSCE process will be presented, with special emphasis on the possibility of benefiting in the Middle East from the European experience.

The Conference on Security and Cooperation in Europe is not merely a conference as such. It is a structure, a system of intergovernmental cooperation and dialogue involving states in Europe and North America. The term CSCE process indicates a continuous effort, a continuation of a set of intergovernmental meetings, conferences, forums, symposiums, which in fact creates a certain self-perpetuating structure or system. It perpetuates itself because it is based on a very simple principle, a simple rule of consensus.

When in the mid-1970s we agreed to the rule of consensus in Europe--although everyone was conscious that consensus protects the sovereign interest of every participating state-- probably no one was fully aware that it created within the CSCE a unique mechanism which assures continuity. At any moment, a given state can exercise its right to refuse agreement, to refuse to join in a consensus; and then the decision cannot be taken. This has happened many times. We have discussed thousands of varied decisions, documents and resolutions in the CSCE that ultimately were not adopted because some states believed these were against their interests.

An assessment of CSCE achievements has always been and continues to be rather controversial. It runs the gamut from approval to criticism. At times, lengthy negotiations were conducted, mainly behind closed doors, until consensus could be reached. This is extremely time-consuming and not easily comprehensible to the press or the public. Moreover, in the past, politicians have not always been very enthusiastic about CSCE because as a rule they also preferred more direct and spectacular bilateral contacts.

There was another troublesome problem. When dealing with such a variety of issues within a nearly all-embracing agenda, certain problems had to be taken up logically; but there were always politicians who preferred to set aside those particular problems for a while. In bilateral politics, this is possible; in the multilateral process, which has its own internal political logic, it is not. Therefore, CSCE has been controversial for years.

Nevertheless, after years of multilateral efforts, the results appear to be so significant that at present the role of the CSCE is not in doubt. At the same time it is also quite clear that following the profound political changes in Europe, the CSCE scope and modus operandi need to be better adapted to new political requirements. 'Scope' refers to the addition of new participating states: post-Soviet republics, three Baltic States, and Albania. This has already been done. Now with the extension of scope, no doubt the CSCE will have to change.

The modus operandi of CSCE constitutes another matter for controversial debate. Is consensus to be maintained in its present form, or is it to be modified? How can the CSCE debates become more efficient? These are subject to further debate in the CSCE, because regular follow-up meetings will soon be held once every three years. The next one will be held in Helsinki, and representatives of all participating states will have to discuss the problems and, hopefully, also address the application of some recent agreements, such as the CFE treaty. This must be done if the CSCE is to fulfill its role in Europe.

Some brief background notes about the CSCE. It was created at the end of the 1960s/beginning of 1970s, and there is still a controversy over who was the first to present the initiative to set it up. Some maintain it was the Soviet Union at the end of the 1950s; others maintain it was Poland in 1964 in the United Nations. The western countries believe Denmark's proposal to the NATO ministerial council in 1966 marked the beginning. This problem may be considered as of secondary importance; yet who took the initiative and how, are important psycho-political questions. This has been avoided in Europe by presenting a variety of proposals more or less simultaneously. However, in the Middle East this issue may not be avoided as easily.

After the CSCE was created, whenever an important political initiative was to be put forward, a way to do so was generally suggested to a group of neutral non-aligned states in Europe, who often acted as "go-betweens." Thus Sweden, Switzerland, Finland, San Marino and other neutral and non-aligned states, that previously did not have much to do with one another, formed a group that played a very important role within the CSCE in the initiation of a new project or the introduction of a new document.

At the beginning of the CSCE, in 1970, long preparatory talks were held among over 200 delegates from 34 European states in Helsinki. They discussed mainly organizational modalities, procedure, objectives of the conference, the agenda, lists of participants and other necessary details. These were termed technical talks.

But later, it became clear that the talks were not so technical. They were in fact political, because what they created during the preparatory talks has survived in its entirety up to now, and in practice is very difficult to change. This came about because of a certain mechanism, the significance of which, as already mentioned, was originally not very clear to the European diplomats and experts. This simple mechanism is the definition of consensus.

Consensus is defined as the absence of any objection expressed by a representative of a participating state, and submitted by him as constituting an obstacle to the taking of a decision in question. This is, as we call it in Poland, a kind of "liberum veto." The absence of objection does not mean full approval. However, when there is an objection, no decision may

156

be taken. This rule of consensus was also defined by the experts at the beginning of 1970 in such a way that once something is decided by consensus, it may be changed only by consensus.

Thus even if you have an objection among many participating states, you cannot change the decision taken. Indeed, this is a universal mechanism that provides for continuity. If Middle East states ever decide to form such a framework, they would also have to determine whether they want a continuous framework, a permanent structure. If so, they have to comprehend something Europeans had to learn from their experience, namely that the principle of consensus not only protects sovereign rights and interests, including security interests; it also affords the extraordinary possibility of maintaining structures, once-created, for the future.

To date--the beginning of the 1990s--no state in Europe has even attempted to violate this continuity. And a state willing to precipitate the breakdown of such a structure would have to assume all the political blame. Therefore, it is completely out of the question.

The agenda of the talks was practically all-embracing. The first item concerned the problem of security in Europe, and the objective was to define basic principles that each participating state would agree to respect and follow. The 'final act' contains ten principles which have sometimes been referred to as 'the ten commandments.' Some may be found in UN documents, but not all. These ten principles guiding relations between the states now serve as a basis for interstate cooperation in Europe.

What may also be important as a lesson for the Middle East, is that in the mid-1970s we realized that there was no chance for disarmament or for arms reduction in Europe. Since at that time there was some opposition by NATO to military confidence building, the set of military confidence-building measures in the 'final act' is very modest, and has often been criticized by the experts. This criticism is largely justified, for those measures are militarily very insignificant.

However, it appears that without this modest beginning, Europe could not have developed them later into the second and third generations of confidence building, and the unprecedented arms cuts, as in the Treaty of Conventional Forces in Europe (CFE), could not have been negotiated. Thus military confidence building and arms control in Europe underwent a very long progressive step-by-step approach, primarily because there was no other way to win consensus.

Only later, at the beginning of 1980, did NATO realize that it could negotiate successfully arms control agreements which would be in its interest. This occurred only after human rights, the other important point on the agenda, had made their extraordinary entrance into the systems of Eastern Europe. Then those two items wrought progressive changes in the political situation and created conditions for progress in arms control.

With regard to the political conditions--of course many barriers had to be thrown down, and the major sources of potential conflict in Europe had to be extinguished before such a European undertaking could be successfully concluded. A series of bilateral agreements on normalizing relations between Germany and Eastern European states were concluded and an important four-power agreement on Berlin was reached. This took place as NATO policy vis-à-vis the Eastern Bloc became more flexible. Altogether, a favorable political environment was created that enabled the CSCE to develop its activities.

So, among the list of topics agreed upon 16 years ago, two dominated CSCE debates: human rights and individual freedoms on the one hand--the western priority--and military security questions, the eastern priority. Yet it must be admitted that at the beginning of this CSCE process, it was not that the East believed in military security. Rather, for the eastern side it comprised a political game: the East knew that the West could not accept real disarmament proposals. Proposals were put forward for propaganda reasons; it was clear in advance that they would not be accepted; and the political propaganda gains were obvious. The same applies to the western proposals for individual freedoms and human rights which were not accepted by the eastern side. Gradually, however, the CSCE mechanism and the changing external situation created a favorable possibility for concrete solutions.

To conclude the discussion of the CSCE, a number of current problems in Central and Eastern Europe, mainly the Yugoslavia crisis and the disintegration of the Soviet Union, should be mentioned. These affect, of course, the activity of the CSCE, because they involve two of its participating states. CSCE cannot act without their full participation, not only in the debate, but also in implementing the decisions in agreements already adopted. Yet they are not able to participate, as the territory between the Bug River and Vladivostok consists of a growing number of sovereign republics, and there is no conception how they could now implement the CSCE treaty.

Europe is currently witnessing a wave of criticism against the CSCE, namely: that the CSCE could not prevent such developments as those evolving in the former Soviet Union or Yugoslavia. This criticism is not justified, because these two important problems are internal in nature. CSCE is not equipped with any instrument to help resolve an internal crisis in a state. It is a structure for interstate, intergovernmental cooperation. Internal situations in the Soviet Union and Yugoslavia took the CSCE negotiators by surprise; they have no instrument by which they could intervene in the internal affairs of a given state.

Currently, of course, the situation is changing in Europe, and the CSCE principle of so-called noninterference in internal affairs is to be reexamined in light of the new situation. The old classic definition of this noninterference is no longer valid; it will have to be modified appropriately.

In drawing lessons from CSCE for the Middle East, there are four extremely important postulates that seem to be universal, as far as the functioning of such a structure as the CSCE or a similar organ is concerned.

First, there should be a political will among states to develop multilateral intergovernmental cooperation. States must see their interest in it, and discover a chance offered by such an effort for their security, dialogue and future cooperation. Those who, in the future, make up their minds that such cooperation is beneficial, would have to learn how the structure operates. What are its advantages? What are the risks? How does the mechanism function and how will it protect their interests?

Secondly, the political will among the states participating in such a system could be expressed or manifested in the Middle Eastern case at a time, I think, when the peace process will be at least sufficiently advanced to indicate that its final success is within reach. At that moment, one could start some informal preparatory discussions.

Third, it is important to know that all participating states must have equal rights. Their interests must be protected by the principle of consensus. If such an attitude were adopted, the consensus could, as in the European case, provide for necessary continuity and protection of the sovereign rights and interests of each participating state.

Fourth, the presence in Europe of the United States and Canada was recognized and considered necessary for the success of the CSCE. This experience could be taken advantage of in the Middle East. One could assume that so-called external participation could be politically important and useful. It could be particularly advantageous as far as implementation of future decisions is concerned.

The agenda for the European CSCE was tailored especially to regional needs. It was all-embracing, but not all of its points were accorded equal priority. The two priorities in Europe were military security and human rights. Military security is undoubtedly extremely important in the Middle East. Yet it may be wrong to concentrate exclusively on military security. Other topics should be recognized as important, including economic cooperation or some universally recognized important environmental project such as a water project, which is broadly recognized as a necessity requiring multilateral cooperation among all the states of the region. It would be wise to begin with something that is not very controversial, in case the military security debate is more time-consuming. Showing some progress in one area could demonstrate the utility of the structure.

Theoretically speaking and perhaps from a purely formal point of view, the states in the Middle East are to some extent in a slightly better situation than the European states were at the beginning of 1970. This is because they have already engaged in peace talks. There are two particular features of the peace talks that suggest that they could be the beginning of such interstate, intergovernmental cooperation: First, although they lack procedural ground rules, they are nonetheless consensus-orientated. Everyone knows that upon the refusal of one of the participants, a decision cannot be taken. So though they may not be consensus-based, they are at least consensus-orientated.

The second particular feature of the Middle East peace talks is that they are multilateral. They constitute a kind of structure which could be developed and extended to include the other states in the region into a future system of cooperation. Of course, ground rules are necessary. The real discussion, however, on such ground rules, procedures and the mechanism as a whole, can be started only when the process is sufficiently advanced politically.

Finally, returning to the realm of military security, in discussing whether arms reductions, conventional disarmament and the like are possible in the Middle East, one needs to be slightly more precise. It is clear that disarmament measures, understood as arms reductions, are not possible at this moment in the Middle East. They are not realistic, so it is better not to have such ambitions.

Another bit of European experience is instructive here, namely that when the states in Europe were in a similar situation in the 1970s, they all understood that real, meaningful, military disarmament measures could not be agreed upon. They started from military confidence building, that is, from agreements between the states that do not affect their military potential, or at least do not affect it directly.

In this context one might suggest for particular consideration in the Middle East one of the most promising among the various kinds of military confidence-building measures applied in Europe, namely, measures directed against surprise attacks and against what we call large-scale offensive action. The problem created by the possibility of such a surprise attack is very real here. One can diminish this possibility in two ways. One way is through military buildup, which is what Israel has been doing. But it is extremely doubtful that Israel could completely diminish or remove the possibility of surprise attack merely by a national military buildup.

If, however, Israel were presented with the possibility that it could diminish the risks through negotiations, agreements, and an entire system of verification and implementation of such agreements, it would be wise to examine such a possibility. This really calls for a multilateral agreement; it could not be done bilaterally, since most of what can be done bilaterally has already been done by the Arab states and Israel.

Hundreds of measures or agreements against surprise attack and large scale offensive action could be concluded. A very long list can be found in the CSCE; another one, in the United Nations Disarmament Committee. It would be advisable to peruse these lists, looking for possible measures of interest to the Middle East. It is also advisable to consider measures not included in these lists. For instance, Israelis suggest that their military forces, combat units and their organization are based on different principles than their counterparts on the Arab side. On the Arab side there are active units, combat-ready military units, and they do not have a reserve system such as Israel has. Shifting to a larger ratio of reserve to regular forces is a measure against surprise attack which would extend warning time. By extending warning time, you do not adversely affect the military potential of the states concerned. If the surrounding Arab states accept the principle of putting part of their forces into the reserves, it could be an effective and significant confidence-building measure which would not affect the military potential of the Arab states or Israel, but would increase over-all military security.

A variety of notification systems, observations, and inspection methods that are more or less intrusive, might be adopted. In negotiating these measures the critical factors are patience, determination and real stubbornness--trying to achieve

162

a result and being prepared to make compromises, so that the other party to the agreement can see its security interests served.

To conclude, the aim of all these efforts could be similar to the one in Europe: a stable military order, possibly of non-threatening character, within the system of cooperation between states.

Two issues remain. First, the idea of how closed societies may be influenced by military transparency which is to some extent created by the system of confidence-building measures. Secondly, the problem of a bilateral option vis-à-vis a multilateral option for the Middle East.

The argument that closed societies may not be good partners for implementation of military-political agreements is not borne out by experience. When we comprised the closed societies of Eastern Europe, we occasionally expressed objections but we had a nearly perfect record of implementation of confidence-building measures and other military agreements. Thus our experience does not suggest that your counterparts in the Middle East could not properly implement the agreements once agreed upon. Nonetheless I have doubts. It all depends on the verification system and the political environment. The possibility of using political persuasion and, to put it quite clearly, political pressure as well as economic pressure in case of violations of agreements, is often helpful. True, military secrecy and lack of transparency in military policies, and military postures in general are elements of totalitarian systems. If through negotiated international agreements a breakthrough is created, then military secrecy will have to disappear, and that will clearly have a political influence upon the whole system.

As for the question of bilateralism versus multilateralism, I have been told by an Israeli that what I am suggesting is a very sophisticated multilateral option, while Israeli foreign policy up to now has been rather bilateralist. "Why," he asked, "should Israel change the pattern of its foreign policy behavior, if to date it has had some degree of success?"

This is a logical argument, and one has to admit that it has had some success. But what should be discussed is whether or not bilateralism in Israeli foreign policy has to some extent, though perhaps not fully, been exhausted.

The multilateral option, although never before experienced, perhaps offers new possibilities, yet unknown, for the states in the Middle East. The peace talks mark the beginning of the multilateral option. One has to think about what will happen upon final conclusion of the peace talks.

The states in the Middle East will have to have at least multilateral intergovernmental mechanisms of implementation. There is a danger that the implementation may not be very smooth. Therefore a mechanism is needed. The question is whether that future mechanism is to be devoted exclusively to implementation, or whether it may include some other elements of cooperative security, economic cooperation, and the like. This is a matter of choice.

11. The Strategic Situation and the Prospects for Confidence Building on the Indian Subcontinent

Shekhar Gupta

India and Pakistan have shared a relationship over the past 40 years of the subcontinent's partition, which is somewhat similar to the relationship between two spouses who are constantly at odds. They fight; there are long periods of tension; they don't speak to one another; they even come close to divorce, then one backs off; occasionally there are also short periods of love, affection and warmth.

The current situation in the Indian-Pakistani relationship somewhat resembles the tense, uneasy, quiet but peaceful phases. The situation has elements that could lead to either extreme--to warmth, or to another sparring phase. Today, unlike a large part of 1987 and part of 1990, strike forces are not on the borders. Nonetheless there is a basic difference between the current situation and the one preceding 1987. The 1987 turning point will be discussed below.

Strike forces have never been far from either side of the border. Pakistani strike forces have always been within 12 hours of the border. But whereas until recently Indian strike forces were always 96-120 hours away, at present they are about 48-72 hours away. Therefore today it takes less time to build up to a military confrontation.

The tensions in Kashmir and Punjab have increased internal pressures within the parliament and within the political setup in India to retaliate against Pakistan. Indians state that they cannot continue allowing Pakistan to bleed them slowly, while they refrain from exercising their option to use their superior military power.

In addition, there are tensions between India and Pakistan with regard to another dimension: the nuclear issue. Pakistani intelligence and the Pakistani establishment are making no attempt to maintain the old pretense and deny that they have the bomb. On the contrary, they have been quite brazen in announcing that they have the bomb, and have been pleading for going "all out" with the nuclear program. At least one of India's major political parties, the Bharatiya Janata Party--which is described rightly as a new party and wrongly as a fundamentalist party--has an election manifesto that very strongly favors going ahead with an overt nuclear program. Therefore nuclear tension continues. This is further complicated by the supply of Chinese missiles to Pakistan, and by the unraveling of the Soviet Union, both of which have caused a lot of concern in India. There is also great concern in India regarding whether an 'Islamic bomb' already exists, and who controls it. Ultimately it might be preferable to have Pakistan control a nuclear bomb than an unfamiliar person or group in some Central Asian republic.

On the other hand, there are also a few positive developments taking place. There is a continuing dialogue at what we refer to as the foreign secretary level. The foreign secretary in India is a bureaucrat similar to the US undersecretary of state. Every three or six months, the Indian foreign secretary and a group of Indian diplomats go to Pakistan, or vice versa, and exchange words and pleasantries with their counterparts. Thus basically, some kind of talking goes on.

In addition, occasionally there are also military-to-military meetings. These take place not exactly between the top brass, but on what is locally referred to as the PSO level, i.e., the principal staff officer echelon of the army, which means the director general of military operations, the director general of military intelligence and the key army commanders and co-commanders. They meet roughly once a year, and exchange notes about exercises.

Another positive factor at the moment is evident in the US policy toward the region. The US seems to have learned over the years that pressure on the subcontinent does not work, because there is a tremendous feeling of anti-Americanism in Pakistan;

indeed, the American embassy was burned down there. In India, anti-Americanism has lessened, but no Indian government could sell a scheme to the parliament if there were any evidence of US pressure on India with regard to the matter.

There are other international factors that have a bearing on what is happening in the region. For example, there is the possibility of bombs going astray in Central Asia. Another alarming possibility that worries not only the Indians but also the Pakistanis is the spread of Islamic fundamentalism in the Central Asian republics. Currently there is a struggle between the regimes which are either fairly progressive or more communist (yet by now have given themselves nationalist names) and the fundamentalist groups, with Saudi Arabia supporting the Islamic movement and flying in a million Korans weekly. Should the fundamentalists win the struggle, serious problems will arise. Pakistan has a large fundamentalist constituency headed by the Jamaat-i-Islami, which has already suggested a confederation of Pakistan, Afghanistan, parts of Iran and Central Asia and parts of India and even Kashgar.

Another concern is how the Indian subcontinent will settle down in the wake of the end of the Cold War and the demise of the Soviet Union, to which it is fairly close geographically. The Soviet Union exerted a balancing influence of sorts on the region. How far will the US go in its current warmth toward India, which is at its highest peak since 1962? Because of the end of the Cold War, Pakistan does not seem to be as important to the US as it was in the past; nor does China. As a matter of fact, China is more of a problem, since people are calculating that within 5-10 years the communist system there will break down. This assessment has led to America's rediscovery of a country called India. But the question remains: How far will the US go?

Another crucial and insufficiently emphasized question is how far China will go in its commitments with regard to the Missile Technology Control Regime (MTCR). Everyone knows, and even the Pakistanis do not deny, that the entire Pakistani nuclear program was built out of the European nuclear free market. For one reason or another much of it was purchased from Germany. The Chinese have sold numerous items, and recently set up a rocket fuel plant in Karachi, which is a cause for great Indian concern, although apparently the Chinese stopped short of selling long range missiles. The Pakistanis are saying openly that they have received M-9s and several M-11s.

Notwithstanding these important international factors, the two countries still seem to be sufficiently mature and experienced to move toward their own regime of confidence-building measures without much intervention or pressure from outside.

Like many others in India and Pakistan, I would suggest that the first prerequisite for any serious confidence-building regime between India and Pakistan is that these two states go overt with their nuclear programs. This may seem a somewhat outrageous proposition, and clearly not one that many would make in either the Indian or Pakistani parliaments, but it nonetheless highlights a necessary condition for progress, and for the following reasons:

First, only when a state admits to having the nuclear bomb can it actually legislate how it is going to be used. As long as the nuclear capability is opaque, there may be bombs lying in the basement, but who can say by whom, how, or when one is to be used? Unless the states--especially Pakistan, as will immediately become apparent--'go open' with their nuclear program, there can be no confidence-building measures, because each side will wonder who controls the button or who carries the briefcase for the red (or green) button, or will wonder about whatever else is context-related. This is a very important prerequisite.

Secondly, if the two countries 'go open' with their nuclear programs, it will help the democratic government in Pakistan to get a better hold on its nuclear program. The Pakistanis as well as the American authorities now suggest that Abdul Qadir Khan, who heads Pakistan's nuclear program, does not report to the military. This naturally raises the question, to whom does he report? The answer is that he reports to the president. But the president was appointed as an active president after his predecessor's death. He was a bureaucrat, and was never formally elected, other than through some kind of an election

168

through the parliament. India also has a president elected by parliament but, unlike Pakistan, India's is a constitutional president with no formal powers. The presidency in Pakistan was fundamentally transformed during the term of Zia ul Haq. Several years prior to his death, Zia passed what was called an eighth amendment to the Pakistani constitution, giving the president (i.e., himself) sweeping powers, usurped from the newly democratically-elected government and the prime minister. The present (elected) Pakistani president inherited exactly the same powers.

It is therefore hardly reassuring that the entire Pakistani nuclear program is controlled by a 76-year old president who is a hawk and very close to the military. If, on the other hand, Pakistan went overt with its nuclear program, this would help democratic governments in Pakistan slowly to attain better control over the program. This development would be quite important, as political parties in Pakistan are believed to have no interest in using nuclear weapons in any military conflict with India.

One other positive consequence of 'going overt' will be the removal of existing ignorance about the bomb in both countries. Lately India and Pakistan have conducted a series of seminars where both sides have met and discussed issues privately. But nothing has been settled. What one hears from the Pakistanis at the conferences very often is: "we have the bomb now; we are not scared of you; we are equals." This is a very dangerous situation because no matter what the balance of power in terms of the number of bombs Pakistan or India has, there is no way that Pakistan would survive a nuclear exchange. India of course would also fare badly. But the Pakistanis, or at least a part of the Pakistani establishment, are badly mistaken if they think seriously that because they have the bomb as ultimate insurance they can go on bleeding India indefinitely, because as long as they have it India will not exercise its military option of initiating war.

Indian history and politics are such that there is no way any Indian government, under any party, would allow Pakistan to exercise control over any part of India through a proxy war. Ultimately, India would have to resort to the military option, despite Pakistan's nuclear capability. In this light one should go back to 1965 and glance at the signals which are now coming out of Pakistan. In 1965 Pakistan would not have gone to war with India and would not have resorted to large scale subversion in sending 10,000 infiltrators into Kashmir in what was called "Operation Gibraltar," had it known that India would escalate.

The Pakistanis were convinced that India would never escalate the war in the plains, hence they went to war with India and Kashmir; but the war escalated. There is real danger of something like that happening again. For this reason 'going overt' with the nuclear program might prove useful, helping the respective populations, parliamentarians, and decisionmakers on both sides to understand the limitations of nuclear weapons.

Setting the nuclear question aside, both India and Pakistan have done a fairly good job of building CBMs at their own levels. The crucial point was 1987, when India and Pakistan were on the brink of war. At the time, India conducted a very aggressive maneuver, called "Exercise Brass Tacks." It moved all its strike formations in the desert next to Pakistan's border, and live ammunition was issued to the strike formations. These actions were accompanied by a psychological buildup which seemed to suggest that at D plus 1 the Indian forces would cross the Indus River; at D plus 2 they would be in Karachi; and at D plus 3 they would be on the border with Iran. The Pakistanis, apparently believing some of this, moved many formations next to the border, and things almost got out of hand.

It was at this time that the first confidence-building measure was initiated by Zia himself who, as a soldier, realized the disadvantages of his situation should war break out. He resorted to what is now called 'cricket diplomacy.' It so happened that when the strike forces of the two were standing muzzle to muzzle, India and Pakistan were playing a cricket test match. So in the midst of all this tension and talk of war, President Zia decided to fly down and watch the cricket match, thereby helping defuse tensions.

In the aftermath of this crisis, a lot of things were done in the area of confidence building. For example, a hotline was set up between generals on both sides of the front. In addition, each side had to notify the other of any movement of one of its brigades within 100 kilometers from its side of the border. This is done through a cumbersome procedure. Rather than the Indian general calling the Pakistani counterpart general or vice versa and informing him, the practice is that a staff officer calls his counterpart. A conversation then takes place using transcribers on both sides, and the information is recorded. Despite its cumbersome setup, the system nonetheless works: most movements since then have been notified, and no side has expressed doubt, except perhaps on one occasion when the Indians lost count of one of Pakistan's divisions, and the Pakistanis lost count of two Indian armored regiments. (But at that point both sides seem to have lost count of their own units as well: the Indians lost track of two regiments for two days; the same thing happened to the Pakistanis.)

Another part of the confidence-building measures instituted between India and Pakistan is the system called "flag meetings," using a colonial term. These occur if there is a clash on the border--particularly in Kashmir, where the forces are very close-- or when someone who goes to steal cattle on the other side is arrested. The local commanders then call for a meeting, and after marking out a neutral area right on the border, each commander puts his flag there and they come unarmed and have a meeting. Many local problems are sorted out in this manner, so that local clashes do not build up into an all-out conflagration.

The real problem is that in both countries the basic mutual fears remain. At this point in time in India the fears are stronger and the anger greater than they have ever been, at least since the liberation of Bangladesh in 1971. The Indians feel that they are being bled in Punjab and Kashmir. While most Indians are aware that there are real indigenous causes for these problems, no one has any or should have any doubt that Pakistanis are also quite actively involved--a fact even the terrorists themselves make no secret of. This state of affairs upsets India considerably, because in these states it is more than the territorial issue that is at stake. In both these territories India has trouble with minorities, and for

171

Indian political leaders this raises fears that the conflicts there could escalate, cutting into the very roots of India's secular policy and society. The frightening prospect is that the Hindu majority might start hitting back.

Let us first consider the case of Punjab, where the Hindus are being killed by Sikh militants in trains, buses, on the streets, or in parks while jogging. So far, except for the one retaliation after Mrs. Gandhi's assassination, there has never been any retaliation by the Hindus in any part of the country. Some 40% of India's Sikhs live outside of Punjab; they are a very prosperous community, very prominently represented in the army and the bureaucracy. Thus far there has been no retaliation against them, but there is genuine fear in India that this situation may not continue forever. Should the Hindus choose to retaliate, a serious deterioration could take place.

The second case is Kashmir. More than four decades after the Indo-Pakistani partition, the Indian Muslims have gained acceptance for the first time as patriotic Indians, because there were always doubts about their loyalty to India. In fact, so much so, that whereas some of India's best hockey players in the 1960s were Muslims, they were not included in the national team; they were not trusted to play Pakistan. So a lot has changed for the better since that time. But the tension in Kashmir and the secessionist movement there, which is Islam-based, undermines the roots of that very integration. The Hindu fundamentalist parties, which have always questioned the patriotism of Indian Muslims, are now in a position to say, "Look, we always told you never to trust the Muslims. You should have treated them the way we told you; it is because you treated the Muslims deferentially that we have such problems in Kashmir."

Thus far nobody has bought this argument of the Hindu fundamentalists, and there has been no retaliation against Muslims elsewhere. Nor have Indian Muslims ever shown any interest in what is going on in Kashmir--so much so that a recent Indian commander in Kashmir was a Muslim. But this situation may not continue indefinitely, particularly if things deteriorate much more in Kashmir, and it comes close to secession. This development is bound to hurt India very deeply. Hence it is a cause for concern.

In Pakistan, on the other hand, there is a continuing fear that India has vast military superiority, and it may simply roll over Pakistan. There is a powerful school in the Pakistani military and in the intelligence agencies, mostly in fundamentalist groups, which believes that Pakistan must not let India relax and build up its strength economically or militarily. India, they believe, is on the defensive today in Punjab and Kashmir, and Pakistan should go on bleeding it there. Because Pakistan has the bomb, they believe that India would not escalate into a full-scale war, and would not be able to use its military potential or advantage over a long period of time. Ultimately, India would cease to be of such importance, as it would lose out to secession. These Pakistani circles also point to the agitation in India by groups like the BJP and groups within the ruling Congress Party and the other parties as a cause for concern. After all, they submit, what is the point of having such a large Indian military machine and spending on it 4% of the Indian GNP, if India is not going to try to use it effectively and teach Pakistan a lesson.

Lately another dangerous trend has grown, associated with what in Pakistan is called "strategic depth." The same "establishment" in Pakistan believes that with the victory in Afghanistan, and with the advances made by Pakistani fundamentalist groups in Central Asian states, Pakistan has acquired strategic depth (i.e., in Afghanistan, the Central Asian republics and Iran). With its strategic depth and its bomb, and given the signs of India breaking up, Pakistan, they believe, has the strength to up the ante a little. This is a very dangerous situation. In reality, what is coming in from Central Asia and Afghanistan to Pakistan may not be strategic strength, but rather a burden, because it is so fragmented and chaotic.

Having described the Indo-Pakistani situation, the question arises what to do about it. Some Americans show great irritation at India and Pakistan for not being able to accept that the world has recently changed. They argue that if Gorbachev could stand up one day and state, "whatever has happened for 40 years is all wrong and I am changing it," why can't this happen in India and Pakistan as well? The answer is that it cannot happen overnight in the Middle East or in the Indian subcontinent because our problems are rooted in the history of our creation. India and Pakistan are not like Germany, which was divided by the superpowers. India and Pakistan were divided by their own people who believed in two conflicting ideologies, and it is impossible to start all over again.

It is this problem, the psychology of partition (more or less voluntary partition--although many in India would blame the British for this), that creates serious psychological stumbling blocks. What are these psychological blocks? The most significant ones have to do with nonacceptance of the ideology of existence. When Pakistan came into being, nobody in India believed that the Muslims would not be disappointed in a separate nation; and nobody in Pakistan believed that a settlers' state could survive in the subcontinent. Then there is the contradiction of ideologies of governments. India chose democracy in the 1947 partition. Pakistan chose a quasi-military Islamic system, and an ideological state. Indians believe that Pakistan will never work out, and vice versa. Such conditions hardly provide the basis for confidence-building measures.

The three wars that India and Pakistan fought in 1947-48, 1965 and 1971 have helped ease the situation somewhat, because each side believes that it has won the ideological battle. How? In 1965 India proved that it was capable of successfully defending itself against Pakistan, despite Pakistan's vast qualitative superiority and preparedness. It demonstrated that a democracy could defend itself, thereby debunking the prevailing Pakistani view at the time, to the effect that a democracy like India whose leaders eat lentils would not be able to defend itself.

In 1971 India won the war against Pakistan, but ultimately Pakistan, too, had something to savor. Although India cut Pakistan into two, Pakistan not only survived that defeat and the loss of more than half of its territory, but it actually emerged much stronger from the 1971 experience.

With regard to ideologies of government, there is also some satisfaction on both sides. Indians believe that despite everything, Pakistan has moved toward democracy. At present the Pakistanis are more democratic than they have ever been, and they will become even more so unless the fundamentalists win. On the other hand, Pakistanis believe that India has fallen behind them, especially in economic development. This is partly true, insofar as Pakistan's per capita income today is almost 50% higher than India's. Indeed, after following the path of socialism and what is called self-reliance for a very long time, India's economy is only now opening up.

Some significant obstacles remain on both sides. At least two of them stand in the way of any long term prospects for peace between these two countries. In India a belief exists among the leadership as well as the intellectuals that the power center in Pakistan consists of the president and the army. Significantly, the Pakistani Army has always believed Zia's doctrine that they are defenders not just of the territorial borders of Pakistan, but also of the ideological frontiers of Pakistan. That view is almost an article of faith for the Pakistani Army. Witness how it sealed the fate of the Pakistani government dismissed on August 6, 1990. Its demise is widely believed to have been determined in mid-March when Prime Minister Bhutto addressed the National Defense College of Pakistan, and said that the Pakistani Army was not the defender of the ideological frontiers of Pakistan, but only of the territorial frontiers of Pakistan. If armies could defend ideological frontiers of nations, then the Berlin Wall would not have crumbled, she said. It seems that it was at that point that the Pakistani Army decided to write her off.

The tug of war in this power structure is connected with the prime minister, who is well meaning, and the democratic setup. The problem is that the three--the president, prime minister, and Army--often work at cross purposes. The real power break comes with respect to relations and to strategic issues, most prominently the nuclear issue. In this context the army and the president are together for all practical purposes. The president never comes out in the open. The army sometimes comes out in the open. For example, it is significant that the negotiations with King Zahir Shah of Afghanistan were held in Rome, not by diplomats but by the army chief of staff.

Consequently, in the Indian government and its decisionmaking establishment there is always the fear when dealing with a democratic Pakistani prime minister that he will not be able to deliver anything. Alternatively, what is the point of talking to the army when by so doing one is legitimizing army rule and enhancing its power in Pakistan, which is not in India's interests. And the Pakistani president is someone who does not even talk to Indians.

Hence the Indians want just to let things drift. This may not be a very sensible policy, although there is some point in these arguments, as evidenced by the experience the one time that India and Pakistan decided to open a political dialogue. This was when Rajiv Gandhi went to Pakistan in the winter of 1988, during the summit of the South Asian Association of Regional Cooperation (SAARC), and after he and Benazir Bhutto had long one-on-one talks. Things seemed to be looking brighter. But as it later transpired, the room had been bugged by the Pakistani Army and the president, and the tapes of those conversations were used against Benazir in the following elections. It turns out she said a lot of things about the army, which, to use a euphemism, were unparliamentary, and these proved devastating for her.

As a result, at present there is a feeling on the Indian side that a dialogue with a Pakistani prime minister is pointless, since he does not control real power, and he cannot deliver anything. Perhaps if he came too close to India or if he seemed to be opening up to India, the army and the establishment would knock him down. Perhaps the answer is that if there are three branches of power in Pakistan, then the Indians should do business with the branch that seems most suitable from the Indian point of view, and nurture it. Nothing can be lost in doing that.

In Pakistan, on the other hand, there is a belief that India's breakup is only a matter of time, and that all that is required is to outlast India. It is well known that India is a settlers' state, composed of people speaking many languages, having many religions, suffering from many other problems. "If India is on the brink of collapse, then why not help the process along, and make it happen." The people of Pakistan, however, surely realize that India's breakup would not be in their interest. Because if India lost territory due to a religious or ethnic secessionist movement, this would only mean that India would be ruled forever by Hindu fundamentalist parties.

What does all this suggest for the future? First, that both countries have to accept the current borders in the subcontinent. If anyone in Pakistan has hopes of getting more of Kashmir, he must realize that it will not work. If anyone in India has hopes of recovering what Pakistan has of Kashmir, he must also reconcile himself to the fact that it will not work. An agreement has to be arrived at at some stage with regard to sharing the boundaries of Kashmir, and retaining each side's holdings there.

Secondly, on the nuclear question, CBMs are urgently needed. One step was taken when the signing of the agreement on non-attack of nuclear installations was followed in December 1991 with the long awaited exchange of the annex containing lists of those installations, although some doubts remain whether each side informed the other in full about all its installations. Now that the exchange of lists has taken place, questions are being raised whether to move on to an agreement on no first attack. Even without each side conceding that it has the bomb, both can still say that any side that has the bomb will not attack the other side first. Indeed, some negotiations along these lines are probably taking place behind the scenes.

Another CBM pertaining to the nuclear programs derives from the fact that these can no longer be rolled back. Now that these programs have acquired momentum and have reached a certain level, there is a need to freeze them, so that if one side has another ten or 15 bombs, they will not be mounted on missiles, and the force will not be militarized. There is no point in continuing to say, "let us have a world without nuclear weapons; let us have a subcontinent without nuclear weapons." The logical step is to try and freeze the situation, which should be possible.

There should be closer military-to-military contacts. Very significant in this context are the observations offered by the Indian prime minister at the annual area commanders meeting of the army in November 1991. He said, "I have come to the conclusion that much can be achieved in professional to professional level talks." A comparison to Indian-US relations is instructive. India and the US tried to do several things over the past four decades. Nothing worked out until a couple of American generals came to India, and General S.F. Rodrigues, Indian army chief, went to the US, and then a lot seemed to happen. At least there are American officers coming to our schools and vice versa.

Concerning Pakistan, the Indian prime minister said that the Indian military should actively try to seek and establish some kind of rapport with their Pakistani counterparts. Much has been said about the interesting Pakistani proposal to have five-nation talks on the nuclear question. It is lamentable that the instinctive Indian official reaction to this proposal, which was naturally negative, continues to dictate the line simply because India became committed to that position. Some kind of talks must start, regardless of whether they are two-nation or five-nation talks.

In any event, the choice of five-nation talks is academic, because it is rather obvious what position Russia now has in the region. However, as far as India is concerned, China is a key player in the region. China is not an outside power that can guarantee an agreement in the region. Indians genuinely fear China; and China is also a country with a very bad nuclear proliferation record. In fact, if American reports are to be trusted, India itself bought tens of tons of Chinese heavy water on the black market. So there are some doubts about China's possible role in such talks.

Some kind of negotiations between India and Pakistan must start. Over the longer term, CBMs between India and Pakistan will also have to take hold at a deeper and less spectacular level. It is unrealistic to expect that, like Europe, things will somehow turn around, there will be a sudden show of statesmanship, and two great leaders will bury past problems.

This cannot happen, because the wounds in the Indian subcontinent are too deep, because people have too much in common, and partition is too recent a phenomenon and has left so much bitterness. After all, in no other part of the world was partition preceded by the massacre of 2.2 million people, as happened on the subcontinent.

Sorting out the Kashmir issue, however, is very difficult. Better to move forward in areas that are not very controversial, such as cultural links and easier travel between the two countries. At present it is almost impossible for an Indian or Pakistani to obtain a visa to travel into the other's country.

India, being the more open and democratic country and having an open society, should not fear permitting Pakistanis to enter without a visa. It need not fear Pakistanis coming in and spending some money, going to Bombay and seeing Kashmir. Indians should open up their country to Pakistan, as this would help to drive the fears of India out of Pakistani minds. They will come and see how disorganized Indians are, and how much poorer Indians are than they, and it will give them a more secure feeling. The fear of the unknown will go away.

In the past, India and Pakistan have talked a lot about such steps, but these have not been implemented. Recall the famous summit in Pakistan between Rajiv Gandhi and Benazir Bhutto. They came up with some good ideas in this realm, such as that judges and members of parliament in all southern countries should be allowed to travel without visas. It was suggested that all SAARC countries be allowed to sell one another's newspapers and magazines. Several years have passed, but none of this has been implemented. The Pakistanis said they will not allow Indian newspapers and magazines to enter because these would comprise a cultural invasion of their country. The Indian parliament has still not ratified the agreement on visa travel for judges and members of parliament, because of a very heavy agenda and time constraints. But these are areas in which a beginning could be made much faster.

At an even deeper, intellectual level, people from both countries have to sit down and clean up school textbooks reciprocally. India began doing this in the 1980s, because of a certain degree of liberalism which came into Indian universities and among intellectuals. But both countries, today much more so Pakistan, have used the teaching of history as an instrument to build hatred for the other country. India and Pakistan, or Hindus and Muslims for that matter, have very different views of the subcontinent's history from the 8th century AD onwards when the first Muslim invader, Mohamed Ben Kassim actually came to India from Iraq, killed the King of Sind and established Islam.

For the Hindus in India the day the foreign invader came and killed the Hindu king and established the first mosque was a black day; in Pakistan, on the other hand, it is a national holiday.

If both countries could sit down and begin to clean up the textbooks, then at least 15 or 20 years from now there might be a generation that will not be so prejudiced about the other country. The ground for this initiative was provided for in the 1973 Indo-Pakistani Simla agreement, which called for ceasing hostile propaganda, cleaning up textbooks, cleaning up the study of history, etc. To that extent, the Simla agreement was far ahead of the Helsinki Final Act, but it was not followed up because of lack of political will as well as simple bureaucratic resistance on both sides. If, at long last, both countries were able to embark on this path, and somehow also managed at the same time to prevent full scale war from occurring, things would only improve as the years passed. Both countries could then move into an era of slightly more solid peace.

Part V

US Non-Proliferation Policy

12. The Bush Administration's Arms Control Agenda for the Middle East

Geoffrey Kemp

The scope and dimension of the Bush Administration's Middle East arms control policy cannot be judged unless it is put in the broader context of American interests in the region and past attempts by the US to control the Middle East arms race. Indeed, judging by the degree of responsibility exercised over the years, the US record on arms control in the Middle East ranks well when contrasted with Soviet, French, Chinese and probably British policies.

During the 1950s, the United States was part of the Tripartite Agreement that restricted and rationed arms to the major countries in the Arab-Israeli dispute. Agonizing decisions were made in the 1960s over supplying Israel with small amounts of arms, though these decisions were made easier after the 1967 war when President de Gaulle cut off French supplies to Israel. Later, in 1972 a major flaw in American policy emerged. The problem began when Henry Kissinger and Richard Nixon agreed in 1972 to sell advanced arms to the Shah of Iran. This decision was taken during their visit to Tehran just after Britain had decided to terminate completely its military presence in the Gulf. The American policy was to replace Britain by supporting a "twin pillar" policy in the region built around arms supplies to Saudi Arabia and Iran. Iran was to receive the lion's share of the arms.

The Shah of Iran was extremely interested in weapons procurement, and the US military and arms producers reacted accordingly. His attitude resulted in open and intense competition between the US Navy and the US Air Force to market their respective front-line aircraft to Iran, in order to reduce unit costs back home. The competition eventually ended, in part because the Pentagon itself became tired of trying to administer arms transfers that were out of control.

With the exception of sales to Iran, most of the other major US arms transfers have been reasonably successful and/or reasonably restrained. In cases like Pakistan where the US seemed less restrained, a more important objective--undermining Soviet military power in Afghanistan--precluded greater restraint. Overall, US restraint on arms supplies can best be demonstrated by listing the weapons, subsystems, and paraphernalia that successive US administrations, including the Bush administration, consistently **rejected** selling despite offers of hard currency. The total value of American military construction and military sales to the region must be considered in the context of the sales that the US turned down.

Requests for US high technology weaponry and subsequent US refusals were common. For instance, in the 1970s Israel was extremely eager to purchase the Pershing surface-to-surface missile. The US refused to sell the Pershing and offered the Lance missile instead. The Saudis have repeatedly requested upgrade components for their F-15s; their requests have consistently been rejected. After the Gulf War no Middle Eastern country, friendly or not, is likely to obtain the very high-tech American equipment that was used in that war, with the exception of the Patriot missile. In future, there will probably be a major debate concerning the timing of Israeli access to new aircraft technologies, including the F-22, since air power is such a critical component of Israel's strategy.

When the Carter administration came to office in 1976, it made a very clear and deliberate attempt to reverse the trends in American arms transfer, arms sales, and military assistance policies globally. In part, this was a reaction to the upsurge of US military assistance and arms sales that occurred during the Nixon/Ford years, particularly to Iran. However, while it was able to articulate a coherent policy of restraint, the Carter administration found that increasingly it had to make exceptions to the rule. The three key exceptions were all Middle Eastern countries. Within a year, the Carter administration reversed itself with respect to arms transfers and military assistance to Israel, Saudi Arabia and Iran. For instance, an extremely bitter fight with Congress erupted over the Carter administration's decision to sell F-15 aircraft to Saudi Arabia.

When the Reagan administration came into office, traditional arms control was not high on the agenda. In addition, references to arms control in the Middle East focused primarily on chemical weapons and missile proliferation. Vice President George Bush launched the Reagan administration's chemical weapons initiative in a speech in Geneva in 1984. Ronald Reagan, in his closing days as president, called for a major chemical weapons conference, which was subsequently held in Paris in January 1989.

Unfortunately, the impact of such a narrow focus on chemical weapons and missiles was predictable in the context of the Middle East. The Arabs all cried "foul." Consequently the most important theme resulting from the Paris meetings was universal Arab condemnation of the selectivity of chemical weapons arms control and the problems of discussing a ban on chemical weapons without placing other weapons of mass destruction, most notably Israel's nuclear weapons, on the agenda. The staunchest supporters of Iraq during the Paris conference were the moderate Arab states, including Egypt. The Bush administration learned its lesson and did not further pursue Middle East arms control until the Gulf crisis.

The first Gulf crisis began in April 1990 with Saddam Hussein's famous statement that he would burn up half of Israel. From then on, new attention was focused on the Middle East arms race. The Bush administration could not ignore the issue without being criticized by Congress. By asking questions and preparing draft legislation, Congress began putting pressure on the administration to take some initiatives.

The Gulf War made the dimensions of the problem more salient, but ironically, the lesson for US arms transfer policy was ambiguous. The war highlighted the dangers of what happens when a Saddam Hussein is allowed access to advanced military technologies. But at the same time it demonstrated that US military operations can derive much benefit from a close military assistance relationship with Saudi Arabia. Had it not been for the massive buildup of military infrastructure in Saudi Arabia during the 1980s, Desert Storm might never have happened.

A breakdown of the total value of all US military assistance and sales to Saudi Arabia during the 1980s demonstrates that some 60-70% was devoted to military construction, rather than to cutting-edge offensive or defensive fighting weapons. The lesson from the Gulf War is that a policy of building up the military capabilities of Arab allies in the Gulf--initiated by President Jimmy Carter in his closing years and adopted by the Reagan and Bush administrations--was sensible and should be continued as long as regional stability remains dependent upon US military power.

Nevertheless, it was clear that in the aftermath of the Gulf War greater pressures would develop to address proliferation and the military buildup in the Middle East. In the spring of 1991, dozens of initiatives were proposed by many sources--the press, public interest groups and Congress--calling for more arms control. The menus included a ban on **all** military sales to every country from Marrakesh to Bangladesh, as well as proposals to stop the supply of sophisticated equipment, including aircraft, to all countries in the Middle East, including Israel. There were two significant problems with this all-embracing approach: it was unworkable, and it was not in the American interest. Yet something had to be done.

The Bush administration outlined a four-pillar post-war Gulf policy that included arms control as a component of Middle East policy. In his March 6, 1991 speech to Congress, President Bush stressed the determination of the administration to produce an arms control agenda. The cornerstone of the administration's arms control policy was UN Resolution 687, the toughest resolution ever passed by the United Nations against a member state. While not quite as all-embracing as the Versailles Treaty which imposed draconian demilitarization penalties against Germany, Resolution 687 provides the mechanism for implementing the disarmament of Iraq.

In addition to UN 687, post-war US policy can be discussed in three contexts. First, the global context, which has significant implications for the Middle East. Secondly, the May 29, 1991 initiative which President Bush outlined in his speech at Colorado Springs. Third, the multilateral arms control talks that began in Moscow in late January 1992.

The global context is crucial in looking at how the Middle East fits into the overall administration view. The concern for nuclear proliferation extends far beyond the Middle East. A successful global nuclear non-proliferation policy would make it more difficult to exempt friends and allies in the region from controls. In pursuit of a more coherent global policy, the Bush administration began a dramatic restructuring of the CIA. Much more emphasis was given to intelligence work on proliferation, and far greater intelligence assets were to be applied to the subject. Indeed, this soon led to bureaucratic skirmishes over control of particular components of the problem. While the end of the Cold War will cause a decrease in the overall size of the intelligence budget, the transfer of assets that used to focus on the Soviet threat to countries like Iran, Iraq, Syria and Libya, will most likely lead to a more forceful, imaginative and, possibly, coercive arms control policy in the Middle East. The coercive element must comprise one of the strands of this multi-faceted policy. Within this context, there has been a shift in US policy from condemnation of the 1981 Israeli bombing at Osiraq to discussions of using similar options against North Korea.

The main themes of President Bush's May 29th initiative were an important part of the arms control framework. First, the president called for a freeze on the acquisition, production and testing of missiles, with the hope that ultimately surface-to-surface missiles with ranges of above 150 kilometers would be eliminated from the region. In a practical sense, this initiative was focused on preventing more missiles coming into the region; no effort to remove missile systems already in place in the region was suggested. But a freeze remained an important goal and could be achieved with the cooperation of China and North Korea.

The nuclear component of the May 29 initiative called for a ban on the production of weapons-usable nuclear materials. It requested all states in the region to sign the NPT. It urged that all nuclear facilities in the Middle East be subjected to the International Atomic Energy Agency safeguards. It also called for the ultimate establishment of a nuclear weapons-free zone.

The new element in this initiative was the clause, clearly directed at Israel, urging a ban on the production of weapons-usable material. Although no specific steps were suggested for implementation, it was one of the most sensitive issues raised by the administration. This stipulation was designed to offset Arab complaints about the lack of evenhandedness, and it is likely to be the major stumbling block in both bilateral and multilateral arms control negotiations in the Middle East. Nevertheless, US policy on this issue is likely to remain constant.

In terms of chemical and biological weapons, the president urged that the countries of the region commit themselves to the about-to-be completed chemical weapons convention as well as to the 1972 Biological Weapons Convention. He also urged that efforts be taken to strengthen the latter.

A second new element, along with the nuclear weapons-material clause, was the initiation of conventional arms supplier talks in Paris in the summer of 1991. Subsequent meetings took place in London and Washington and included representatives from the United States, China, Britain, France, and Russia. In London in October 1991 and in Washington in May 1992, the participants agreed to restrain global, conventional arms sales; exchange data on sales to the Middle East of tanks, aircraft, certain missile systems, helicopters, naval vessels, and armored vehicles; and stop exports of technology, equipment or services that could be used for the manufacture of nuclear, chemical, or biological weapons.

Based on the texts from these supplier meetings, it is easy to be cynical about the language used in statements released following these meetings. This included such phrases as "not attempting to interfere with the legitimate defense needs of recipients"--a statement open to many different interpretations. Indeed, definitions of which weapons are offensive or destabilizing have plagued analysts for generations. Generally, those texts represented an effort to reach the lowest common denominator

188

while avoiding damage and interference with the independent policies of the five major suppliers. At the very least each government could then explain to its respective legislatures--and, more specifically, the Bush administration could explain to the US Congress--that a suppliers' initiative was underway. That is the cynical explanation.

A more charitable explanation suggests that the initiative was unique and extremely complicated. Obtaining an agreement between the five powers will not happen overnight; it may take years or even longer. Indeed there are some serious questions about the extent to which pushing hard to obtain supplier restraint is in America's interests.

American interests were bound to be the focus of the Bush administration's policy. Until Americans stop driving large automobiles and reduce consumption of Middle East oil, the Persian Gulf will remain a critical strategic asset; it must be protected by the US since no one else will perform this task. In turn this requires continued arms sales to key Gulf Arab countries. Also, until peace between Israel and the Arab states is concluded, it is highly unlikely that any administration will change the policy of providing Israel with a qualitative military edge, though there will be debates about the interpretation of that policy. Not all US arms sales to the Gulf threaten Israel, and Israeli policy should be sensitive to the stability and security of the Gulf.

The Bush administration policy on arms sales and arms control was similar to that of previous administrations and reflected a multi-faceted, multi-track approach. A survey of current actions and initiatives taken on arms control produces an impressive list. Within the cooperative realm, obtaining the agreement of key suppliers on certain restraints was essential. It was preferable if this could be done with the blessing of key regional allies. Hence, before the talks on conventional arms restraints of the five permanent members of the UN Security Council were convened in London, the United States held discussions with Israel and Egypt about their interests and agenda. In addition, tough unilateral policies of selected restraint had to be pursued.

Saudi Arabia presented a problem that combined many of these issues. For example, the US could agree to ban the sale of advanced combat aircraft. But its reliance on the Saudis suggested that it wanted them to have efficient armed forces, not a combination of weapons from multiple sources. Therefore a ban on combat aircraft would have hurt US interests in Saudi Arabia.

The real problem is dealing with recipients of non-US arms. This is especially important when dealing with countries that are clearly committed to policies that are inimical to American interests. The new republics of the former Soviet Union create a new dimension of cash-strapped states in possession of valuable assets: military hardware and technology. They could supply a US foe for financial, non-ideological reasons. The four countries that are most troublesome in this context are Iran, Iraq, Libya and Syria. The first three may soon have greater access to hard currency than they have at the moment. In the future this may also apply to Syria, thus allowing all four states to purchase large amounts of weaponry.

In the absence of effective regional arms control, there are two things a country needs in order to acquire the types of technologies that may threaten American interests, and in many cases Israeli interests as well: money and skilled workers. Once they recover from their present status, Iran and Iraq possess a potent combination of both indigenous skills and major oil revenues. One of the more frightening lessons of the Gulf crisis was not the skills the Iraqis showed at weapons manufacturing. These skills were crude: they had some useful marsh-clearing equipment, but their surface-to-surface Scud missiles were not top of the line models. Yet the Iraqis **did** show remarkable skills at manipulating the world financial markets, working within the gray area of technology transfers and setting up dummy companies.

The lessons of the Versailles Treaty and the extent and manner in which the Germans circumvented its stipulations have been compared to Iraq's situation today. The Germans set up dummy companies, produced steam rollers in Sweden and, essentially, built an undercover air force in the Soviet Union. Those who worry about Iraq must be aware of the various ways in which Saddam Hussein, or his successors, can bypass the restrictions currently being imposed by the UN and the major suppliers once he or they have access to hard currency. This includes not only what they can smuggle in or smuggle out without detection, but also the manner in which they might cooperate with other countries. During the interwar years, the Germans cooperated with Sweden, Argentina and the Soviet Union in order to build up their military capabilities. Similarly, the Tehran-Khartoum axis points to the possibility of an Iraqi military alignment with other Arab or Muslim countries in the future.

The Iranians will never forgive the Iraqis for their conduct during the Iraq-Iran War, and this explains why the Iranians are rearming. Also, a generation of Iraqi officers will probably never forgive the United States and Saudi Arabia for their conduct during the Second Gulf War. Addressing these high-priority issues, the Bush administration correctly decided to begin a very focused arms control effort. In order to obtain the cooperation of Russia, China, France and Britain, it seemed better to focus on the especially dangerous categories of weapons, rather than to attempt implementing across-the-board restrictions. But dealing with these weapons in the framework of the Middle East multilateral arms control talks is very difficult. Invariably, the issues of nuclear-free zones and bans on weapons of mass destruction are brought up. As a result, the most promising arms control agreements in the Middle East will result from the bilateral meetings. More specifically, once a breakthrough between Syria and Israel is achieved, arms control will become extremely important in the bilateral context.

In sum, the central US dilemma concerns the need to reconcile security assistance to friends in need, while at the same time advocating a policy of arms restraint. These two goals are not incompatible, provided that arms control initiatives are carefully crafted for the unique security environment of the region. Most important, this requires a thorough understanding of the sources of regional conflict and their impact on the security perceptions of the local states. Unless these concerns are taken into account, external arms control initiatives will fail.

13. International Defense Business and Restraint of Conventional Arms Transfers to the Middle East

William W. Keller

In May 1991 President Bush announced a set of proposals to ban weapons of mass destruction and limit trade in conventional arms.[1] The Bush initiative included a plan for multilateral restraint of conventional arms transfers to the Middle East. The new approach arose from a realization that Iraq had acquired a vast arsenal of advanced weapons, which it could not have produced indigenously. From 1983 to 1988, Iraq imported $40 billion of conventional weapons, with the largest shares coming from the Soviet Union, France and China. None of the major arms-supplying states appeared to be troubled by the buildup of Iraq's military power. It was only after Saddam invaded Kuwait, threatening access to Persian Gulf oil, that the major arms suppliers, who were also the five permanent members of the United Nations Security Council, began to question their arms transfer policies. In the aftermath of the Persian Gulf War, there was a flurry of proposals to restrain the transfer of arms to the region, to ensure that such an arsenal would never again be handed over to any despot bent on regional conquest.

These proposals must be understood both in the context of the arming of the Persian Gulf and in relation to expanding international defense business activity. Both processes have long been underway, and are now being propelled forward as domestic procurement budgets collapse. Many defense companies must either increase foreign sales or stop making major weapons like the M1 Abrams tank and the F-16 fighter aircraft. In the former Soviet republics and Eastern European states, bleak economic conditions make it difficult to resist mounting pressures to dump quantities of sophisticated weapons onto arms markets worldwide, especially the Middle East, at fire sale prices. At the same time, increasing levels of deployed and planned armaments in the Persian Gulf region decrease the likelihood that states facing antagonistic or potentially hostile neighbors will voluntarily forego additional acquisition of arms.

A set of unilateral national policies led first to the arming of Iraq, second to mounting a multilateral invasion to disarm that country, and third to unprecedented large transfers of advanced weapons to a variety of the Persian Gulf states, all in the space of a few years. History will sort out whether it was short-sighted and even dangerous. It has been catastrophic for the peoples of that region. While there is much discussion of a new world order characterized by international cooperation and multilateralism, the increase in unilateral international arms transfers belies that vision. In the fiscal year 1991, the United States alone transferred $16.6 billion in foreign military sales and $5.9 billion in commercial military sales to the Middle East for a total of $22.5 billion.[2]

The persistence of the US policy of arming the Middle East can be explained in part as an unintended consequence of the failure to bring together two different policy arenas--the defense industrial base community and the foreign policy community. Each has a separate legislative history, a separate stream of documentation, its own language, lobbyists, experts and expectations. In the United States, this separation is administratively enforced because the responsibility for arms transfer policy resides in the Department of State, while implementation of the policy, and the overall direction of the defense industrial base, is administered by the Department of Defense.[3]

Similarly, in the US Congress, most defense industrial issues are handled by the Armed Services committees and in the context of economic, technological, and administrative factors.[4] There is a strong constituency in favor of keeping domestic weapons production facilities open, even where the policy is to reduce defense procurement and overall defense budgets. On the other hand, foreign policy issues, such as arms transfers, arms control and proliferation, usually fall under the jurisdiction of the committees on Foreign Affairs and Foreign Relations, and are more often associated with diplomatic and strategic concerns. The question of whether to permit the export of tens of billions of dollars of US-made weapons comes before these committees, but the overall structure and regulation of the defense industries does not. These separations and differences are important because they are symptomatic of the disconnect between the internationalization of defense industries and markets and the quest for governmental stability and world peace.

This chapter, which draws on the work of the US Office of Technology Assessment, attempts to bridge this gap and to draw the connections between expanding international defense industrial activity, the proliferation of conventional weapons, and the policy of arming the world.[5] These topics are now being forced together by gradual changes in the conduct of international defense business and by momentous changes in international relations leading to very different perceptions of the defense requirements of the United States, Europe, the former Soviet Union and elsewhere.

For the first time, the major suppliers of advanced weapons to the Middle East met in July 1991 to discuss multilateral controls on arms transferred to the region. At the same time, significant legislation to limit arms proliferation was introduced in the US Congress. While these events are encouraging, it is nevertheless likely that well-established trends in the evolution of the world's defense industries will lead to greater proliferation of conventional arms and technology on a global scale.

In the most simple and direct formulation, the defense industries of the West are internationalizing. Companies from different countries have entered into strategic alliances, joint ventures, licensed production and codevelopment activities, and many other forms of joint R&D and dynamic technology transfer. This process has been in train for at least a decade, and is accelerating today. The result is the building up of new centers of defense industry, the proliferation of powerful weapons, and the diffusion of increasingly advanced defense technology to developing countries. In the future, it will be more difficult, not easier, to control arms exports to the Middle East.

Is this surprising? Possibly not. Many defense manufacturers, especially in Europe and Asia, also produce sophisticated goods and equipment for consumer markets. Indeed it is possible to view defense as just another sector of the economy, and in the corporate context, as an extension of existing business operations. Some companies export a substantial percentage of their defense production; others enter into international collaboration to spread the costs of R&D and production of big-ticket defense items. Such arrangements are common among the major European arms producers. From this perspective, it looks as though the defense industries are undergoing a process of multi-nationalization similar to that which got under way in many other economic sectors 25 years ago.

But here the comparison between civil and defense industry is too facile. Questions concerning the appropriate extent of defense trade, the permissible levels of international transfer of defense technology, and the emerging structure of a global defense industrial base are all matters of public policy. To date, these policies have been handled in the United States and elsewhere in the West on an ad hoc, inconsistent, and largely unilateral basis. The result is a state of affairs in which advanced defense equipment and technology has proliferated beyond the control of any single state or group of states, with profound implications for the future of the Middle East.

The end of the Cold War and associated reductions in global defense spending have exerted, and will continue to exert, a strong influence on the structure of the defense industries and on the international arms trade. Many defense companies find themselves in a tough bind. They have pursued a number of adjustment strategies: massive layoffs, reducing the number of subcontractors, extensive restructuring in the form of mergers, acquisitions, and divestitures, and concentrating corporate activity on the most profitable product lines. In addition, many defense companies in the West are increasing their emphasis on international business. This is being pursued through selling advanced conventional weapons to foreign governments, joint ventures, foreign direct investment, and increasingly, through licensed production of advanced equipment and international codevelopment of new defense products.

The European states and the United States routinely transfer a great deal of advanced defense technology among themselves[6] and to developing countries.[7] Until recently, the former Soviet Union also transferred a significant, although smaller, amount of defense technology to its allies and client states. At any given point in the decade of the 1980s, approximately 180 major weapons systems were being produced under license by countries that did not design or develop them, about half by developing countries.[8] Extensive international collaboration in defense technology has contributed to the emergence of numerous centers of advanced defense industry and technology, first in Europe, next in the Western Pacific,[9] and increasingly among developing countries around the globe.[10]

In 1988, for example, Brazil, Egypt, India, Indonesia, South Korea and Taiwan were producing 43 different major weapons under international licensing agreements. Several of these states have attained significant defense industrial and technological capabilities, and have entered the arms export business. Between 1978 and 1988, the arms exported by Brazil, Israel, South Korea and Spain amounted to $16 billion.[11] Each new center is capable of transferring technology and selling weapons to additional countries. The primary result is the proliferation of defense industrial capacity in both the advanced and developing countries. The collateral effect is the gradual and collective loss of control over the destination and disposition of potent weapons emanating from many different parts of the world. The multiplicity of sources has produced a buyers' market in which a range of modern defense equipment is generally available to anyone who can pay for it. It has also produced ubiquitous overcapacity in the global defense industries.

On the political side of the arms transfer equation, wide and increasing diversity of supply from both advanced and developing countries has degraded the use of arms transfers--and their denial--as instruments of foreign policy. When the US Congress blocked the sale of F-15 fighters to Saudi Arabia in the mid-1980s, for example, the Saudis were able to buy large numbers of advanced strike aircraft, the Tornado IDS, from the United Kingdom. Diversity of supply has also decreased the likelihood that supplier states can somehow establish a balance of military power in the Middle East. If the goal of creating such a balance is to deter war, the historical record for the Middle East is bleak indeed.

The problem might be framed as a simple game. If a single country were the only supplier, it would be able to dictate the allocation of weapons, assuming the absence of domestic arms industries, a significant black market, and nuclear weapons. Where there are two suppliers, it is more difficult, because the second supplier can upset the balance, and intelligence about his actions is unlikely to be perfect. This is the simplified version of US-Soviet surrogate confrontation. As the number of suppliers increases, and regional powers develop defense industries and acquire weapons of mass destruction, the value of any single transfer in promoting (or upsetting) a military balance becomes indeterminate.

The Gulf War has provided support for the view that the United States and its allies must maintain a collective capacity to respond to large-scale military crises in distant lands. But at the same time, the crisis confirmed the growing danger of putting advanced weapons in the hands of governments that may use them for nefarious purposes. Nevertheless, between August 2, 1990 and November 1, 1991 total worldwide arms sales to the Middle East reached approximately $14.8 billion, of which about $12.8 billion were sales by the United States.[12] These sales and others now being contemplated take on the character of a self-perpetuating cycle. In this cycle, the United States, the Europeans, and possibly elements of the former Soviet Union continue to export high volumes of weapons to reestablish regional balances of power either upset by war or by the last round of weapons sales.[13]

European arms producers, and those of the developing world, export a substantial proportion--often more than one third--of the weapons they produce.[14] In the past, European governments have been willing to export high-technology weapons to a wide range of countries, and they have tended to view arms transfers as commercial rather than political transactions. Although they were not used effectively in the Persian Gulf War, some of the most advanced weapons in the Iraqi arsenal were made in France.[15] European governments often conduct extensive diplomacy in support of arms sales. In the past, this has provided strong competition for US arms exports, especially in the Middle East, but also in the Western Pacific.

In recent years, a distinctly economic component has entered US international military sales policies. In a departure from long-standing practice, high-ranking officers of the United States Army and Air Force have advocated foreign sales of US equipment as a means of increasing production to keep lines open.[16] The US Defense Security Assistance Agency, the agency responsible for carrying out the US Foreign Military Sales (FMS) program, reported to the Congress that "the long term survival of a number of important domestic arms programs are tied to foreign sales: M-1 A1 Abrams battle tank, Blackhawk helicopter, HAWK surface-to-air missile, Boeing 707 aircraft, to name a few."[17] In addition, the US government has directed its embassy personnel to increase the level of assistance provided to US defense companies selling in foreign countries,[18] created the Center for Defense Trade within the State Department, and proposed a "defense GATT" that would allow free and open trade in arms and defense technology within the NATO Alliance, and with other US allies.[19] Most recently, the US government has helped to pay the expenses of US arms manufacturers marketing their weapons at international trade shows.

Countries that export advanced weapons to the Middle East have many different motivations, but some of the most important reasons may not be political or strategic in nature, even if the consequences often are. The motivations of suppliers are important because they contribute to the root causes of proliferation. In the 1970s and 1980s, a principal stated purpose of US arms exports to the Middle East was to counter and balance Soviet arms exported to client states in the region. Now that the Cold War is over and the Soviet Union no longer exists, the new US policy appears to be to support regional governments that joined in the coalition against Iraq. US arms (and those of many other states) continue to flow to the region at record levels.

It is certainly possible that new political and strategic motivations may have replaced the old ones. But there are also economic and industrial factors in play. The dynamics of defense production and the emerging global structure of the defense industries encourage arms exports, and may directly impede efforts to restrain the arms race in the Middle East and elsewhere. Most major defense equipment-producing countries, for example, have adopted policies, first, to collaborate with other countries to share the development costs for major new weapons, and secondly, to export top-of-the-line defense equipment to reach affordable economies of scale. Many states find they must export arms to keep the unit price of weapons tolerably low. As the former French Minister of Defense Pierre Joxe stated, "If you want to be able to afford to make your own weapons, you have to be able to sell them."[20] Indeed, the French procurement executive funds between 40-70% of the R&D costs for new weapons systems; and companies are expected to ante up the rest drawing largely on profits from foreign sales. In the United States, market conditions have deteriorated to the point where foreign buyers of advanced US weapons can demand to produce some of the weapons in question, even though it requires the transfer of underlying manufacturing technology to foreign governments and companies.

In an ongoing case, the Republic of Korea benefited from a competition between two US companies, McDonnell Douglas and General Dynamics. In 1989, South Korea agreed to buy 120 twin engine F-18A fighter aircraft from McDonnell Douglas for $5 billion, with 12 planes to be purchased off-the-shelf, 36 assembled from US-built kits, and 72 produced under license in Korea. But by 1991, the price had risen to $6.2 billion, and the

Koreans demanded sophisticated radar, software, and composite materials technologies that the company was reluctant to release. After nearly two years, South Korea broke off negotiations and decided to acquire the General Dynamics F-16 fighter technology instead. The ability of the latter to offer the F-16 at a lower price and add additional technology, an advanced radar, and air-to-air missiles were decisive factors.[21]

In the final analysis, it is difficult to avoid the conclusion that international arms business, in which the United States is first among several prominent suppliers in the West, is building up a dangerously armed world.[22] In the Middle East, arms imported to the region have raised the stakes associated with political instability and have figured prominently in the calculations of militant religious regimes and regional strong men. As the Islamic revolution in Iran demonstrated, once transferred, modern weapons can outlast the governments they were intended to support. As the most recent Persian Gulf War has shown, arms may outlast the good will of the leaders to whom they were supplied. Moreover, the accumulation and potential hostile deployment of enormous arsenals threatens neighboring countries and can invoke costly reprisals by supplier states. Recent wars in the Persian Gulf have been a boon to the defense industries but not for the citizens of the affected countries.

What then are the prospects for restraining the transfer of arms to the Middle East? In the months following President Bush's May 1991 non-proliferation proposals, there was optimism, both domestically in the United States and in the international community. The buildup of Iraqi armaments and the most recent Gulf War focused sustained attention on arms transfers to the region. Over 50 bills were introduced in the 102nd US Congress that would affect US policies on the export of arms and defense technology.[23] In June 1991, President Francois Mitterrand of France issued a comprehensive "Plan for Arms Control and Disarmament," and Prime Minister John Major called for an arms registry at the United Nations.[24] In July the five permanent members of the UN Security Council met in Paris to discuss arms transfers and non-proliferation.[25]

Two weeks later, the efforts of "the five" were explicitly supported at the London Economic Summit by the leaders of the seven major industrial democracies (G-7), who issued a "Declaration on Conventional Arms Transfers and NBC Non-Proliferation." Among other measures, the G-7 called for a "universal registry of arms transfers under the auspices of the United Nations."[26] In October 1991, "the five" met again, this time in London. They issued a set of "Guidelines for Conventional Arms Transfers," agreed to inform each other of arms exports to the Middle East, and supported the "early establishment" of the UN registry.[27]

These meetings and proposals represent an unprecedented stream of activity to control proliferation directed toward the Middle East. On the other hand, and in parallel with these meetings, a different and more sobering set of events also took place. In the US Congress, most of the significant legislative proposals to restrain US (and other) arms transfers to the Middle East were combined into HR 2508, the International Cooperation Act of 1991. Different versions of the bill were passed by the Senate and by the House of Representatives requiring that the legislation be submitted to a conference committee for reconciliation. As printed in the report of the conference committee, this legislation would have committed the United States to a multilateral arms transfer and control regime, placed limits on US arms transfers to the Middle East, and required the president to submit to Congress detailed reports on arms transfers to, and the military balance in, that region. But on October 30, the House of Representatives rejected the conference report by a vote of 262 to 159 and the legislation was dead.[28]

The meetings of the five powers in July and October of 1991 were indeed historic because it was the first time that representatives of the United States, the Soviet Union, China, France, and Great Britain met to consider any aspect of proliferation or conventional arms control in the Middle East. However, the US opening position in those talks decreased the possibility of a real breakthrough. On June 6, several weeks prior to the first meeting, the US delegate to the talks, Undersecretary of State for International Security Affairs Reginald Bartholomew signaled the intention of the US to resume transfers of arms to the Middle East. In testimony before the Senate Foreign Relations Committee he stated, "We will not seek a regime that halts arms transfers.... We will resume sending to the Congress over the next few weeks those defense-related and weapon system transfers which we believe are in the best interests of the United States, the recipient states, and the cause of peace and stability."[29]

In the months following the July 1991 talks, the United States sold M-60 A3 tanks to Bahrain; Hawk anti-aircraft missile upgrades and ground based communications equipment to Egypt; F-15A/B fighter aircraft to Israel; M1 series tanks and F-18A fighter aircraft to Kuwait; F-16A/B fighter aircraft and military trucks to Morocco; V-300 Commando armored wheeled vehicles and missile corvettes to Oman; HMMWVs, BMY trucks, Peace Shield air defense system, MK-84 bombs, CBU-87 cluster munitions, AIM-7M Sparrow air-to-air missiles and laser guided bomb components to Saudi Arabia; and F-16C/D fighter aircraft to Turkey.

In contrast, the other four members of the UN Security Council appear to have made far fewer sales to the Middle East during the same period.[30] In February 1992, however, Russian President Boris Yeltsin announced a policy to export Russian weapons for profit. Commenting on the decision, Andrei Kokoshin stated, "If other countries would have started reducing arms deliveries, this would have had some effect, but it turned out that most democratic countries are not stopping arms sales, but increasing them. Naturally, it's very disappointing to our arms producers to see...other countries advancing on our markets."[31]

These sales, and prospective future sales of F-15 fighters and other US arms to Saudi Arabia, suggest that in their initial meeting in July, the five powers intended to leave wide latitude and discretion to the individual states. This position was made explicit by Ambassador Bartholomew on March 24, 1992 in testimony before the House Foreign Affairs Committee. He stated, "The Guidelines themselves are **not** a formula for determining who gets what. Again, we are not trying to create an international arms cartel. Rather, the Guidelines give us wide berth to question and be questioned on such matters. This is exactly what we intended when we proposed the Guidelines."[32]

Indeed, the language of the October 1991 communique explicitly subordinates the transfer Guidelines to "the national control procedures [for] conventional arms transfers" of the participating countries. In this respect, the multilateral Guidelines recognize the priority of unilateral arms transfers. While the principles advanced by the Guidelines are constructive, their meaning and application are open to interpretation. For example, "the five" have agreed to avoid transfers that would be likely to "increase tension in a region or contribute to regional instability." The extent to which arms transfers contribute to political instability has been the subject of sustained debate in the United States. There is no magic formula. Another example--transfers should not "introduce destabilizing military capabilities to a region." This often involves a difficult calculation. For instance, would the acquisition by Israel of submarines capable of firing nuclear weapons introduce a destabilizing military capability or would it enhance deterrence? A final example--a given transfer should be avoided if it is likely "to be used other than for the legitimate defense and security needs of the recipient state." This again is a judgment call, as the US experience with Iran and the French experience with Iraq suggest.

The United States could assume a leadership role by adopting a radically different course than the present one of increasing arms exports to unprecedented levels. It could, for example, prohibit the planned sale of 72 McDonnell Douglas F-15 fighters to Saudi Arabia on the grounds that such a sale would violate provisions of the Guidelines. This could be accomplished either by executive branch action or by introducing a successful resolution of disapproval in the United States Congress. Such an action would send a powerful diplomatic signal to the other four permanent members of the UN Security Council. It would generate strong pressure within the international community for all arms exporting countries to join in a multinational action to

203

prohibit the sale of advanced fighter aircraft to the Saudis, and ultimately to other states in the region.

Accordingly, the Guidelines represent a beginning because they enunciate general principles that could, if implemented, lead to dramatic reductions in conventional arms transfers to the Middle East. At a minimum, they have committed five of the major arms exporters--who together account for more than 80 percent of global arms trade--to the principle of multilateral action to restrain the transfer of weapons to the Middle East. Moreover, the multilateral talks made progress by establishing a universal arms registry and a forum for ongoing consultations. The Guidelines do not, however, constitute anything resembling a coherent and effective trade reduction regime. No limits as to numbers or kinds of weapons that can be sold or otherwise transferred to the Middle East have been set. No mechanism enables one state to challenge a proposed sale by another. There are no agreed definitions, no channels for arbitration, and no verification or enforcement provisions. Unless these missing elements are added, and added quickly, it is likely that disagreements over the type, volume, and destination of permissible arms transfers will erode the progress made to date.

In that case, the historic opportunity to reduce the traffic in conventional arms to the region will have slipped away. Once again, the dynamics of international defense business will exert pressures on even the most reluctant suppliers to resume high-volume, high-technology weapons sales to the Middle East.

Notes

1. *Washington Post, New York Times*, May 30, 1991, p. 1.
2. United States Congress, *Congressional Record*, January 24, 1992, p. E-67. The detailed tabulation, placed in the *Congressional Record* by Representative Lee H. Hamilton, was provided to the Committee on Foreign Affairs on January 9, 1992 in a quarterly report in compliance with section 36(a) of the Arms Export Control Act.
3. Within the Defense Department, the Defense Security Assistance Agency (DSAA) has overall responsibility for carrying out foreign military sales. DSAA charges a 3% administrative fee for its services which funds over 80% of the agency's budget. If all of the $22.9 billion in foreign military sales made in FY 1991 were delivered, the DSAA fee would be approximately $690 million.
4. There are exceptions such as the Defense Production Act which falls under the jurisdiction of the Subcommittee on Economic Stabilization of the House Committee on Banking, Finance and Urban Affairs.
5. U.S. Congress, Office of Technology Assessment, *Global Arms Trade: Commerce in Advanced Military Technology and Weapons*, OTA-ISC-460 (Washington, DC: U.S. Government Printing Office, June 1991).
6. Among many other examples, the United States has transferred highly advanced production technology for the Stinger missile to Germany, Belgium, Greece, Italy, the Netherlands, and Turkey; for the Patriot to Japan and Italy; and for the AIM-9L Sidewinder air-to-air missile to Japan, Germany, Norway, Italy, and Taiwan.
7. Major systems transferred have included the US M-1 Abrams tank (to Egypt), the US F-16 fighter and Multiple Launch Rocket System (to Turkey), the German Type 209 submarine (to Brazil and South Korea), the French Alpha Jet (to Egypt), the Soviet MiG-27 fighter (to India), the British Jaguar fighter (to India), the UK Swingfire Anti-Tank Missile (to Egypt), the French Super Puma helicopter (to Indonesia), the French Milan Anti-Tank

Missile (to India), the German BK 117 helicopter (to Indonesia), among others.

8.   *Global Arms Trade*, figures 1-7 and 1-9, pp. 7 and 9.

9.   Defense Science Board, "Defense Industrial Cooperation with Pacific Rim Nations," October 1989, p. viii.

10.   U.S. Congress, Office of Technology Assessment, *Arming Our Allies: Cooperation and Competition in Defense Technology*, OTA-ISC-449 (Washington, DC: U.S. Government Printing Office, May 1990), pp. 3 and 24.

11.   *Global Arms Trade*, pp. 4, 5, 9, and 10.

12.   Calculated from unofficial data provided by the Congressional Research Service. See Richard F. Grimmett and Alfred B. Prados, "Near East Arms Transfers, August 2, 1990 - November 1, 1991," Rpt. No. 91-839 F, December 2, 1991, pp. 5-13.

13.   For example, following the October 1973 war, from 1974-1978, the Soviet Union transferred $2.7 billion in military equipment to Syria largely in an effort to resupply equipment lost or damaged in the war. See U.S. Library of Congress, Congressional Research Service, "Middle East Arms Control and Related Issues," 91-384 F, May 1, 1991, p. 10.

14.   In 1984, for example, Brazil, France, Israel, Italy, Spain, and the United Kingdom exported over 40 percent of their weapons production. U.S. Arms Control and Disarmament Agency, *World Military Expenditures and Arms Transfers*, 1989 (Washington , DC: U.S. GPO, 1990), and Stockholm International Peace Research Institute, SIPRI Yearbooks 1986, *World Armaments and Disarmament* (Oxford: Oxford University Press, 1986), p. 336.

15.   From 1980 through 1987, the French sold $6.7 billion (current dollars) worth of advanced weapons to Iraq, including 143 Mirage F-1C fighters and 734 AM-39 Exocet missiles. U.S. Arms Control and Disarmament Agency, *World Military Expenditures and Arms Transfers, 1988* (Washington, DC: U.S. Government Printing Office, 1989) p. 22.

16.   *Defense News*, Dec. 17, 1990, p. 16.

17.   U.S. Department of State and U.S. Defense Security Assistance Agency, *Congressional Presentation for Security Assistance Programs*, fiscal year 1992, p. 6.

18.   Cable from Acting Secretary Eagleburger for Ambassador/Chargé on "Guidance Concerning Embassy Role in Support of U.S. Defense Exporters."

19.   On the "defense GATT," see "The Future of Defense and Industrial Collaboration in NATO," a speech presented by Ambassador William Taft to the German Strategy Forum and the Institute for Foreign Policy Analysis in Bonn, Germany, Mar. 15, 1990.

20.   Quoted in *The Washington Post*, April 6, 1991, p. A17.

21.   *The Washington Post*, Mar. 29, 1991, p. F1; *Wall Street Journal*, Mar. 29, 1991, p. A3; *Defense News*, Apr. 1, 1991, p. 4. National policies which permit the transfer of advanced fighters and associated production technologies will ultimately have to be reconciled with multilateral arms control regimes such as the Missile Technology Control Regime and the Australia Group which seek to ban the spread of technologies associated with the production of ballistic missiles and chemical weapons. See *Assessing Ballistic Missile Proliferation and Its Control*, Center for International Security and Arms Control, Stanford University, pp. 7-10.

22.   In the 1970s and 1980s, countries in the Middle East alone imported more than $200 billion in conventional armaments. Congressional Research Service, "Middle East Arms Control and Related Issues," p. 1.

23.   For details of the various legislative proposals see United States Congress, Congressional Research Service, "Weapons Nonproliferation Policy and Legislation," CRS 91-536 F, July 3, 1991, updated August 30, 1991.

24.   Presidence de la Republique, *Plan de Maitrise des Armaments et de Desarmement*, Paris, le 3 juin 1991.

25.   Communique, "Meeting of the Five on Arms Transfers and Non-Proliferation," Paris, 8th and 9th of July 1991.

26.   U.S. Department of State, *Dispatch*, "Group of Seven (G-7) Summit Declarations," July 22, 1991, p. 526.

27.   "Meeting of the Five on Arms Transfers and Non-Proliferation: London 17/18 October 1991," Commonwealth Office, Press Release, No. 172, Friday 18 October 1991.

28.   Alfred B. Prados, "Middle East Arms Supply: Recent Control Initiatives," Congressional Research Service, IB91113, Updated November 1, 1991, p. 8. Congress did, however, pass the P.L. 102-138 (the Foreign Relations Authorization Act, Fiscal Years 1992 and 1993). Section 322 does contain language regarding the transfer of defense articles to the Middle East, but it is far less detailed and less restrictive than related provision in H.R. 2508.

29.   Prepared statement, "Testimony of Ambassador Reginald Bartholomew, Under Secretary of State, International Security Policy, to the Senate Foreign Relations Committee," June 6, 1991, pp. 8-9.

30.   The former Soviet Union sold SA-5 surface-to-air missiles to Iran. *Congressional Record--Senate*, November 19, 1991, pp. S 16980-S 16982; and *Arms Sales Monitor*, Federation of American Scientists, Issue No. 7-8, 102 Congress, September-October 1991, p. 1. According to the Arms Control Association in Washington, DC, the United States transferred $21.4 billion in arms to the Middle East in the 20 months following the Iraqi invasion of Kuwait. Of that, roughly $8.5 billion was transferred after President Bush announced his "Middle East Arms Control Initiative" in May 1991. Arms Control Association press release, April 13, 1992, Washington, DC.

31.   *New York Times*, February 23, 1992, p.1.

32.   Testimony of Ambassador Reginald Bartholomew, Undersecretary of State for International Security Affairs, Before the House Foreign Affairs Committee, March 24, 1992, p. 3.

14. Controlling the Proliferation of Missiles

J. Lise Hartman

This presentation provides an overview of a number of issues involved in assessing some of the uses and dangers involved in the proliferation of ballistic missiles and evaluating the efforts to control their spread. Outside of NATO, the former Warsaw Pact and China, some 12 countries have deployed ballistic missiles; and of those that have deployed them, Iran, Iraq, Egypt and Israel, and both Koreas have production capabilities. Libya has a program to develop its own. Another six countries that have not deployed their own, have programs or in the past have attempted to establish programs to produce them. This category includes Argentina and Brazil. Altogether, some nine countries have chemical weapons programs, and one, Israel, has a nuclear capability. Seven countries have, to one degree or another, nuclear aspirations.

The Significance of Ballistic Missiles

One of the questions that constantly arises is the military significance of ballistic missiles as compared with other forms of weapons delivery, particularly aircraft. Very briefly, here are some of the advantages and drawbacks of ballistic missiles compared with aircraft.

With regard to the operational criteria of range, payload, accuracy, speed, and the ability to penetrate defenses, missiles are clearly superior only in speed and the ability to penetrate defenses.

Particularly in the Middle East theater, the need for range is highly dependent on geography. At any rate, only the Indian Agni and the Israeli Jericho missiles exceed the range of most combat aircraft in the region.

In terms of payload, aircraft typically carry greater and more diversified ordnance, especially of nuclear and chemical weapons. Therefore, a country with a relatively unreliable missile system would probably be well advised to stick to aircraft. Efficient warhead design for chemical weapons is still beyond the competence of the majority of countries that have chemical weapons programs. Proximity fuses to detonate warheads at the proper altitude, and burster charges to disperse the agents so that they do not all collapse in one place, are fairly unknown indigenous products in the region.

In terms of accuracy, most Third World missiles are very inaccurate compared with those in the industrialized world. An unmodified Scud-B has a CEP of 980 yards, and the CSS-2 of 1.5 miles. Only the SS-21 in Syria is considered relatively accurate. Many have maintained that this inaccuracy necessarily implies an intention to use the missiles only with nonconventional weapons, or against troop formations, or to terrorize civilian populations. That, of course, is ominous enough. But again, bear in mind the utility of such technologies as the GPS and its Soviet equivalent, in improving the accuracy of even very inaccurate missiles.

Speed and ability to penetrate defenses are the characteristics which, in the current context, favor ballistic missiles for Third World countries. While aircraft can, in some circumstances, penetrate air defenses, the equipment to do so is expensive, and the air operations must be supported by redundant and specialized aircraft. Furthermore, given that a number of Third World countries actually possess sophisticated air defense systems and assuming that they can find the sellers to sell them what they need, for many of them the use of aircraft is prohibitively expensive. They have to be prepared to sustain a large number of losses to successfully complete a mission.

Seth Carus has cited the example of the US attack on Libya as having required 70 aircraft, only 14 of which actually dropped bombs. Other aircraft were committed to defense suppression, electronic jamming, command and control, tanker support, and air cover.[1] Third World countries tend to lack the reconnaissance and intelligence capabilities to coordinate some of these activities. If you consider that even the United States actually lost some aircraft in the course of that Libyan attack, you

210

realize that notwithstanding our capabilities to pull off something fairly sophisticated, it can be very expensive to operate against a country with air defenses.

This brings us to the issue of relative cost. If you add to the loss ratio for aircraft the relative cost of a million dollars say, for a Scud, and maybe 20 million for a not-so-sophisticated aircraft, in addition to the requirement of properly-trained pilots, runways, airfields, storage facilities for the aircraft, operation and maintenance costs--then it is higher still. These are some of the factors which weigh in judging the operational military threat in the regional context. An excellent study by Stanford University's Center for International Security and Arms Control, on the subject of trade-offs and relative benefits and costs of using ballistic missiles versus aircraft,[2] should be consulted for further analysis of the military utility of such missiles.

The extent to which ballistic missiles change the operational functioning and planning of the militaries involved, is extremely relevant to the Middle East, and the decisionmaking process in a democracy demands that it be taken into account. One can see the reflection of the intensity of this issue in the debate over whether to spend money now on upgrading the Patriot, or whether to use every resource on the Arrow. Part of the explanation for the intensity of the debate is that it actually means something in Israel. Similarly the ABM debate may well have turned out differently had America's population suffered several days of ballistic missile bombardment by a country that possessed chemical weapons. In this respect, a country such as Israel is unlikely to forego incorporating the consequences of even militarily insignificant ballistic missiles into its military planning, and obviously then into its passive civilian defense program.

In the case of missiles of great range, the periphery has vastly expanded, increasing the difficulties of planning for every country within that periphery. The US is part of that periphery. At a minimum, the United States must safeguard its military facilities overseas, possibly hardening command centers, sheltering aircraft, building additional runways, and increasing intelligence-gathering capabilities.

Evaluation of the Missile Non-Proliferation Regime

Several events which occurred in the course of the 1980s raised US interest in ballistic missile proliferation. To cite just a few: the attempt by Libya to use missiles off Lampadusa against US installations there; the provision by the Soviets over time of large numbers of missiles to Iraq and Syria; China's sale of CSS-2 missiles to Saudi Arabia; and evidence that a joint ambitious program by Argentina, Iraq and Egypt was, in fact, progressing quite nicely. In addition, the war of the cities between Iran and Iraq, the deployment of the US Navy in the Gulf during the reflagging of the Kuwaiti tankers, and the stationing of Iran's Silkworm missiles within range of the United States fleet--all helped to raise the consciousness of the United States military establishment and, to a certain extent, of the political establishment as well--as it was rather closely involved in most of the deployment decisions just mentioned--regarding ballistic missiles. The political establishment indeed raised the problem on the political calendar. The prospect of US troop concentrations falling within range of these countries' missiles, and concern regarding the consequences for Israel's security as well, contributed to greater attention in this sphere.

During the last year or two of the Carter administration, the question of ballistic missiles came up for more serious consideration. The Carter administration had begun the term focusing on other kinds of conventional weapons, as well as on nuclear proliferation; but in the end it also began to focus on ballistic missile proliferation.

In 1982 the Reagan administration, no doubt as a result of an NSC staff recommendation, instituted the NSDD-70, which comprised an examination of the ways in which ballistic missiles might be controlled. This culminated the following year in negotiations between the United States and Canada, Italy, France, Japan and the United Kingdom essentially to formulate the Missile Technology Control Regime (MTCR).

But already by 1982 the USSR had provided hundreds of Frog-7 Rockets and Scud-B missiles to the Third World--perhaps to as many as ten countries. And until the early 1970s France had provided technology to Israel's Jericho Project, as well as to India's and Pakistan's propulsion system development, to which Germany too, contributed technology.

At the same time, through the Nike Hercules Program, the United States had inadvertently contributed to the development of the NHK missile in South Korea. It was some combination of these factors, and possibly other considerations as well, that led the United States to follow-up the NSDD-70 by beginning discussions with the six countries on curbing the proliferation of missiles. These discussions culminated in 1987 in the MTCR.

What was included in the MTCR, and what was not? How was it implemented? To what extent did it succeed? The final MTCR document that emerged in 1987 in the elegant form of a press release and an unclassified annex of equipment that was controlled, revealed much about what separated the parties that signed it, and what united them.

To begin with, the very fact that it was a consensual agreement rather than a formal treaty demonstrated the deep ambiguity felt by some of the countries over the propriety of selective denial. States were to incorporate the guidelines of the MTCR into their own statutes and to enforce them as sovereign nations. Decisions as to whether to export technologies in any grey area to a marginal country were to be put to other members, and once a decision not to export a technology to a certain country had been taken by one member, the others were expected to abide by it.

The MTCR covers missiles and unmanned airborne vehicles with payloads in excess of 500 kilograms, and ranges of 300 kilometers or more. The articulated goal of the MTCR was to limit the risks of nuclear proliferation by controlling transfers that could contribute to nuclear weapons delivery systems, other than manned aircraft.

This nuclear nexus inherent in the MTCR system has been the cause of many disputes among its members. But for now it is relevant only to explain why the 500 kilogram minimum weight yardstick was chosen; it was assumed that no Third World country would be able to build a nuclear weapon of a lighter weight. The 300-kilometer yardstick was chosen possibly to accommodate one of the members' contemporaneous arms export practices, although whether that is indeed the case is uncertain.

The MTCR established a two-tiered system of review: within the first year, with regard to items such as complete ballistic missiles, space launch vehicles and sounding rockets, and also complete subsystems, such as rocket stages, reentry vehicles, guidance sets, rocket engines, fusing and firing mechanisms and the production facilities to build any of those--regarding them, export requests were to be scrutinized very closely, with the presumption of denial among the members.

The second tier category was meant to include dual-use goods, such as rocket casings, staging mechanisms and, more recently, cruise missile technology, the GPS system itself, and aircraft navigational systems that could be useful for missile systems. Category Two items are meant to be the subject of close scrutiny to ensure that they are not diverted for use in missile programs.

Before dealing with the issue of the strengths and weaknesses of the MTCR, both inherent and as practised, it is worth touching briefly on why there is any hope that the entire regime might succeed. To begin with, building ballistic missiles is expensive and very difficult. This holds true especially for a developing country--as Israel, as much as anyone, could probably confirm. When there are other pressing domestic needs, it is an extremely taxing endeavor. The production, assembly and deployment of ballistic missiles tax a nation's resources in different ways at different levels. The personnel needs dig into other national aspirations, as engineers, computer scientists, and experts in specialized materials are peeled away from civilian sector needs. Expertise in design manufacturing, testing and systems integration is diverted into this, most often no-return asset.

Under these circumstances, marginal difficulties which in any way delay the acquisition of key components of the ballistic missile system can drastically increase the costs of having already diverted this enormous national wealth into one of these missile programs. An excellent complete study of this phenomenon is provided by Janne Nolan.[3] Moreover, though many countries will achieve self-sufficiency in any one of these areas, whether in propulsion systems or reentry vehicle technology, certain components remain completely inaccessible to all but the most highly industrialized countries.

Adding an appreciation of the difficulty that even the most advanced states had in building successful ballistic missile programs, the case becomes yet more arresting. Recall some of the catastrophic failures of the US industrial machine in this field, despite the wealth of the richest treasury in the world, and the most sophisticated military industrial complex already underway. Unfettered by a legal international conspiracy to deny it the world's most sophisticated technology--which is what the MTCR comprises--the US missile program had some embarrassingly bleak moments at different times. If this experience is overlaid on some of the countries that are attempting to develop ballistic missiles, then the marginal success that the MTCR can have in producing delays, can be rather debilitating. These are some of the reasons why there has been hope that the MTCR could work.

Given these expectations, what nonetheless are the MTCR's strengths and weaknesses as a system? The weaknesses are hardly fatal ones. In some cases they are necessary; in others, they ought to be reexamined in future joint reviews of the MTCR. Some of these weaknesses are:

The nuclear nexus. For all practical purposes this weakness is now obsolete. At the outset the US had some difficulties on this issue with France, because France said, "Well, if we are transferring ballistic missile parts of this capability to countries that do not have a nuclear program, then it does not count, because the introduction to the MTCR says that it aims 'to control ballistic missile proliferation.'"

Yet when a country like Brazil actually plans to share technology with a country like Libya, it becomes apparent that there need not exactly be a nuclear program for missiles to constitute a dangerous program. Therefore, this exception should simply be excised from the language of the regime.

Range. The applicability of the MTCR to missile systems with a range over 300 kilometers has caused a number of problems as well. Again, the French had a case when they wanted to assist Egypt despite evidence that the Egyptians were diverting technology from the Sakr-80 to the Condor program. The argument was, "why be so precise about limiting exactly where the technology goes, when basically it all ends up in the same kind of program." So it is necessary to examine whether the 300-kilometer yardstick is actually a useful distinction. The Bush proposal to freeze missiles of a much lesser range, may be a step in that direction.

Space programs. Another, perhaps inherent, weakness in the MTCR stems from a sort of ambivalence or ambiguity over space programs. Consider in this regard President Mitterand's announcement that France would like to help people with their peaceful space programs, and then look at a country like Brazil or India, whose space and ballistic programs work hand-in-glove. Thus there are some ambiguities that must still be clarified. Parenthetically, in November 1991 the MTCR members did produce another annex, which settled other difficulties and differences of opinion among the regime's members. This new annex is a useful step.

There are, of course, obvious benefits to the MTCR system. For one, it established a system for international consultation and joint review of various kinds of exports. And, perhaps more importantly, it committed a number of countries with the greatest capability in this sphere to observing a set of guidelines. Once commitment of the countries is secured, what remains is primarily oversight and averting embarrassing situations of being caught doing something one promised and subscribed not to do.

The record on implementation and enforcement since the informal observance of the MTCR in 1985, and even since the formal observance in 1987, has been very uneven. Each country undertook to incorporate into its national laws the enforcement

216

mechanisms necessary to halt the export of ballistic missile technologies. In countries like France this was extremely well done. The French system is rather unique, where many of the companies involved are partially owned by the government, and the idea of one of these companies doing something behind the back of the government is somewhat preposterous. In such countries the regime was extremely well enforced.

Germany, on the other hand, is at the other extreme. It had the export regulations on the books, but next to no interest in enforcing them in any of their parts, and virtually no legal means to do so. This was due to the German constitution, which guarantees the right to trade. In order to issue just a subpoena to obtain company documents in Germany, the case virtually has to be proven before the judge. This is a process that in some cases has taken a number of years.

The legal burden had been on the party that wanted to infringe on the right to trade. This included the customs officer personally, and dated from Allied-imposed constitutional obligations which ensured that the individual bore responsibility for his own actions. It filtered down to the customs officer who was personally and financially responsible for any loss, any unfair or undue loss of money from trade. So a customs officer, looking at one of these cases, would say, "If I stop this sale and I'm wrong, I have to be financially liable in a court of law for whatever money is lost due to the loss of the transaction." It is hardly surprising that no customs office in Germany took the trouble to stop anything.

These legal obstacles stood in the way of the enforcement of the MTCR in Germany and, in fact, that was one of the cases where the US legislation--Missile Technology Control Act (MTCA)--had decisive results. Within two months of introducing a bill that would have sanctioned companies which exported ballistic missile material in defiance of the MTCR guidelines, two companies that were major contributors to the Condor project inquired in the Congress exactly how the law worked. Then they explained that there was absolutely nothing that was going on in either of the companies that could possibly be interpreted as in defiance of the MTCA.

The Italian law was merely mystifying; it was most difficult to understand how it worked. The MTCR Annex was considered a classified document, making it virtually impossible for a company to sit down and assess its exports. Apparently the Italian law is that if you are exporting anything, go to the government and ask. If they say yes, it is all right. So the companies would lie. They would say they would export something else; and the customs officers, who were probably not given a copy of this classified document, had no idea what they should do, so everything was exported.

In any event, the inconsistency in implementation and enforcement of the MTCR, and the record of its many specific failures--among the most prominent of which was the Condor-2 program--inspired Congress to write the sanctions legislation: the MTCA.

The novel feature of the MTCA legislation was its "extraterritoriality." The legislators were told in unambiguous words by various lobbyists that if we put certain clauses into law and implement them, the European Community would break relations with the United States. Yet this did not happen. The MTCA stipulated for the first time that if a foreign company does something which is or is not necessarily proven to be in violation of the national law in the country in which it is operating, but which, in the US view, is contrary to the MTCR, the US would take action against that company.

In the US view, the MTCA does not involve any extraterritoriality. It protects its own rights, by stipulating that the US will not export sensitive technologies to that company, and will not grant it the benefit of contracts which are paid for by US taxpayer money. This is, in the US view, a completely independent decision which it has every right to make. Neither of those things is extraterritorial, and at the end of the day the countries and companies involved also realized that was the case. Later, the entire system was incorporated into the enhanced Proliferation Control Initiative, not just for ballistic missiles, but

218

for chemical weapons proliferation, nuclear proliferation, and biological weapons proliferation as well.

Finally, as a score card of the successes and failures of the MTCR vis-a-vis individual projects and countries, the following are a few examples which do not comprise an exhaustive list, but are demonstrative of some of the patterns. Caution is in order, however, in interpreting these examples since these outcomes are not strictly the result of the MTCR. Thus, these outcomes should also be viewed in light of other factors and other events, illustrating that to be successful the MTCR need only be a catalyst for failure of missile proliferation, and need not be the sole reason for such failure.

In Argentina and Brazil there were fairly similar cases. **Argentina** had the Condor-2 program, with Iraq and Egypt, and the clandestine assistance of several European companies. But Argentina wanted to sell the Pampa trainer to the USAF and the Navy. Its economy was in desperate straits and its new president was less beholden to the military and less committed to the project. The combination of slowing it down, making it more expensive, denying certain key technologies, and public exposure-- all combined to kill Argentine participation in the Condor-2. This was an outright success.

Brazil's case was also a success. It had two companies developing missile technology. One, Averbros, developed missiles; the other, Orbita, developed the space program--the Sonda 1 through 4. Both of those programs became bankrupt for a number of different reasons. They were also denied a lot of technology along the way and, therefore, were not able to start any kind of export promotion activity. At the same time, however, Brazil also had a new president, who was not committed to the military or to the projects. Both companies fell into economic difficulties because of the collapse of the conventional arms market for the types of conventional arms they sold. And one of the companies had problems because Iraq reneged on its debts for artillery that it had bought from it.

Brazil, however, was also an example of a different kind of effort. As of 1989, it attempted rather creatively to acquire a complete rocket motor. In a rather clever offset deal, it stated that any company that wanted to launch its satellite would have to deliver to its doorstep a complete rocket motor. Orion Space was considering the deal, and was on the verge of offering it the rocket motor, when all the other companies came crying to their masters and said, "How come I don't get to do that?" After two years France withdrew the offer. Several other specific components were denied Brazil over the year. Thus, Brazil is really an unqualified success, although the space program sort of chugs on. There is little likelihood of the missile program being very successful.

India, on the other hand, has been untouched by the MTCR. Things have slowed down, but India has industrial depth, scientific depth, and a commitment and a reason to have a robust space program interrelated with its civilian economy. It is therefore unlikely that much headway will be made there. The most one can hope for is to slow down India's program.

Iran is a case of a country that is entirely dependent on other countries like China or North Korea. If the latter can be prevented from exporting missiles and related technology to Iran, then Iran's acquisition of ballistic missiles can be stopped.

Iraq signals a failure, and provides the blueprint for how to beat the system. It is a case where money triumphed. If a country has the money, it is going to be very, very difficult to stop it from acquiring ballistic missiles. The only thing one can hope for is universal participation by the sellers in missile nonproliferation efforts.

Saudi Arabia constitutes another regional failure--it has sufficient financial resources. Libya and Pakistan should probably be counted as successes, because they have been slowed down, and they do not contain any kind of depth: any industrial and scientific depth in the case of Libya, and any money in the other case.

In the final analysis, what the MTCA represents is power politics by a new means. And so it should be. The US does not go to China and say, "You and I, we're white knights; and these guys, Iraq and Syria, they are bad guys. Let's not sell them anything." The US applies its leverage by saying to the PRC, "You have a ten billion dollar trade surplus with us. You don't earn more than two billion dollars on arms sales every year. And we're going to deny you Most Favored Nation status if you sell missiles to Syria and Iran." With certain countries, that is the only way to succeed: China and North Korea are two prime examples. The point of the matter is for the US to say to potential proliferators: "Whether it's in your interest to do this or not is your problem, but it is not in the US interest, and the US is going to do absolutely everything within its power to punish you unless you come to agree with it." There is nothing moralistic about it.

Finally a word on the reason why the MTCA sanctions legislation is aimed at suppliers, rather than at recipients. At least some of the sponsors of the legislation on missile non-proliferation said that they were not going to tell a country not to do everything it could, that it thought it needed to do, for its own security. But they were going to do everything in their power to stop it from happening, "if the US does not think it is in its own interest." That is why the supplier route was taken. This may seem like a distinction without a difference, but it is at least a passing nod that what the US is seeking is not to tell other nations how to live, but rather to do what it can to ensure that how other people behave is in its own security interests.

Notes

1.   Seth Carus, *Ballistic Missiles in the Third World: Threat and Response* (New York: Praeger Books, 1990).
2.   "Assessing Ballistic Missile Proliferation and Its Control," A Report of the Center for International Security and Arms Control (Stanford University: November 1991).
3.   Janne E. Nolan, *Trappings of Power: Ballistic Missiles in the Third World* (Washington DC: Brookings, 1991).

15. America's Non-Proliferation Policy: A Congressional Perspective

Zachary S. Davis

The US constitution invests the president with primary responsibility for charting the course of American foreign policy. Thus, arms control and non-proliferation are mainly the domain of the Executive Branch of government. Past Middle East arms control initiatives left little room for congressional input beyond providing the funds for proposed arms sales and assistance to the region. However, Congress has become increasingly active in efforts to shape US arms control and non-proliferation policy, particularly in the Middle East. The large volume of weapons proliferation bills introduced in the first session of the 102nd Congress, many of which contain special provisions regarding the Middle East, are evidence of intensified congressional interest and assertiveness in this regard.

This chapter reviews some congressional mechanisms for shaping US policies, assesses the effectiveness and appropriateness of these mechanisms, and concludes with a few words about the status of US non-proliferation policy.

Legislative Mechanisms for Influencing Non-Proliferation Policy

Congress sometimes behaves like a nervous back seat driver who shouts directions at the president while he decides on the direction of the nation's foreign policy. Despite the fact that Congress owns the car and pays for the gas, a tension exists between the president and Congress over the ends and means of non-proliferation policy.

The legislative process provides a myriad of ways for Congress to influence the president's policies. Legislation can and does serve many political objectives, and is introduced for a variety of reasons with different expectations for results. For example, a very hard-hitting non-proliferation bill--full of restrictions, conditions, controls, and sanctions--may be introduced to ignite public debate and attract attention to the problems associated with an existing policy, even if the bill has little chance of ever becoming law. This kind of bill can be a shot across the bow of the administration; it is intended to send a signal. There are a few bills in this category in the 102nd Congress. Another possibility is for a seemingly bland bill to be transformed into a very aggressive piece of legislation. Bills are often chopped into parts which can be reconstituted, mixed with other bills, hidden in totally unrelated measures, and transformed from caterpillar to butterfly and back again. Non-proliferation legislation in the 102nd Congress underwent such changes. Six legislative approaches that comprise the congressional component of US non-proliferation policy will be reviewed here.

Hearings are used by Congress to examine policies, draw attention to problems, discuss proposed changes in policy, and set the stage for legislative action to remedy perceived problems.

Proliferation and Middle East arms control were a hot topic on Capitol Hill in 1991-92. The end of the Cold War, and Operation Desert Storm, caused the Congress to focus more attention on proliferation issues. Hearings in the 102nd Congress examined the full range of proliferation issues, including all countries of concern, successes and failures of US non-proliferation policy, and the possibility of nuclear leakage from the former Soviet Union. Hearings on Iraq focused on US and western exports to Iraq, Iraq's imports of dual-use technology, US policy toward Iraq prior to the war, and intelligence estimates of Iraqi capabilities. Hearings serve an oversight function by providing a forum for administration officials and expert witnesses to explain policies and to engage in debate with legislators about their merits and shortcomings.

Reporting requirements. One of the legislative tools used by Congress to encourage transparency, or openness, on the part of the Executive Branch is to require periodic reports to the

223

appropriate congressional committees on particular policies. Such reports are intended to facilitate oversight by reminding agencies of the need to justify their actions. Ideally, reports provide those in Congress who track a particular issue with information about the goals of policy, how policy is being implemented and by whom.

Several of the proliferation bills in the 102nd Congress contain extensive new reporting requirements on such things as the president's efforts to convene a conference of arms suppliers (S.1435, S.1046), on the names of countries known to be involved in proliferation activities (S.309), and on US efforts to enforce existing non-proliferation norms.

It should be noted that in practice these reporting requirements number in the thousands and are regularly ignored by those in Congress who ask for them as well as by the Executive Branch agencies that are required to submit them. They are often viewed by the administration as a punitive measure intended to harass officials who have better things to do with their (or their interns') time. Often the reports satisfy the bare minimal requirements of the law and contain little substantive information. The annual non-proliferation policy report required by the Nuclear Nonproliferation Act of 1978 is a good example of such a report.

Conditions on aid. The power of the purse may be the most effective non-proliferation leverage available to the Congress. Congress can attach conditions to proposed military and/or economic assistance. Conditions are generally of two types. The first type may require the president to take certain actions before providing aid, such as convening an international conference to discuss multilateral controls on arms transfers, or certifying to the Congress that a particular transfer is consistent with legislative guidelines. This is the type imposed on aid to Pakistan. The second type of condition may also require the country that is to receive the aid to certify that its policies are consistent with US standards on such issues as its human rights or non-proliferation policy.

Problems often arise from linking unrelated issues, such as foreign aid and non-proliferation. The Bush administration

224

strongly opposed this type of linkage, as in the case of China. There is, nevertheless, considerable interest in the Congress in continuing to put conditions on assistance. Some members have suggested linking assistance to membership in the NPT.

Changes in legal authorities: reorganizing the government. This is an option that strikes fear into the federal bureaucracy: Congress can reorganize government agencies, shift responsibilities from agency to agency, or create new ones. One complicating factor in nuclear non-proliferation policy is that responsibility for formulating and implementing the administration's policy is dispersed among at least seven agencies--the departments of State, Defense, Commerce, and Energy, the Arms Control and Disarmament Agency, the Nuclear Regulatory Commission, and the CIA. Director of Central Intelligence Robert Gates has indicated that his agency is prepared to focus more resources on proliferation issues. Lately there has been talk of creating a new office of strategic trade, although there are no provisions for creating a new agency in current legislation.

Congress can also amend or pass new laws to loosen and/or tighten controls on exports. Several bills of this type are before Congress. The Export Control Act is the main arena for non-proliferation legislation intended to expand restrictions on nuclear and nuclear-related dual-use exports.

Sanctions are one of the most contentious issues between Congress and the president. Several bills in the 102nd Congress target sanctions against US and foreign violators of US non-proliferation laws and policies. On the eve of the Gulf War (November 1990) President Bush pocket-vetoed chemical weapons legislation that contained provisions for mandatory sanctions. The lessons of the Gulf War convinced many more members of Congress of the dangers of proliferation and the need to punish those who endanger world security by seeking profits from trade in weapons of mass destruction. Much of the focus is on suppliers. Knowledge of Iraq's nuclear, chemical and missile programs created an environment in which it is more difficult for President Bush to veto tough non-proliferation legislation. The White House has been more willing to negotiate sanctions and

President Bush has signed some sanctions bills based on the MTCR legislation. It simply does not make sense to continue to conduct business as usual with countries and companies that undermine your non-proliferation policy objectives.

Strengthening international regimes. Congress has lately become enamored with the concept of non-proliferation regimes, and is seeking to apply it broadly. This intensified interest is manifested in the unprecedented volume of non-proliferation legislation before Congress, much of which contains language intended to promote multilateral efforts to control the spread of conventional and nonconventional weapons and dual-use technology. This interest in regimes is one of the most promising, and in some regards also one of the most awkward areas of congressional activity.

Regimes are popular, but they are delicate diplomatic enterprises which function according to the rules of international diplomacy, not the rules of torts and contracts. Groups such as the Nuclear Suppliers Group, the Australia Group, and the MTCR are informal in nature. Their members are neither bound by formal legal commitments nor is their compliance officially policed or enforced. The IAEA comes closer to being a formal institution, but operates on many of the same principles as the less formal regimes. In attempting to ,strengthen the suppliers' regimes, Congress should avoid imposing formal measures that could make participation distasteful.

Congressional influence on non-proliferation regimes is manifested through indirect efforts to persuade, cajole, or if need be blackmail the administration into undertaking more visible and energetic efforts to use the existing regime structures to achieve the non-proliferation objectives favored by Congress. A number of bills before the Congress would urge the president and the Secretary of State to hold meetings to discuss ways to strengthen supplier controls and to expand the scope and authorities of existing regimes. These bills fall into the "shot across the bow" category mentioned earlier. While the president warily protects his foreign policy prerogatives by resisting congressional interloping in non-proliferation diplomacy, there exists a creative tension between the president and the Congress that may ultimately strengthen the utility of the regimes.

Some Comments on the Utility of Non-Proliferation Regimes

It is now appropriate to move from the practical issues of building, using and maintaining non-proliferation regimes to a more theoretical analysis of the regime phenomenon. Hopefully the regime concept will be studied intensively by scholars to bring greater understanding to the inner workings, potential uses, and inherent limitations of security regimes in international politics. We are in need of new and expanded concepts for arms control in the post-cold war era, and the regime concept may have significance for this endeavor.

Regimes may indicate the evolution of a new type of actor in international politics--a new type of actor that is uniquely appropriate for certain of the challenges we face. Regimes are not equivalent to international law, despite arguments to the contrary presented by academics who question the validity of the concept of security regimes. These somewhat informal multilateral groupings have more in common with the CSCE process than with the formal bilateral arms agreements between US-USSR, although the regimes may benefit from their association with formal treaties such as the NPT or perhaps the CWC. In practice, non-proliferation regimes are powerful tools for shaping the global and regional security environment. They cannot replace existing means of securing national interests, but have proven effective in US and multilateral diplomacy to control the spread of the most dangerous weapons.

Israel's accommodation to the MTCR could strengthen the missile non-proliferation regime. With the help of its allies, Israel should find a way to accommodate the nuclear non-proliferation regime as well, because it is one of the few tools available to ward off the emergence of a multi-nuclear Middle East. President

Bush's proposal for a ban on the production of nuclear weapons materials may offer some useful options in this regard.

Regimes are an example of theory being outrun by events. Policymakers did not envision the emergence of non-proliferation regimes as we have come to know them, yet they are quite comfortable with the concept. In practice, regimes are composed of the full range of unilateral, bilateral, and multilateral efforts aimed at the goal of non-proliferation. The nuclear regime is composed of US and other national laws, formal and informal bilateral and multilateral agreements, international treaties such as the NPT and its supporting institution, the IAEA, as well as the nuclear suppliers groups: the NSG, and the Zangger Committee. Together this web of formal and informal agreements constitutes a new actor in international politics. Although creating and maintaining the regime was not originally identified as a policy goal by the US Congress, US presidents, diplomats, or national leaders, it has become the main focus of US and international non-proliferation policy. In this case, policymakers seem to be forging ahead of scholars. If the regime is to remain our frontline of defense against nuclear proliferation, a deeper theoretical understanding of regime politics would be extremely useful to help guide non-proliferation policy in the future.

16. The Nuclear Agenda: The Middle East in Global Perspective

Lewis A. Dunn

The nuclear agenda, both at the global level and in the Middle East, has figured prominently in public debate since the collapse of the Soviet Union and the discovery of Saddam Hussein's "mini-Manhattan Project." In reviewing that nuclear agenda, this chapter makes six points:

First, the global nuclear order, which provides the basic context for the nuclear agenda in the Middle East, is in the midst of fundamental change; this change has mostly encouraging, but some discouraging characteristics;

Secondly, the familiar Middle East nuclear status quo of the past two decades--an Israeli nuclear monopoly--is increasingly unstable;

Third, a multi-nuclear Middle East quite probably would be very dangerous, unstable and with less security for all countries in the region;

Fourth, unilateral or coercive nuclear non-proliferation measures, whether export controls or military intervention, will not suffice by themselves to prevent a multi-nuclear Middle East;

Fifth, arms control, and in particular unilateral actions by the government of Israel to indicate nuclear restraint, can buttress coercive measures in useful ways; and

Sixth, a long-term solution to head off a multi-nuclear Middle East calls for dealing with the underlying political disputes and confrontations of the region; but there may not be enough time to wait for the long-term.

The Changing Global Nuclear Order

The basic defining feature of the post-war global nuclear order was the US-Soviet nuclear competition. This competition

was driven by a number of factors: conflict of interests; ideology; and the US commitment to Europe's defense via a posture of extended deterrence. In particular, once the United States committed itself to deter a Soviet/Warsaw Pact attack on Western Europe, this commitment dictated a US nuclear posture which included a significant theater nuclear force, a robust strategic nuclear force, and a capability for prompt and rapid escalation in response to such an attack.

But bureaucratic factors and technological momentum also played a part in affecting the nuclear competition. American engineers over-designed the first nuclear reactors in the post-war period. Thus, in the mid-1950s, the US Atomic Energy Commission found it could produce much more nuclear weapons-grade material than had been anticipated. Moreover, the shift from fission weapons to thermonuclear weapons during that period made more efficient use of that nuclear material possible. Thus, US officials discovered in the mid-1950s that they had lots of bomb material, and that it took a lot less than anticipated to make a bomb. As a result, the original US arsenal, and eventually the Soviet arsenal, steadily expanded.

Finally, the nuclear competition of the post-war period was driven, at least to some extent, by missed opportunities. For example, some observers believe that during the Khrushchev years, political opportunities to constrain the US-Soviet nuclear competition were ignored. On the technical side, had there been more foresight, the United States and the Soviet Union might have managed to avoid the deployment of multiple independently retargetable warheads (MIRVs) in the late 1960s and 1970s. Failure to do so led to a sharp technical escalation of the East-West nuclear arms competition.

The Nuclear Order Today

By the early 1990s, this global nuclear competition, like the broader East-West political order it helped to define, has radically changed. First, retaining deterrence of a Soviet threat to Western Europe and the United States as the driving concept of

American strategy--a position it occupied for the better part of four and a half decades--no longer makes sense. It is not clear whom the US is deterring, from what it is deterring them, and under what circumstances deterrence is expected to function.

Moreover, a strategy of nuclear deterrence does not help addressing the current real threats from the East. Nuclear deterrence cannot contain the proliferation spillovers of Soviet collapse. It does not provide an effective means to lessen the risk that one or more former Soviet republics might decide to retain former Soviet nuclear weapons or seek nuclear weapons indigenously.

A second and equally important change of the global nuclear order is underway. During most of the past 40 years, there has been a steady East-West nuclear buildup. Nuclear postures, doctrine, systems, production infrastructure, and testing infrastructure have been put in place and expanded. From the western perspective, these capabilities made sense in that postwar world. But those same East-West nuclear postures are no longer necessary or desirable in the post-Cold War world. Thus, an accelerating roll-back of those US and Russian nuclear postures can be expected. President Bush's September 27th 1991 initiative to eliminate ground-launched tactical nuclear weapons, and Gorbachev's favorable response, were but the first steps in this process.

Consider some possible specifics. Eventually, the numbers of warheads on both sides may be reduced to the low thousands--two or three thousand. In terms of production capabilities, the United States and Russia may agree formally to cut off the production of nuclear weapons-grade material. In addition, a ban on the testing of nuclear weapons may be concluded within the next several years. Finally, an eventual shift away from the doctrine of first-use of nuclear weapons may well take place. Thus, at the global level, fundamental political, military, and strategic changes are evolving.

An Unstable Middle East Nuclear Status Quo

The Middle East nuclear status quo is unstable. It is likely to be very hard to preserve Israel's unacknowledged but publicly assumed nuclear monopoly in the decade ahead. There are many reasons for thinking that the pressures on Israel's nuclear monopoly would increase rather than decrease.

First, the Iraqi nuclear weapons program is badly damaged but not eliminated. No more than in 1981, after Israeli aircraft destroyed the Osirak research reactor, has Saddam Hussein given up his desire for nuclear weapons. Although the United Nations Special Commission eliminated the known components of Iraq's nuclear weapons, the know-how remained. It must be assumed that Saddam Hussein, his generals, and whoever might succeed him, will continue the quest for nuclear weapons. Given a chance, Iraq's pursuit of the bomb would accelerate again.

Elsewhere in the region, Iran comprises what might be called an up-and-coming contender in the nuclear realm. It is probably motivated most by concerns about Iraq. But a desire to deter outsiders and perhaps to threaten Israel may also figure in its calculations. On the sidelines are Syria, Algeria and, as a long-shot, Turkey. If the Turks are not admitted to the European Community, and if they face a resurgent nuclear Iraq, Ankara's proliferation incentives could jump sharply within the coming decade. Ties with former Soviet republics and with Muslim countries could help to "jump-start" pursuit of nuclear weapons.

Another long-shot is Egypt. There appears to be growing uneasiness in Egypt, about "What are the Israelis really up to in the nuclear realm?" This may comprise rhetoric--an effort to score diplomatic points with outsiders; but it may also signal a new debate in Cairo about the wisdom of President Sadat's decision not to pursue nuclear weapons. Further, there is a danger that the Egyptians' current push for greater transparency in the Israeli program may succeed and then backfire. This is so since greater transparency will likely make it harder for the Egyptian government to resist popular and elite pressures, which would in any case jump with open confirmation of Israel's capability, to reverse the decision not to seek nuclear weapons.

Impact of Soviet Breakup

Yet another reason for being concerned that the Israeli nuclear monopoly is unstable is the risk of proliferation spillovers from the breakup of the Soviet Union. In this regard, it is important to distinguish four aspects of this problem. Strategic nuclear weapons are probably under excellent command and control. It is unlikely, therefore, that former Soviet strategic weapons would be successfully diverted to a Middle East country. By contrast, diversion or theft of tactical nuclear weapons is a greater threat. These weapons are more moveable, and technical measures of control probably vary from weapon to weapon.

Perhaps the greatest threat, however, is the illegal or simply irregular export of nuclear-weapons-related components, machinery, and equipment. For instance, Iranians might open contacts with a company in Kazakhstan and buy numerically controlled machine tools useful in a nuclear weapons program. Or Iran might seek to purchase other components that would allow it to follow Iraq's example and build calutrons to produce weapons-grade uranium. Another issue--the brain drain problem--has been widely discussed. Yet even with access to outside brainpower, a country would still have to obtain the needed equipment, components, material, and other inputs. Seepage of the latter is the real threat.

One final reason for concern about the stability of the regional nuclear status quo should be mentioned. This is the possibility of nuclear weapons cooperation among the countries within the Middle East and Gulf regions. For instance, the Iraqis might take their know-how, trained manpower, and skills and set up shop elsewhere, perhaps in Algeria. A science and technology cooperation agreement between the two countries already exists. Another possibility would be the establishment of an Islamic consortium in which the Pakistanis and the Iranians cooperate. Throughout the first decades of the nuclear age, such assistance or cooperation between states has been the norm and not the exception: all of the first five nuclear weapon states provided aid to another country.

Dangers of a Multi-Nuclear Middle East

There are good reasons for concern about the likely instability and dangers of a multi-nuclear Middle East. At best, the transition to a situation of stable nuclear deterrence in this region will be slow and subject to breakdown; at worst, that transition may not be made successfully.

Concern about the dangers of proliferation has little to do necessarily with whether the Arabs or the Iranians are irrational, although one experienced "Saddam-watcher" suggested that Saddam Hussein would be prepared to use nuclear weapons even if this were to lead to his country's destruction. Setting aside the argument about the possibility of "crazy leaders" or "crazy states," two reasons for concern stand out: First, the conditions of stable deterrence may not be met in the Middle East; and secondly, "rational" national nuclear-forcebuilding choices may lead to unstable regional strategic outcomes.

A series of conditions--some political, some technical, some related to the overall context--underpinned the stable nuclear balance that eventually evolved between the United States and the Soviet Union. At the political level, for example, the stakes--what each side was after--were basically low. By contrast, in the Middle East the stakes are existential: who is going to live on this one little strip of land next to the Mediterranean. Ultimately, national survival is the issue.

Technical factors also contributed to the stability of the Cold War nuclear balance. For example, the United States spent a lot of money to ensure the safety of its nuclear warheads. As a result, when a technician dropped a wrench down a Titan-2 missile silo back in 1980, leading to explosion of the missile fuel and the throwing of a ten-megaton warhead 400 yards down the road, an accidental nuclear detonation was avoided.

234

By contrast, other new nuclear powers may pay less attention to safety, putting top priority on building the bomb. Consider how the Iraqis stored chemical weapons: they simply kept chemical agents in 55 gallon drums that were thrown around. At the very least, Iraq clearly had a very different safety culture.

With regard to the context, the fact that the East-West competition was a bipolar confrontation, also mattered. With clear dividing lines, it was easier to calculate relative military advantage and the risks of action. In the Middle East, the confrontation is multipolar in two ways. First, there are several different sets of countries confronting each other: Israel vs. Syria, Israel vs. Iraq, Iraq vs. Iran, Syria vs. Iraq, and so on. In addition, there are different weapons of "mass destruction" in the region. This too complicates calculations and increases the risk of miscalculation and escalation. Can nuclear weapons deter chemical weapons? Can chemical weapons deter nuclear weapons? What deters BW? And how do these all fit together?

Thus one reason for concern is that some of the key conditions that were essential to the eventual emergence of a relationship of stable East-West nuclear deterrence may be absent in the Middle East. There is a second reason for concern, related to the choices likely to be made by new nuclear powers.

Nuclear-Forcebuilding Choices

Any country that has a nuclear weapons program faces a number of nuclear forcebuilding choices. For example, does it emphasize readiness, or does it emphasize safety? There is a trade-off between these requirements, since one effective way to have safe nuclear warheads is to keep them disassembled. But if they are kept disassembled, they might not be ready for use in a crisis or conflict. Another example is the choice between survivability (e.g., by dispersion of mobile missiles) and controllability (e.g., by centralized deployments).

At this force-building level, some countries in the Middle East have very good reasons to make choices that will be less, not more, stabilizing. For instance, mobile Scuds with nuclear warheads deployed in the Iraqi western desert would probably be very survivable, but at a considerable price in terms of security and safety. In turn, keeping warheads disassembled would assure the weapons' safety. But some countries in the region may be unwilling to take that approach if they want a highly ready force or if it is a time of crisis. As a result the dangers of unintended escalation would be high. For all these reasons, a prudent policymaker, observer, or analyst must conclude that the emergence of stable nuclear balances in the Middle East would at least take a long time, and may well be subject to breakdown. Hence the need to prevent nuclear proliferation in the Middle East.

To Acknowledge or Not To Acknowledge

A particularly important choice which confronts new or emerging nuclear weapon states is between acknowledgment or non-acknowledgment of that nuclear capability. Does a country's leadership acknowledge possession of nuclear weapons or does it refrain from such acknowledgment?

So far, all of the new nuclear weapon states (after the first five) have basically chosen not to acknowledge. There are costs and benefits of making that choice, for the country in question as well as outsiders, but the distribution of these costs and benefits favor non-acknowledgment. Specifically, continued Israeli nuclear ambiguity makes it easier to work the problem of heading off a multi-nuclear Middle East, not least by damping domestic political pressures to seek the bomb in other countries. More broadly, it would not be desirable, as some observers have proposed, to amend the Nuclear Non-Proliferation Treaty (NPT) to allow Israel, India, and Pakistan to adhere to the treaty as nuclear weapon states. This would stimulate proliferation and could lead to the NPT's collapse, especially by triggering withdrawal from the Treaty by Arab countries.

The Limits of Unilateral Measures and Coercive Actions

Unilateral measures and coercive action will probably not suffice by themselves to block the emergence of a multi-nuclear Middle East. Several different types of unilateral action or coercive measures stand out. These include export controls, enhanced inspections, covert action, and military action. Also, such action must be backed up by effective intelligence and complemented by responses to the threat posed by Soviet nuclear breakup.

There are, however, important limits to the likely effectiveness of unilateral measures or coercive action. Some of these limits are practical. Export controls can be circumvented, and in any case only buy time. Successful direct military action depends on very precise intelligence. But as the Iraqi case indicated, although the United States and others knew a lot about Iraq's nuclear and missile program, there were important sites that were not known or were misidentified. The gradual acquisition of sufficient indigenous capabilities by countries within this region is another limit to the effectiveness of unilateral measures, including military action. In that regard, Soviet nuclear breakup is a wild card: components, equipment, materiel--or even a bomb--might seep out to the region.

Questions about the legitimacy of unilateral export controls and especially of direct military action also limit the feasibility of such actions. Such questions could especially affect the prospects for successful coalition-building, whether for export controls or for United Nations sanctions, as well as the likely political staying power of the United States in pursuing unilateral measures. In the past, for instance, support for tough non-proliferation measures was somewhat undermined by continued expansion of the American nuclear arsenal. This expansion made it tougher for US diplomats to convince other countries to refrain from exporting to problem countries or to argue the case against acquiring nuclear weapons with officials from these problem countries. More generally, that expansion eroded the credibility of the US non-proliferation policy.

This global dimension, however, is changing. US officials can now point to the rollback of US nuclear weaponry to give greater legitimacy to non-proliferation efforts. These efforts include export controls, pursuit of sanctions, and even possible direct military action.

By contrast, recent revelations have reinforced the widespread perception that there are no restraints on Israel's nuclear program. To outsiders, the Israeli program seems pretty much to steam ahead on its own. This makes it tougher to call for new initiatives to restrain the nuclear programs of Arab countries and of Iran, such as the application of special conditions on nuclear supplies for this region. It also makes it harder politically for outsiders to build domestic and coalition support for tough non-proliferation measures in this region, including military or covert action. This is another reason why unilateral measures and coercive action may become less effective over the next decade.

Payoffs of Unilateral Israeli Restraint

Unilateral signals of Israeli nuclear restraint could buttress current efforts to avoid a multi-nuclear Middle East. Consider each of the following questions related to unilateral restraint: Why self-restraint? Of what sort? In return for what? How to package restraint? And, when to do it?

"Why nuclear self-restraint?" As has been suggested, some sign of restraint of the Israeli program would enhance the political legitimacy of unilateral measures, including covert or direct military action, to block proliferation in the Middle East.

In this context, signs of Israeli restraint would make it less difficult to sustain global coalition support for intrusive inspections in Iraq for the long term. For instance, if Saddam Hussein were to be overthrown, Arab countries would likely argue that the sanctions against Iraq must be lifted, and the inspections of Iraq must end. Arab countries would also contend that, unlike in the case of Iraq, nothing is being done to contain "an ever-expanding

238

Israeli nuclear threat." If US and other officials could point to Israeli restraint, it would be easier to deflect that charge and to convince some European countries to pay the political price of continuing tough inspections of Iraq. For similar reasons, a signal of Israeli nuclear restraint would make it easier to build a coalition against Iran--the next problem. More generally, should covert or direct action against those countries become necessary, Israeli restraint would help to contain the resulting political side effects.

Unilateral Israeli restraint could also influence the debate about whether to acquire nuclear weapons in one or two countries in the Middle East. (Similarly, a signal of restraint could make it easier for Arab governments to adhere to a global Chemical Weapons Convention, in effect severing their earlier linkage between such adherence and elimination of Israel's nuclear capability.) This could be especially important if allegations about Israel's expanding nuclear arsenal trigger a growing debate in Cairo about whether to reassess Egypt's non-nuclear status. Algeria could be another case in point: statements by senior officers of the Algerian military suggest that one motivation for seeking a nuclear capability could well be political and ideological resentment of what is seen to be outsiders' acceptance of an unfettered Israeli nuclear capability. That said, Israeli restraint would have little direct effect, of course, on such countries as Iraq, Iran, Libya, or Syria.

The next question concerns "**What restraint? And what not?**" What could be done as a signal of Israeli nuclear restraint? One possible measure to signal Israeli nuclear restraint would be for the Israeli government to announce a readiness to consider an eventual freeze on production of nuclear weapons-grade materials. Another step would be a commitment not to test nuclear weapons. A call for technical discussions of how to verify a regional nuclear materials production ban would be still another. Or a maintenance stoppage at Dimona might be announced: the plant is getting old, and like an automobile, Dimona could go into the shop for servicing and maintenance.

On the other hand, such restraint is not--and is not intended to be--the first step to the complete elimination of Israel's nuclear capability. Even assuming progress in the peace process, and greater political harmony in the Middle East, Israel should not be expected to give up its nuclear capability. But with progress over the long term, it might make sense for Israel to reduce that capability, particularly if public allegations about its scope are anywhere near true. This would be similar to the situation in which the United States finds itself today: the world has changed and the United States no longer needs such a robust nuclear posture. That day might come in the Middle East--but not for quite some time. Therefore, it must be clear that suggestions for unilateral nuclear restraint are not aimed at the elimination of Israel's capability.

The next question, likely to be raised by this proposal for unilateral restraint, is: **"In return for what?"** Are there any quid pro quos? What can Israel obtain in return for such restraint?

One possibility in this context might be a tacit or explicit understanding between Washington and Tel Aviv that the US would block any UN Security Council decision to end inspections in Iraq unless both the US and Israel agreed to that step. Another quid pro quo might be a similar understanding on Washington's part to take all necessary steps to block Iran's pursuit of nuclear weapons. Intelligence sharing, cooperation in next generation missile defense, and strong responses to third-party troublemaking (e.g., Chinese sales of missiles to Syria) are other possible quid pro quos.

Ultimately, however, the issue is, does unilateral restraint--with or without a quid pro quo--serve Israel's interest? The answer is yes, for reasons already discussed.

Regarding the **"how,"** it is important that such restraint comprise unilateral Israel action. Restraint cannot be seen to be the result of American pressure.

"When?" Probably not right away, but soon enough to do some good. When will pressures arise to lift Iraqi inspections? How soon will the crunch come with Iran? When will it be useful to be able to say that there is some evidence of restraint in the Israeli nuclear program? These aspects of timing are very much a matter of judgment. Another important aspect of timing concerns the relationship between nuclear restraint and the evolving Middle East peace process.

The Long-Term--and How Long Can We Wait?

Any long-term solution to head off a multi-nuclear Middle East calls for successful political efforts in the peace process. For long-term stability in the region it is essential that the underlying insecurities, ambitions, and conflicts that have been driving this proliferation process be addressed. But two of the key countries, Iran and Iraq, are not part of the peace process. At best, substantial progress among the current participants will take considerable time. The danger is that given current Middle East nuclear developments, enough time may not be available. The pace of events may outrun the peace process.

Thus, a long-term solution clearly requires that politics change, just as occurred in the US-Soviet confrontation. Moreover, as so graphically demonstrated by the collapse of communism and the end of the Cold War, surprising things do happen. But while working for surprises, our primary efforts to avoid a Middle East of four or five nuclear weapon states must focus elsewhere. Those efforts must emphasize a mix of unilateral measures, from strengthened export controls to possible coercive actions.

Conclusion

The line of argument presented here began by reviewing the far-reaching changes of the nuclear order at the global level. The reasons for pessimism about the stability of today's Middle East nuclear status quo have been highlighted; the limits on unilateral measures and coercive action have been considered; and it was suggested that some sign of Israeli nuclear restraint would strengthen the legitimacy, feasibility and, ultimately, the likelihood of success of such measures and actions. Over the long-term, however, unilateral measures--even direct military action--can only buy time. Over the decade ahead, whatever time becomes available must be used to foster a change of political realities via an expanding peace process.

What are the prospects for success? It is difficult to say; there are too many uncertainties. What seems clear, however, is that such a combined approach--combining short-term unilateral actions and longer-term political steps in the context of Israeli nuclear restraint--provides the best alternative to avoid an increasingly unstable and dangerous multi-nuclear Middle East.

17.   Concluding Remarks

Ariel Levite

This first Ginosar conference took place when arms control in the Middle East was about to shift from a somewhat sterile academic exercise into a real political process. The opening of the Madrid peace process in October 1991 had created the conditions in which erstwhile Arab and Israeli foes began formally talking to one another. Then, the follow-up initiation of the multilateral peace process, formally launched a few weeks after the Ginosar conference, established for the first time a regional forum--the Working Group on Arms Control and Regional Security--where such issues could be formally discussed among many of the Middle East states. These developments combined to render the Ginosar conference more than an intellectual exercise. It had become, as Shai Feldman aptly notes in the introduction to this volume, an educational endeavor designed to acquaint the audience with the arms control experience in other regions and contexts, as well as with the factors that were likely to influence the regional arms control process about to get underway.

Part of the audience arrived at the Ginosar conference believing that arms control in the Middle East was a contradiction in terms--an oxymoron. Even among those who were less certain that this was indeed the case, few were convinced that many valuable lessons could be learned from the experience of others. Most subscribed to the viewpoint that the Middle East was *sui generis*--a truly unique case--at least as far as arms control was concerned.

Many factors were mentioned in support of the argument regarding the unique nature of the Middle East. These commonly referred to the climate of belligerency and suspicion, as well as to multiple asymmetries existing between Arabs and Israelis both in the military domain (force structures and size, doctrine) and in other areas pertinent to security such as natural resources, geography, demography, numbers of states and their alliances, and types of regime and political culture, not to mention the track record in honoring past agreements.

Both sets of beliefs were quite understandable, if one takes into account that the peace process had barely gotten underway when the conference took place. They clearly reflect the bitter legacy of the century-old conflict between Arabs and Jews in Palestine, reinforced by the wars and other forms of bitter struggle since the establishment of the State of Israel in 1948, and especially since 1967. During this period there was virtually no experience with cooperative multilateral and, in most cases, even bilateral security arrangements of any kind between Arabs and Israelis. The historical residue, reinforced by profound ignorance about arms control matters, combined to produce a massive dose of skepticism regarding arms control arrangements and their applicability to the Middle East.

It is against this background that one should look at the presentations of the Ginosar conference. These did not break new theoretical grounds--they were not intended to. But they did shed light on experiences, as well as other factors, that have relevance for assessing the prospects and desirability of arms control in the Middle East.

One striking insight that emerged from the Ginosar conference is that the present circumstances in the Middle East are not so fundamentally different from those that characterized the onset of arms control processes in other regions. True, even when one bloc faced another in Europe, each consisted of multiple parties, whereas Israel stands alone against an Arab bloc. Moreover, even at the lowest point of their relationship, mutual recognition and diplomatic relationships did exist between the parties. Ignorance about arms control was not as prevalent in Europe, the US, and the Soviet Union, as it presently is in the Middle East. Extra-regional parties were of little relevance to the European or bilateral superpower accords, which is clearly not the case in the Middle East, not to mention the uniquely acute challenge of delineating the Middle East region for arms control purposes.

These significant differences notwithstanding, many important commonalities also exist with other arms control processes, be they between the superpowers, in Europe, or in Latin America. In many of those contexts multiple asymmetries had also existed between the parties along multiple dimensions. Skepticism regarding both the viability and desirability of arms control was also clearly evident in these other contexts. In fact, even when skepticism evaporated regarding viability, it remained regarding desirability, and in some circles it is very much apparent to this day.

Bearing in mind the inherent limitations of analogies, one may still be able to generate some useful insights into the Middle East arms control process by examining processes elsewhere. In order to do so with any utility, however, one critical challenge ought to be met, namely identifying the time frame in the other processes which could serve as a basis for comparison. The presentations and discussions at Ginosar led us to conclude that, as far as the analogy to Europe was concerned, the point of reference is the period beginning with the Harmel Report (December 1967) and leading into the Helsinki Final Act (August 1975). Additionally, Ginosar offered a useful analogy with the superpowers' experience, where the appropriate point of reference probably is the period between the seminars on surprise attacks in the late 1950s and the first set of bilateral and bilaterally-sponsored multilateral arms control accords and treaties in the early 1960s.

If one looks at the evolution of arms control processes at these points in time, several conclusions emerge. First, arms control processes are inherently slow and time consuming. Multilateral arms control negotiations are even more problematic in this respect. Parties commonly enter formal arms control negotiations for multiple or diverse reasons. In some cases they do so with no initial desire to reach any concrete agreement, but rather to attain other--exogenous--gains, e.g., in the public relations or propaganda spheres, or to acquire some intelligence on the adversary. Moreover, even when agreements are actually sought by the parties, these commonly reflect the desire to concede no assets other than those one was planning on giving up in any event, and to gain in exchange valuable concessions from the other side.

Interestingly enough, judging by experience, it appears that negotiations that do get underway are quite likely to produce agreements, irrespective of the original motivations that guided either or both of the parties when entering them. In all cases, the attainment of an agreement is preceded by a breakthrough in the political relationships between parties. In fact, where no such breakthrough has taken place, as is the case between India and Pakistan, the two countries have not been able to make much headway in the area of arms control. The jury is still out, however, as to whether the dynamics of arms control can somehow contribute to a change in the political climate (as some suggest it has done in Europe), or whether, on the contrary, the causal link must be strictly the reverse.

Finally, the historical analogies suggest that if and when early agreements are arrived at, they usually do not attain two of the three classic objectives of arms control: they neither produce savings in peacetime, nor limit the horrors of war. In fact, some early arms control agreements are even said to have merely rechanneled and to an extent also reinvigorated an arms race, rather than having curbed it. The primary utility of such arms control accords is, therefore, as confidence-building measures that help reduce the likelihood of war.

One outcome of the Ginosar conference was thus to generate, on the basis of the experience of others, some useful general insights into arms control processes. These help calibrate expectations regarding the path such negotiations are likely to follow in the Middle East, especially in their early stages. These insights were complemented by another layer of contributions from Ginosar, namely those that map the global agenda that may affect the prospects as well as the process of arms control in the Middle East. Here, three additional sources of insights were considered. First, domestic developments in the US, most prominently the role the US Congress plays in global non-proliferation policy. Secondly, the impact of tightened export control policies and even more prominently, supplier regimes, on the global marketplace for weapons, in both the conventional and nonconventional realms. And third, the impact the ascendance of global multilateral arms control treaties (such as the CWC) was likely to have on the Middle East.

Presentations at the Ginosar conference suggested that US non-proliferation policy (including legislation), supplier regimes, and new or reinvigorated global arms control treaties were already having a growing impact on the Middle East proliferation and arms control scene. It was suggested that their impact was rising further in the aftermath of the Second Gulf War. This ascendence is attributed, at least in part, to the trauma of the Gulf War, which has produced a greater assertiveness by the US and other powers in promoting the global non-proliferation and arms control agenda. This development marks a sharp contrast even from the near past, when supplier regimes were either nonexistent or ineffective, and the few global and multilateral arms control treaties in existence were mostly targeted elsewhere and were either ignored or disregarded by most Middle East parties, including by member states. Still, it seems clear that these factors have and will continue to have only a marginal impact on the conventional arms trade and accumulation in the region. No real comprehensive effort to regulate conventional transfers has been or presently is in the cards.

Interestingly enough, presentations at Ginosar suggested that extra-regional players might also affect the way Middle East arms control and regional security negotiations are undertaken. It was noted that they might emulate the role played in the European process by the 'neutral group.' Just as the latter was instrumental in enabling the opposing blocs to overcome a zero-sum situation, the former, especially but not exclusively the cosponsors of the Middle East process (the US and Russia) might play a similar role in the Middle East.

The final layer of contributions by the Ginosar conference are those that pertain to the understanding of factors specific to the regional arms control scene. The presentations at Ginosar manifested a remarkable degree of consensus regarding not only the diagnosis and prognosis for Middle East arms control, but also regarding the prescriptions for action. This broad consensus may conveniently be summarized in the following five points.

First, the Middle East is not yet politically ripe for meaningful military disarmament measures, deep cuts, foreclosure of options, and the like. Some moderation of the conflicts permeating the Middle East will have to precede regional arms control. Easing of tensions and significant movement toward political openness and normalization of relations are necessary, if insufficient, conditions for arms control. The primacy of the political context implies that the nature of the arms control process in the region will necessarily be long and incremental. Given that this is the case, it has been suggested that it is preferable to scale down expectations for rapid progress, as these are likely to be counterproductive.

Secondly, not only the overall prospects, but also the objective as well as subjective incentives for pursuing region-wide arms control measures are presently considered to be rather weak, in some cases even negative. No powerful economic incentives for arms control presently exist, nor is arms control likely in the short to medium term to free any significant resources for civilian activities. Moreover, presently some arms control measures may actually prove harmful to regional security and stability.

Third, until region-wide arms control becomes feasible, it is important to engage in the building of a cooperative inter-state arms control and regional security architecture. Each of the regional parties will have to learn to understand how it operates, what its advantages and risks are, and how it could be made to serve the cause of regional stability without undermining its national security requirements.

Fourth, in the interim the policies pursued by regional parties should emphasize a combination of regional confidence-building measures (moving from lesser to more significant military steps), limited bilateral agreements, and modest unilateral restraints. Given the level of ignorance, misunderstanding, and

248

suspicion, improving the understanding of the sensitivities and concerns of all regional parties will have to be an essential part of the early phase of the process. All of these will have to be coupled, at least initially, with targeted arms control (supplier restraint) initiatives against specific troublemakers in the region such as Iraq, Iran and Libya. These targeted efforts will have to persist until these countries are fully and reliably integrated into the cooperative regional process.

Fifth, when ambitious arms control negotiations ultimately are undertaken, the agenda will have to be comprehensive. It will probably have to cover all the sources of conflict (Arab-Israeli, intra-Arab, and Iran-related) as well as all categories of arms. It will also have to cover many other security-relevant factors, ranging from force structures and states of readiness to political commitments and their verification and enforcement. The comprehensive agenda must, nonetheless, allow for some sequencing in implementation as well as for certain sub-regional variance.

All in all, the outlook for Middle East arms control may not be as optimistic as some would have hoped. Yet judging by past experience (including in the Middle East) as well as present conditions, the opportunities for progress are there. A realistic assessment of the prospects for moving ahead as well as the path to follow is clearly important to realize these new opportunities, irrespective of whether one is an ideological fan or foe of arms control. We hope that our readers will share our assessment that this first Ginosar conference indeed proved useful on both counts.

Contributors

Christophe Carle is director of the International Security Program at the Institut Français des Relations Internationales (IFRI) in Paris. At the time the conference was held, he served as deputy director of the program.

Patrick L. Clawson is professor at the National Defense University. At the time the conference was held, he was Editor of ORBIS and Director of Research at the Middle East Council of the Foreign Policy Research Institute (FPRI) in Philadelphia.

Anthony Cordesman is a fellow at the Woodrow Wilson International Center for Scholars, Washington DC. At the time the conference was held, he served as senior foreign policy advisor to Senator John McCain (R-Arizona).

Zachary Davis is an analyst of international nuclear affairs and non-proliferation policy at the Congressional Research Service (CRS), Library of Congress, Washington DC.

Lewis A. Dunn is Assistant Vice President and Manager of the Negotiations and Planning Division, Science Applications International Corporation, McLean, Virginia.

Shai Feldman is a Senior Research Associate and director of the Project on Regional Security and Arms Control in the Middle East at Tel Aviv University's Jaffee Center for Strategic Studies.

Dore Gold is a Senior Research Associate and director of the Project on US Foreign and Defense Policies in the Middle East at Tel Aviv University's Jaffee Center for Strategic Studies.

Shekhar Gupta is senior editor for foreign affairs of *India Today*, New Delhi.

J. Lise Hartman currently lives in France. She is former Staff Director of the Subcommittee on International Operations, Committee on International Relations, US House of Representatives, Washington DC.

Ephraim Kam is a Senior Research Associate at Tel Aviv University's Jaffee Center for Strategic Studies.

William W. Keller is a senior analyst and project director at the Office of Technology Assessment (OTA) of the US Congress, Washington DC.

Geoffrey Kemp is Director of the Middle East Arms Control Project at the Carnegie Endowment for International Peace, Washington DC. He is former director of Middle East Affairs at the National Security Council.

Wlodzimierz Konarski is ambassador at the Ministry of Foreign Affairs in Poland. He is the former head of Poland's delegations to the Conference on Security and Cooperation in Europe (CSCE) and to the Conventional Forces in Europe (CFE) negotiations in Vienna.

Ariel Levite is a Senior Research Associate at Tel Aviv University's Jaffee Center for Strategic Studies. He is a member of Israel's delegation to the multilateral talks on Middle East Arms Control and Regional Security (ACRS).

Jerome Paolini is senior advisor to the Minister of Research and Higher Education in the government of France. At the time the conference was held, he served as director of the International Security Program at the Institut Français des Relations Internationales (IFRI) in Paris.

Barry Posen is professor at the Department of Political Science and member of the Center for International Studies at the Massachusetts Institute of Technology (MIT).

The Jaffee Center for Strategic Studies (JCSS)

The Center for Strategic Studies was established at Tel Aviv University at the end of 1977. In 1983 it was named the Jaffee Center for Strategic Studies in honor of Mr. & Mrs. Mel Jaffee. The objective of the Center is to contribute to the expansion of knowledge on strategic subjects and to promote public understanding of and pluralistic thought on matters of national and international security.

The Center relates to the concept of strategy in its broadest meaning, namely, the complex of processes involved in the identification, mobilization and application of resources in peace and war, in order to solidify and strengthen national and international security.

JCSS International Board of Trustees

JCSS Publications

JCSS Publications present the findings and assessments of the Center's research staff. Each paper represents the work of a single investigator or a team. Such teams may also include research fellows who are not members of the Center's staff. Views expressed in the Center's publications are those of the authors and do not necessarily reflect the views of the Center, its trustees, officers, or other staff members or the organizations and individuals that support its research. Thus the publication of a work by JCSS signifies that it is deemed worthy of public consideration but does not imply endorsement of conclusions or recommendations.

Editor
Joseph Alpher

Editorial Board

The Jaffee Center for Strategic Studies
Recent Publications in English

1993-1994 Subscription Series

Study no. 21   Aryeh Shalev, *The Israel-Syria Armistice Regime 1949-1955*.

Study no. 22   Aharon Klieman and Ariel Levite, eds., *Deterrence in the Middle East: Where Theory and Practice Converge*.

Study no. 23   Shai Feldman and Ariel Levite, eds., *Arms Control and the New Middle East Security Environment*.

Study no. 24   Aryeh Shalev, *Israel and Syria: Peace and Security on the Golan*.

Study no. 25   Shai Feldman, ed., *Confidence Building and Verification: Prospects in the Middle East*.

The Middle East Military Balance 1993-1994
Edited by Shlomo Gazit; with Zeev Eytan.

1991-1992 Subscription Series

Study no. 18   Mark A. Heller, *The Dynamics of Soviet Policy in the Middle East: Between Old Thinking and New*.

Study no. 19   Dore Gold, *Israel as an American Non-NATO Ally: Parameters of Defense-Industrial Cooperation*.

Study no. 20   Karen L. Puschel, *US-Israeli Strategic Cooperation in the Post-Cold War Era: An American Perspective*.

War in the Gulf: Implications for Israel
Report of a JCSS Study Group. Edited by Joseph Alpher.
The Middle East Military Balance 1992-1993
Edited by Shlomo Gazit; with Zeev Eytan, and Amos Gilboa.

Books
Abraham Ben-Zvi, *The United States and Israel: The Limits of the Special Relationship* (New York: Columbia Univ. Press, 1993).